Rhythms

Modern French Identities

Edited by Peter Collier

Volume 68

PETER LANG

Oxford · Bern · Berlin · Bruxelles · Frankfurt am Main · New York · Wien

Elizabeth Lindley &
Laura McMahon (eds)

Rhythms

Essays in French Literature, Thought
and Culture

PETER LANG

Oxford · Bern · Berlin · Bruxelles · Frankfurt am Main · New York · Wien

Bibliographic information published by Die Deutsche Bibliothek
Die Deutsche Bibliothek lists this publication in the Deutsche
Nationalbibliografie; detailed bibliographic data is available on the
Internet at ‹http://dnb.ddb.de›.

British Library and Library of Congress Cataloguing-in-Publication Data:
A catalogue record for this book is available from *The British Library*,
Great Britain, and from *The Library of Congress*, USA

ISSN 1422-9005
ISBN 978-3-03911-349-1

© Peter Lang AG, International Academic Publishers, Bern 2008
Hochfeldstrasse 32, Postfach 746, CH-3000 Bern 9, Switzerland
info@peterlang.com, www.peterlang.com, www.peterlang.net

Printed in Germany

Contents

III   Disruptive Rhythms

IV   Everyday Rhythms

V   Cinematic Rhythms

Acknowledgements

This publication emerged from the tenth annual French Graduate Conference, held at Selwyn College, Cambridge in April 2006. The conference would not have been possible without generous financial assistance from the Department of French, University of Cambridge, for which we are most grateful. We are indebted to the invaluable inspiration, support and guidance of Peter Collier, Emma Wilson, Philip Ford, Miranda Gill, Esther Palmer and Jacky Graves. We would also like to thank Graham Speake and all at Peter Lang for their assistance. We dedicate this volume, on behalf of the Department of French in Cambridge, to the memory of Malcolm Bowie.

ELIZABETH LINDLEY AND LAURA MCMAHON

Introduction

From the regular pulse of blood around the body to the uneven distribution of stresses in speech, rhythms are central to our life-world and our interaction with others. In art, rhythms emerge through particular combinations of words, images, notes and movement (rhyme in verse, montage in film, timing in music, gesture in dance), thereby determining structures of tension and affect in our relation to the artwork or performance. Yet rhythms also ground us in the concrete physiology of the body, in collective social ritual, and in patterns of everyday experience, such as the to-and-fro of transport and multi-media communication. Rhythms shape our work and leisure time, lending contours both to the recurrence of scheduled routine and to the sporadic release of activities such as dance, sport and music. As they oscillate between action and aesthetics, and flow between habit and creativity, rhythms appear to be vital to our understanding of how subjectivities are constructed upon the shifting borderlines between life and art.[1]

Yet as Henri Meschonnic has observed, the more we attribute to rhythm, paradoxically, the more vague our understanding of the term becomes. Rhythm as a concept is inherently slippery and difficult to define.[2] As Meschonnic observes in *Critique du rythme*, to refer to

---

1   Examples of recent studies of rhythm, ranging from poetry to dance, include: Clive Scott, *Reading the Rhythm: The Poetics of French Free Verse 1910–1930* (Oxford: Clarendon Press, 1993); David Evans, *Rhythm, Illusion and the Poetic Idea: Baudelaire, Rimbaud, Mallarmé* (Amsterdam and New York: Rodopi, 2004); Dee Reynolds, *Rhythmic Subjects: Uses of Energy in the Dances of Mary Wigman, Martha Graham and Merce Cunningham* (Alton: Dance Books, 2007).

2   Kathleen George notes for example that everyday use of the term tends to be vague and is often confused with 'tempo'. See George, *Rhythm in Drama* (Pittsburgh: University of Pittsburgh Press, 1980), p.3.

cardiac rhythms of the body or to iambic rhythms in poetry is to speak of two very different kinds of rhythm.[3] He argues that although cosmic rhythms (such as the cycle of day and night, or the movement of the tides) and biological rhythms (such as the breathing and heart-beat of the body) seem to affirm the notion of rhythm as a regular pattern, the disjunctive rhythms of spoken and written discourse necessarily subvert any such idea of rhythm as strictly regular, metrical or measured. Meschonnic seeks to develop a theory of rhythm which shifts away from the traditional concept of rhythm as metrical.[4] For Meschonnic, rhythm is always in excess of regularity; it is 'sans mesure' – not because it necessarily opposes measure, but because '[c]'est toujours autre chose qu'on a mesuré'.[5]

One key move that Meschonnic makes in his work is to disrupt the myth of any *unity* to the concept of rhythm; rather he seeks to celebrate rhythm in all its distinctions and disjunctions, flux and instability. It is this injunction to explore rhythm in its many diverse manifestations – as both regular and irregular, as flow and dispersal, yet also as a mode of recurrence, organisation or structure – that this collection of essays takes as its point of departure. Meschonnic's work seeks to draw rhythm into a more complex analysis than an under-standing of it purely in terms of regularity, measure or metre would allow; similarly, as the essays in this volume think through questions of temporality and the everyday, poetry and autobiography, tech-nology and the city, space and the body in performance, what emerges is a wide-ranging and complex engagement with the notion of rhythm, one which probes the possibilities of the concept – both as theme and as critical tool – across a range of historical periods (from Medieval to

3   Henri Meschonnic, *Critique du rythme: anthropologie historique du langage* (Lagrasse: Verdier, 1981), p.146.
4   Here the work of Émile Benveniste provides a key point of reference for Meschonnic. In his study of the etymology of the word 'rythme', Benveniste demonstrates its gradual mutation from the Platonic definition as regularity (*rythmos*) to a more fluid model based on the organisation of movement (*rhuthmos*). See Benveniste 'La notion de « rythme » dans son expression lin-guistique', *Problèmes de linguistique générale*, 2 vols (Paris: Gallimard, 1969–74), Vol 1, pp.327–335.
5   Meschonnic, *Critique du rythme*, p.143.

contemporary) and an array of artistic media (poetry, literature, music, dance, painting, architecture and cinema).

What follows here then, as an introduction to these essays, is a brief outline of the ways in which a number of contemporary French thinkers have engaged with the theme of rhythm in order to test out its potential as a conceptual tool for analysis and thought. As the work of Meschonnic suggests, the potential of rhythm may lie in its very resistance to definition: despite the fact that rhythm is everywhere, it remains difficult to fix in any precise terms. It is in this sense that rhythm has acted as a key figure of interest not only for Meschonnic, but for thinkers such as Julia Kristeva, Henri Lefebvre and Gilles Deleuze (whose works serve as important points of reference for the essays in this volume).[6] Like Meschonnic, these thinkers have challenged the conventional concept of rhythm as a regular, metrical pattern. As means of an introduction, it is these thinkers we focus on here, with the aim of sketching a theoretical consideration of rhythm in its simultaneous construction and dispersal, tension and release, of the subject.

A theory of rhythm

We begin then, in a move which marks the first of many rhythmic cycles in this volume, with a return to Meschonnic. His work suggests that the rhythms of language are at once both irregular and organised.

6   For a deconstructive approach to the question of rhythm see Philippe Lacoue-Labarthe, *Le Sujet de la philosophie* (Paris: Aubier-Flammarion, 1979), in particular the chapter entitled 'L'Écho du sujet'. For a detailed discussion of Kristeva and Lacoue-Labarthe in relation to rhythm and poetry, see Amittai F. Aviram, *Telling Rhythm: Body and Meaning in Poetry* (Ann Arbor: University of Michigan Press, 1994). For a succinct analysis of the figure of rhythm in Kristeva, Lacoue-Labarthe and Meschonnic, see Aviram, 'The Meaning of Rhythm', in *Between Philosophy and Poetry: Writing, Rhythm, and History*, ed. Massimo Verdicchio and Robert Burch (New York and London: Continuum, 2002), pp.161–170.

Arguing that 'le rythme est irréductible au signe',[7] Meschonnic considers rhythm as a disruption of the Saussurean relation between the signifier and signified. Whilst semantic meaning is seen to reduce the internal free play of rhythms in language, conversely the rhythms of spoken and written discourse have the potential to destabilise lexical meaning. As Meschonnic shifts away from an understanding of language in structuralist terms as the pure operation of signs, rhythm becomes central to his discussion of the relation between subject and discourse:

> Si le sens est une activité du sujet, si le rythme est une organisation du sens dans le discours, le rythme est nécessairement une organisation ou configuration du sujet dans son discours. Une théorie du rythme dans le discours est donc une théorie du sujet dans le langage. Il ne peut pas y avoir de théorie du rythme sans théorie du sujet, pas de théorie du sujet sans théorie du rythme. Le langage est un élément du sujet, l'élément le plus subjectif, dont le plus subjectif à son tour est le rythme.[8]

The rhythmic organisation of the discourse of the subject overlays (and potentially exceeds) the already inherently rhythmed structures of language. For Meschonnic, any theory of the subject is necessarily also a theory of rhythm: the subject lives, occurs, speaks, listens *as rhythm*. The writings of Victor Hugo, for example, inscribe their own subjective history of rhythm (the personal rhythm of what Meschonnic calls a 'devenir-sujet'), superimposed upon the discourse of the historical moment in which Hugo writes.[9]

In an ongoing circuit of reciprocal flow and exchange therefore, 'c'est le rythme qui produit, transforme le sujet, autant que le sujet émet le rythme […]'.[10] Though Meschonnic clearly recognises rhythm as a vehicle for sense and communication ('le rythme est une organisation du sens dans le discours'), by emphasising the ways in which rhythm also exceeds the limits of the sign, he simultaneously gestures to something in rhythm which may be before or beyond signification. Poetry becomes exemplary of the way in which rhythm

7   Meschonnic, *Critique du rythme*, p.705.
8   Ibid., p.71.
9   Ibid., p.100.
10   Ibid., p.83.

poses a challenge to semantic constraints: through the patterning of its beats, cadences and rhymes, a poem is much more than the pure sum of its signs. To highlight this, Meschonnic cites an observation by Valéry: 'Quand le vers est très beau on ne songe même pas à comprendre. Ce n'est plus un signal, c'est un fait.'[11] For Meschonnic, the possibility of responding to the pure facticity of the poem's sound signals a kind of pre-reflective receptivity to rhythm: 'le rythme installe une réceptivité, un mode de prendre qui s'insère au défaut de la compréhension courante, celle du signe [...]'.[12] This receptivity to rhythm opens the subject onto a non-symbolic space anterior to sense: 'Ni copie du sens ni symbolisation, le rythme est un représentant non sémiotique du sujet qui est antérieur au sens.'[13]

Disruptive rhythms

Resonating with Meschonnic's reflections, rhythm in the work of Kristeva is similarly that which disturbs semantic meaning. In *La Révolution du langage poétique*, Kristeva privileges the rhythms of the semiotic over the symbolic, locating the source of semiotic rhythm in the *chora*.[14] The term *chora* is borrowed from Plato's *Timaeus* in order to denote the free play of semiotic rhythm in the space of the womb, defined as 'une totalité non expressive constituée par ces pulsions et leurs *stases* en une motilité aussi mouvementée que réglementée [...]'.[15] This rhythmic site – 'cet espace rythmé, sans thèse, sans position'[16] – is a space of pre-Oedipal drives, organised and

11 Valéry, cited in ibid., p.83.
12 Ibid., p.83.
13 Ibid., p.98.
14 Julia Kristeva, *La Révolution du langage poétique: l'avant-garde à la fin du XIXe siècle, Lautréamont et Mallarmé* (Paris: Seuil, 1974). It is important to note here that the term 'semiotic' corresponds to *le sémiotique*, which Kristeva distinguishes from *la sémiotique* (the study of signs).
15 Kristeva, *La Révolution du langage poétique*, p. 23; original emphasis.
16 Ibid., p.25.

ordered yet also, paradoxically, chaotic and free of any (symbolic) law. The infant's entry into the symbolic order relies upon what Kristeva refers to as the 'thetic' break – the suppression of semiotic rhythm in a rupture which establishes linguistic and social structures. It is thus the repression of the chaotic, rhythmic motility of the *chora* which enables the thetic subject to assume an enunciatory position in language. For Kristeva, rhythm is the essential supplement to discourse, an element as vital as it is suppressed:

> la *chora* elle-même, en tant que rupture et articulations – rythme – est préalable à l'évidence, au vraisemblable, à la spatialité et à la temporalité. Notre discours – le discours – chemine contre elle, c'est-à-dire s'appuie sur elle en même temps qu'il la repousse [...][17]

Here, as for Meschonnic, rhythm plays an organisational role whilst simultaneously threatening to exceed the constraints of signifying discourse. The *chora* is the ordering of pre-symbolic rhythms, 'antérieure à la position du signe',[18] thus resonating with Meschonnic's model of rhythm as a non-symbolic space, 'antérieur au sens'. What is specific to Kristeva's model, however, is that semiotic rhythm denotes a feminine space, inextricably linked to the maternal body: 'indifférent au langage, énigmatique et féminine, cet espace sous-jacent à l'écrit est rythmique, déchaîné, irréductible à sa traduction verbale intelligible [...]'.[19] For Kristeva, the feminine rhythms of the *chora* ripple below and through the symbolic, allowing the semiotic, even after the thetic break, to haunt discourse with its potential for interrupting reason and logic. Kristeva finds examples of such disruption in the poetry of Mallarmé and Lautréamont. In readings of their work, she privileges an analysis of non-metrical aspects (for example, accidental rhymes, alliteration, repetition), drawing out rhythmic sound patterns which resist meaning and thereby potentially fracture the symbolic. Yet at the same time, she argues that the semiotic and symbolic cannot be seen as separate entities: they co-exist in a dialectical relation which structures all processes of signification. For Kristeva, the dis-

17   Ibid., p.23.
18   Ibid., p.26.
19   Ibid., p.29.

junctive, chaotic rhythms of the *chora* thus perpetually threaten to burst through the symbolic whilst remaining essential to its very functioning.

Rhythms of the everyday

Whilst Kristeva emphasises the importance of rhythm in poetry, Henri Lefebvre's *Éléments de rythmanalyse* is a manifesto for the centrality of rhythm in analyses of the urban and the everyday, themes which recur throughout his corpus.[20] *Éléments de rythmanalyse* opens with the claim that 'ce petit livre [...] ne se propose rien de moins que de fonder une science, un nouveau domaine du savoir: l'analyse des rythmes; avec des conséquences pratiques.'[21] Heralding rhythm-analysis as an innovative approach which would combine theory with practice, 'ce petit livre' roams across a vast range of subjects: the media, the manipulation of time, the city, the workplace, dressage and the body. Here Lefebvre seeks to unearth the secret, unsung rhythms of the everyday, highlighting intersections between individual rhythms (patterns of waking, watching, sleeping) and collective rhythms (such as festivals, fêtes and celebrations).

Rhythms for Lefebvre are an essential tool for the analysis of lived experience as they operate at the intersection between rational, mathematical categories and the chaos of the visceral human body. Both natural and logical, rhythms structure encounters between the bodily and the social, between the personal and the collective, be-tween chaos and law. Though the tempo of everyday experience is measured according to the 'law' of clock-time, it is traversed by cosmic rhythms (day and night, the seasons) and biological rhythms

20 Henri Lefebvre, *Éléments de rythmanalyse: introduction à la connaissance des rythmes* (Paris: Syllepse, 1992). On Lefebvre and the everyday see Michael Sheringham, *Everyday Life: Theories and Practices from Surrealism to the Present* (Oxford: Oxford University Press, 2006), pp. 134–174.
21 Lefebvre, *Éléments de rythmanalyse*, p.11.

(heartbeats, blinking); the everyday emerges in the interplay between these two sets of rhythms.[22] Yet this interplay is also a battleground, a site of struggle and disruption. As night-time leisure activities become more popular, for example, circadian rhythms are upset. In the workplace, where repetitive rhythms dominate, the struggle between clock-time and biological rhythms (such as hunger or fatigue) becomes even more marked.

Lefebvre argues that rhythm always involves a certain mode of regulation: 'Partout où il y a rythme, il y a *mesure*, c'est-à-dire loi, obligation calculée et prévue, projet.'[23] This model of rhythm as measure, obligation or calculation, differs significantly from both Meschonnic, who aims to define rhythm away from the metrical, and Kristeva, who seeks to define rhythm away from any law. For Kristeva in particular, rhythms are precisely the opposite of obligation: defiant of the symbolic, they are utterly lawless. By contrast, Lefebvre sees rhythm as inseparable from a form of organisation defined as rule, project or obligation. Yet the apparent divergence between Lefebvre and Kristeva here also reveals a point of resonance. Lefebvre notes that this organisation of rhythm in and by social regulation is always in contact with – and potentially undercut by – the irrational and unpredictable rhythms of the human body: 'Le rythme apparaît comme un temps réglé, régi par des lois rationnelles, mais en liaison avec le moins rationnel de l'être humain: le vécu, le charnel, le corps.'[24] Here the Marxist thrust of Lefebvre's rhythmanalysis becomes apparent: numerical, rational rhythms are always vulnerable to destabilisation by the chaotic, natural rhythms of the body. As rhythms assume a subversive role in Lefebvre's model, this appears to echo Kristeva's theorisation of the semiotic as a rhythmic, potentially disruptive (dis)organisation of the symbolic, anchored in corporeality.

The body and the senses assume a central role in rhythmanalysis; the body is described as 'un paquet de rythmes, différents mais

---

22   See Henri Lefebvre and Catherine Régulier, 'Le projet rythmanalytique',
       Éléments de rythmanalyse, p.191.
23   Ibid., p.16.
24   Ibid., p.18.

accordés [...] une *gerbe* de rythmes.'[25] Lefebvre draws a distinction between psychoanalysis, which privileges the verbal, and rhythm-analysis, which listens to the murmuring of the world, responding to unexpected beats and noises. The rhythmanalyst is attentive to sounds, to smells, and even to his or her own breathing and heartbeat: 'il pense avec son corps, non dans l'abstrait, mais dans la temporalité vécue [...]'.[26] In this sense, Lefebvre's project appears close to Maurice Merleau-Ponty's *Phénoménologie de la perception*, a work which seeks to attend to the lived experience of the body by analysing sense perception in philosophical terms.[27] At the same time, as Lefebvre points out, rhythmanalysis differentiates itself from phenomenology through its primary focus on rhythm. Crucial for Lefebvre is the sense that rhythm is not only a question of analysis but also one of abandon: 'pour saisir un rythme, il faut avoir été saisi par lui; il faut se laisser aller, se donner, s'abandonner à sa durée.'[28] Grasping a rhythm means also being grasped by it, letting oneself go, abandoning oneself to the beat and flux of its movement.

Visual rhythms

The work of Deleuze provides an interesting point of comparison here, as it shifts our analysis of rhythm away from writing and the everyday towards a consideration of rhythm as a property of the visual. In his discussion of the work of the painter Francis Bacon, Deleuze, like Lefebvre, seeks to privilege a relation between rhythm and sensation.[29] In his reading of Bacon's works, he locates a contrac-

---

25 Lefebvre, *Éléments de rythmanalyse*, p.32.
26 Ibid., p.33.
27 Maurice Merleau-Ponty, *Phénoménologie de la perception* (Paris: Gallimard, 1945).
28 Lefebvre, *Éléments de rythmanalyse*, pp.41–2.
29 Gilles Deleuze, *Francis Bacon: Logique de la sensation*, 3rd edn (Paris: Éditions de la Différence, 1994).

tion or 'spasm' within the paintings, a movement denoting the action of invisible forces upon the painted figures, designating something which is inscribed at once both within and beyond the visual. According to Deleuze, Bacon's work articulates this force or contraction through a direct appeal to the senses: to view a painting by Bacon is to hear the sound of hooves, to smell or feel the weight of meat, to touch the quivering of feathers and skin. For Deleuze, this synaesthetic effect is fundamentally a question of rhythm:

> cette opération n'est possible que si la sensation de tel ou tel domaine (ici la sensation visuelle) est directement en prise sur une puissance vitale qui déborde tous les domaines et les traverse. Cette puissance, c'est le Rythme, plus profond que la vision, l'audition, etc. [...] Une « logique des sens », disait Cézanne, non rationnelle, non cérébrale. L'ultime, c'est donc le rapport du rythme avec la sensation, qui met dans chaque sensation les niveaux et les domaines par lesquels elle passe. Et ce rythme parcourt un tableau comme il parcourt une musique. C'est diastole-systole: le monde qui me prend moi-même en se fermant sur moi, le moi qui s'ouvre au monde, et l'ouvre lui-même.[30]

Deleuze locates a rhythmic pulse in the paintings of Bacon, one which would be akin to the movement of contraction and relaxation in a heartbeat. This rhythm effects a direct sensorial impact upon the viewer which bypasses rational or cerebral functions (it is for this reason that Deleuze describes Bacon's paintings in terms of a 'logic of sensation', replacing a logic of narration). As it traverses but also exceeds each sensory domain, rhythm becomes the fundamental element in the painting's impact upon the viewer.

What can be drawn from Deleuze's remarks? Rhythm here is powerful, belonging to the senses yet also somehow overwhelming them; rhythm denotes a simultaneous movement of relaxation and contraction, a relation of opening-closing between self and world. As for Lefebvre's rhythmanalyst, here the viewer of Bacon's art is abandoned to the rhythm of the paint: taking up the rhythm means also being taken up by it. For Deleuze, as for Meschonnic, Kristeva and Lefebvre, rhythm makes an appeal to something which potentially exceeds the verbal and the rational. Yet these domains of experience

---

30   Deleuze, *Francis Bacon*, p.31.

are always already invested in, shaped by and traversed by rhythm and thus remain open to (rhythm)analysis in whichever form this may take. As rhythm opens onto the limit of the sign (Meschonnic), the rupture of the symbolic (Kristeva), the tension between chaos and law (Lefebvre), and the movement of opening-closing between world and self (Deleuze), its refusal to be brought fully to representation gestures to its potential for a simultaneous dislocation and shaping of thought, both echoing and redistributing that which precedes it.

Introducing the essays

The five chapters of the book map sites of rhythmic movement, vibrating loosely around poetic, narrative, disruptive, everyday and cinematic rhythms. In Chapter One, 'Poetic Rhythms', the first essays explore the use of rhythm in poetry for communicating a sense of musicality and meaning beyond semantic restrictions. Helen Abbott investigates the relationship between word definitions in Mallarmé's poetic language. The term 'rhythmic sensation', where 'rhythmic' deliberately incorporates both regular and irregular patternings, describes an encounter with words that possess a shifting meaning. As Mallarmé seeks to *déchiffrer* the irregular patternings of the meanings, the process allows for the possibility of attaining sense beyond words. Abbott contends that Mallarmé privileges a strategy of murmuring poetic language by allowing words to speak rhythmically in irregular ways.

Exploring the poetic translations of Yves Bonnefoy, Matthias Zach draws on Meschonnic's understanding of *signifiance* to describe the translator's attempts to recreate the poem's original rhythm. Zach argues that translating poetry constitutes a dialogue with another author: the translator transforms the rhythm of the original into his own, bestowing new expression on the poem. Analysing Bonnefoy's translation of a sonnet by Shakespeare, Zach claims that rhythm in poetic translation is simultaneously a dialogue and a creative process.

Rhythms of the creative poetic process are considered in the next essay, as we return to the work of Mallarmé. Here Ariane Kossack suggests that, as Mallarmé makes recourse to the mythological tale of the Orphic journey, Orpheus' descent into and departure from the underworld, and the poem's rising and setting sun, pose as rhythmic poles of creation and destruction. Mallarmé's poetry underlines the relationship between poetry and music through the rhythms of the Orphic song.

Surveying the narrative structure of Medieval writings and twenty-first century literary works, Chapter Two, entitled 'Narrative Rhythms', develops and exemplifies the concept of rhythm as offering the narrative its movement and progression. Brenda Garvey and Luke Sunderland place the conflict between linearity and cyclicity within the tale's structure, shaping the narrative in equal force as both development and conclusion. Garvey traces how a sparse text describing the passage of time captures biological rhythms, daily rhythms and cyclical rhythms. The movement of the text is recurrent while remaining progressive: the narrative rhythm advances the text, yet Ernaux's narrative repetitions and rewritings prove cyclical as an obsession with memory causes the author to relive times past.

Sunderland charts the rhythm of narrative at a macro-level, also contrasting the repetition of cyclicity with the development of linear narrative. As youth is echoed in adulthood and as the past returns in future events, the cyclicity of an imaginary 'future perfect' conflicts with the linearity of lived time. Sunderland argues that rhythms of repetition dominate the Medieval cycle, achieving the linearity of progression while reiterating notions of the body's cyclical time.

Chapter Three's 'Disruptive Rhythms' considers rhythm through the lens of theory, dance, painting and poetry, examining its tendency to alter or disturb the subject's position in time and space. By abandoning expected rhythmic regularities, interruptions destabilise elements of sound and movement as well as temporal subjectivities. Dee Reynolds explores the effort rhythms of movement via the concept of kinesthesia, a sensory experience orienting our position and movement in space and time. If movement is characterised as the potential for action – such as conventional musical rhythms which encourage anticipation of the next beat – then kinesthetics potentially destabilises movement by disrupting rhythmic expectations. Reynolds engages with examples from poetry, painting and dance, all involving the experience of rhythm in time and space, replacing modulation with rhythmic dislocations.

In investigating Joseph Zobel's 1946 short story 'Laghia de la mort', Louise Hardwick considers the irregular rhythms of the tambour. Through the author's social realist approach to Caribbean plantations, the tale interprets the laghia dance as two quarrelling men rhythmically communicating their rage to a Creole drumbeat. Hardwick explains that, owing to irregular changes in tempo and the ultimate stumbling of the tambour, an anticipated violent climax dissipates as dancers and audience members alike return to the regular rhythms of quotidian reality.

Gerald Moore's essay considers how participating in the rhythm of community allows the modern subject to locate a position within the space and time of a social order. As past rhythms enter the present through an exchange of gifts, songs or myths, the unknown future is mitigated through the repetitions of rhythm and heritage. Aligning Walter Benjamin's diagnosis of the modern subject with Lefebvre's model of *arrhythmia*, Moore sketches a subject abandoned by the rhythms of history, adrift in the present. For Moore, disruptions of rhythm shape the modern subject's temporal experience and identity.

Surveying the movement of individuals across the urban landscape, the authors in Chapter Four's 'Everyday Rhythms' observe how subjects assume new routes and routines by breaking rhythmical movements and expected journeys. Michael Sheringham argues that rhythm plays a central part in shaping everyday experience, and can thus be seen to feature prominently in theoretical and literary accounts of the *quotidien*. He reads Gilles Deleuze and Félix Guattari's *Mille Plateaux* and Jacques Réda's *Les Ruines de Paris* as texts linking issues of rhythmicity, subjectivity and the everyday: 'they identify rhythm less with repetition and return than with momentum, divergence, and a constant traversing and subverting of fixed codes, articulations and contexts' (p.148). The subject becomes paramount in marking territory by remaining distinct from the city's routines of modernity. As Sheringham contends, a parallel space exists within the city landscape because of the mobile movement of a city stroll.

In Sophie Fuggle's essay, the subject also challenges traditional manners of perceiving urban spaces, as 'le parkour', or 'l'art du déplacement', becomes a way of marking dissident rhythms against the routines of city life. Rejecting regular modes of access, the 'traceur' ruptures rhythms of everyday movement by discovering new pathways across the urban landscape, confronting ideas of text and authorship. Creating distinct, interruptive movements, 'le parkour' both constructs and deconstructs rhythms of the city, enabling individuals to articulate unique rhythms by reading and writing the space in which they live.

In the next essay, Lisa Villeneuve considers the body's relation to the city environment by following the protagonist of Georges Perec's *Un homme qui dort* as he wanders aloofly through the Parisian metropolis outside the beat of urban social behaviour. If, according to Lefebvre, space implies a cognisance of particular rhythms, a conventional journey denies the subject the purposeless travels dictated by the body's rhythmic sensations. Focusing on Perec's text and film, Villeneuve examines the subject negotiating space through mundane experiences, allowing the placeless rhythms of the body to blend with the urban rhythms of the everyday.

Discussing 'Cinematic Rhythms' in Chapter Five, the essays examine ideas of rhythm and subjectivity in film, reconfiguring notions of cinematic continuity and temporality. In the opening essay, Ian James considers how modern technologies of cinema and television have impacted upon our collective understanding of life's temporal rhythms. According to Paul Virilio, film offers an unstable, fleeting presence through a succession of still images. Rhythms of lived, temporal experience are shaped by the technology of the cinematic image; for James, the body responds to the pace and speed of technological alteration as it distorts everyday rhythms of the passing of time.

Jennifer Valcke examines how avant-garde French filmmakers and theoreticians of the 1920s engaged with problems of tempo and rhythm in film, investigating the rhythm of movement, form and colour perceived through a succession of filmic images. Valcke contends that, by drawing a parallel between music and cinema, certain French filmmakers and theorists foreshadowed the principles of

Soviet montage. As avant-garde artists searched for a visual equivalent of music, their exploration led them to envisage film as a symphony of visual rhythms.

In the final essay, Jenny Chamarette examines Chris Marker's *La Jetée* (1962), a film composed of a series of predominantly static images, described as a visual 'photo-roman'. The rhythms of still images, dynamic sounds and voiceover narration create both a linear narrative and a disrupted subjectivity. Chamarette's reading underlines how halting rhythms – of fragmentation and reassembly, and of dynamism and stillness – move the film beyond illusions of time, fleeing the fixity of regularity and allowing a fluctuating subjectivity to surface.

These essays constitute a set of intersecting conversations, addressing a range of diverse and generative interpretations of rhythm. Theoretically-oriented approaches confront many of the slippery connotations of rhythm, often undermining accepted notions. The final result reveals the difficulty of specifying any single, distinct definition of rhythm. Yet, by assessing the presence of various forms of rhythm across a series of media, the authors seek to forge a more fertile, interdisciplinary understanding of the term. The aim of these readings is not to limit the use of rhythm, but rather to lead readers and artists alike to unknown ways of incorporating rhythm and pursuing its myriad of possible meanings.

Suggested Reading

Amittai F. Aviram, *Telling Rhythm: Body and Meaning in Poetry* (Ann Arbor: University of Michigan Press, 1994).

Gilles Deleuze, *Francis Bacon: Logique de la sensation*, 3rd edn (Paris: Éditions de la Différence, 1994).

Julia Kristeva, *La Révolution du langage poétique: l'avant-garde à la fin du XIXe siècle, Lautréamont et Mallarmé* (Paris: Seuil, 1974).

Henri Lefebvre, *Éléments de rythmanalyse: introduction à la connaissance des rythmes* (Paris: Syllepse, 1992).

Henri Meschonnic, *Critique du rythme: anthropologie historique du langage* (Lagrasse: Verdier, 1981).

Dee Reynolds, *Rhythmic Subjects: Uses of Energy in the Dances of Mary Wigman, Martha Graham and Merce Cunningham* (Alton: Dance Books, 2007).

Michael Sheringham, *Everyday Life: Theories and Practices from Surrealism to the Present* (Oxford: Oxford University Press, 2006).

I Poetic Rhythms

HELEN ABBOTT

Reading and Deciphering:
Mallarmé's Rhythmic Sensation

Mallarmé's celebrated poetic 'difficulty' – a charge which he famously rebuffed in the Huret interview – is, of course, what characterises the potential rewards that can be gained from reading and re-reading his work.[1] He seeks to create meaning not through the direct means of the dictionary meaning of words, but through a particular indirect means which he characterises as the 'sensation' of poetic language. Mallarmé's use of the term 'sensation' in his discursive writings is, however, far from unequivocal in meaning, and I suggest that Mallarmé's understanding of 'sensation' is one which is closely governed by his attitude towards the problematic of rhythmicity.

In 1865 he explains to Cazalis that poets resonate by being touched by different sensations: 'un [...] poète – c'est-à-dire un instrument qui résonne sous les doigts des diverses sensations.'[2] Poetic experience is defined, then, by a range of sensations. In 1887, defining himself as a 'lettré' who experiences language in a particular way, he suggests that such experiences are rhythmically patterned: '[il] n'existe à l'esprit de quiconque a rêvé les humains jusqu'à soi qu'un compte exact de purs motifs rythmiques de l'être [...]: il me plaît de les partout déchiffrer' (II, p.294). Does this imply that the kind of sensations elicited by a poet can be measured and 'deciphered' according to a model of rhythmicity? In his poetic works, Mallarmé posits himself as someone who is able to 'déchiffrer' the patternings that occur not simply as a result of the metrical verse line, but also in the interstices between meanings of words. These patternings are,

---

1   I refer, for example, to Malcolm Bowie, *Mallarmé and the Art of Being Difficult* (Cambridge: Cambridge University Press, 1978).

2   Stéphane Mallarmé, *Œuvres complètes*, ed. Bertrand Marchal, 2 vols (Paris: Gallimard, 1998–2003), I, p.675. All subsequent references are to this edition.

however, imbued with an uncertain status because of Mallarmé's predilection for the more mysterious and complex moments of poetic language. Through an analysis of the prose poem 'Le Démon de l'analogie' and its relationship with four verse poems ('Apparition', 'Sainte', 'Don du poème' and 'Cette nuit'), I suggest that the nature of the relationship between meanings of words is dynamic, palpable and immanent: it is in the interstices of poetry that he discerns a profound 'sensation' which is imbued with rhythmicity because it encounters words within the context of a suspended vibration of meaning.

For a consummate wordsmith to famously declare (in a letter to Cazalis in October 1864) that 'toutes les paroles [doivent] s'effacer devant la sensation' reveals what seems to be astonishingly poor business acumen. It would fundamentally imperil the future of his trade, since it does away with the very tools of that trade. Mallarmé's use of the word 'sensation' in this context (which is closely allied with the notion of an 'effet produit') reveals the potential to uncover a more profound meaning beyond the meaning of the specific words which constitute a verse line:

> Peindre non la chose mais l'effet qu'elle produit. Le vers ne doit donc pas, là, se composer de mots, mais d'intentions, et toutes les paroles s'effacer devant la sensation. (I, p.663)

The paradoxical power-struggle between words within the poetic line and their effacement from it dissolves into an aesthetic quandary for Mallarmé, and I suggest that he begins to resolve this in his poetic compositions through an exploration of rhythmic patternings and relationships which are structured by the problematic of meaning. In order to explore what Mallarmé expresses through his use of the term 'sensation', I shall elaborate the relationship, first of all, between 'sensation' and meaning, before moving on to the relationship between 'sensation' and rhythm (which also recalls the problematic status of the meaning of rhythm itself). A notion of 'rhythmic sensation' begins to emerge from Mallarmé's use of language through the way that he privileges the palpable patternings of poetic language, which open themselves up, in particular, through the physical act of speaking or murmuring.

'Sensation' and meaning: the role of the voice

In 1869 Mallarmé writes in his fragmentary notes on language:

> Enfin les mots ont plusieurs sens, sinon on s'entendrait toujours – nous en profiterons – et pour leur sens principal, nous chercherons quel effet ils nous produiraient prononcés par la voix intérieure de notre esprit, déposée par la fréquentation des livres du passé. (I, pp.508–9)

It seems that what defines the most important meaning of words is the sensation evoked ('effet produit') by trying out different possible meanings according to experience. In this respect, the 'effacement' of words that Mallarmé had longed for in the October 1864 letter to Cazalis is part of a process which explores words in their most transitory, ephemeral state ('prononcés par la voix intérieure'); that is to say, they must always be able to offer the potential for differing, even conflicting, meanings if the more profound 'sens principal' of the 'effet produit' is to be achieved.

This is mirrored in Mallarmé's comments to Cazalis in 1868 with regard to the 'Sonnet en *yx*':

> J'extrais ce sonnet, auquel j'avais une fois songé cet été, d'une étude projetée sur *la Parole*: il est inverse et je veux dire que le sens, s'il en a un, (mais je me consolerais du contraire grâce à la dose de poésie qu'il renferme, ce me semble) est évoqué par un mirage interne des mots mêmes. En se laissant aller à le murmurer plusieurs fois on éprouve une sensation assez cabalistique. (I, p.731)

By trying out how the poem sounds and feels, murmuring it 'sotto voce', like an incantatory prayer, the relationship between the 'sensation' and the 'sens, s'il en a un' calls upon the words themselves, because it is 'évoqué [*ex* + *vocare*] par un mirage interne des mots mêmes'.[3] This latent ability within language to somehow 'speak for

---

3   That Mallarmé has frequently likened his poetry to a spiritual or incantatory act has been explored extensively in Bertrand Marchal's *La Religion de Mallarmé* (Paris: Corti, 1988). For more on the idea of 'sotto voce' language, see Roger Pearson's chapter in *Mallarmé and Circumstance: The Translation of Silence* (Oxford: Oxford University Press, 2004).

itself' becomes an increasingly recurrent theme in Mallarmé's poetic aesthetic. For example, in 'Le Démon de l'analogie', he famously allows the words in the phrase 'La Pénultième est morte' to speak for themselves: 'elle [la phrase] s'articula seule' (I, p.417). In order for words to take on this evocative potency of being able to speak for themselves, they must first be brought to voice ('prononcés' or 'murmurés') by the poet and his reader. Moreover, Mallarmé does not expect to attain this 'sensation' on a first reading; rather he actively seeks to repeatedly murmur words of a poem to himself 'plusieurs fois', thereby disengaging his own agency by placing that responsibility on the words themselves:

> je résolus de laisser les mots de triste nature errer eux-mêmes sur ma bouche, et j'allai murmurant avec l'intonation susceptible de condoléance: 'La Pénultième est morte, elle est morte, bien morte, la désespérée Pénultième.' (I, p.417)

The relationship between meanings of words and poetic sensation in the Mallarméan aesthetic thereby becomes a quasi-ritualistic rite-of-passage as the reader travels through a range of different ways of experiencing the words of poetic language and – as the words themselves begin to take over – leaves dictionary meanings behind, uncovering the more profound meaning of sensation itself.

What becomes clear in 'Le Démon de l'analogie' in particular is that any attempt to specifically verbalise a sensation is inevitably superseded by a different verbal experience which distances itself from descriptive meaning:

> Je sortis de mon appartement avec la sensation propre d'une aile glissant sur les cordes d'un instrument, traînante et légère, que remplaça une voix prononçant les mots sur un ton descendant: 'La Pénultième est morte.' (I, p.416)

Here Mallarmé's verbalised description of a lingering sensation of a wing softly strumming a stringed instrument (the 'winged sensation') is quickly superseded by a 'voix prononçant les mots' of a haunting four-word phrase. This suggests that the initial attempt to describe a sensation is precarious, perhaps even impossible. However, since the actual words of the description of the sensation remain on the page ('traînante et légère'), the very drawing attention to the notion of a 'voix prononçant les mots' requires the reader to turn his focus once again towards the described sensation of the wing gliding over the instrument. It is no longer merely a figurative, verbalised description of a sensation, but a sensation waiting to be re-explored through the process of pronouncing the words themselves. As Roger Pearson has outlined in *Unfolding Mallarmé*:

> As readers we are not merely being asked an anodyne question about our psychological experience of language, we are being given a hint as to how to understand what is coming. We must, like the poet, let the words of the text play upon our own lips, murmur them, adapt them, 'remember' their past, try placing unexpected silences between them.[4]

The 'sense' that is to be made of Mallarmé's poetic language, then, is one which fundamentally relies on the sensation of the words themselves. Mallarmé's idealised strategy for attaining a profound poetic 'sensation' is to murmur the words so persistently that the words are no longer a hindrance in themselves; words are 'effaced' by the trying-out of language in its differing guises, on the page, 'prononcés' or 'murmurés', in order to 'remember' their past so that the various meanings of different words dissolve into a more significant meaning (or 'sens principal'): that of the 'sensation' of language.

'Sensation' and rhythm: the suspension of meaning

Remembering that the description of the 'winged sensation' in 'Le Démon de l'analogie' is replaced by the incessant, vocalised repetition of a four-word phrase, Mallarmé also posits these words as ones that are governed by metrical constraints:

de façon que
                    La Pénultième
finit le vers et

4   Pearson, *Unfolding Mallarmé* (Oxford: Clarendon, 1996), pp.78–9.

> *Est morte*
> se détacha de la suspension fatidique plus inutilement en le vide de
> signification.   (I, pp.416–7)

The use of the term 'suspension' here is, in typical Mallarméan fashion, ambiguous. It implies the interruption (and breathing space) created by the verse line-end; the interruption, in rhetorical terms, is also an interruption of sense or direction; it has musical connotations created by the context of musical vocabulary (a musical suspension is a delayed resolution where a dissonant note is tied over from the previous chord before resolving); and this specific connotation also implies the broader sense of delay or uncertainty. But the 'suspension' is 'fatidique', and is itself fatally killed off by the words 'Est morte' which are granted the agency of the verb 'se détacha'. That Mallarmé places the verb in the past historic, as an irrevocably completed past action, leaves the suspension hanging in mid-air and complicates the implications of the relationship between the terms 'morte' and 'fatidique'. What has died remains suspended or hanging in the air in the 'vide de signification'.

The 'vide de signification' is not, however, a negative emptiness. It is filled, instead, by the sensation that something more profound lies beyond the surface meanings of words. This notion preoccupied Mallarmé right through to the end of his career. In 'Le Mystère dans les Lettres', published in the *Revue blanche* two years before his death, he writes:

> Les mots, d'eux-mêmes, s'exaltent à mainte facette reconnue la plus rare ou
> valant pour l'esprit, centre de suspens vibratoire. (II, p.233)

Words (once again of their own accord) raise themselves up towards a suspended position within the mind. The vibrating nature of this suspension is derived from the exploration of meaning, implied here by terms such as 'mainte facette' or 'valant'. For Mallarmé, words themselves are 'à facettes', that is to say that they are 'difficile[s] à déchiffrer'.[5] In trying to evaluate and decipher the effect of words, Mallarmé senses that the inevitable consequence of allowing poetic

5   *Le Nouveau Petit Robert.*

language to persistently speak for itself will be that of a suspended, vibrating, trembling sensation. The interruptions and delays in meaning caused by poetic language create a model of rhythmicity where the continual repetition of words leads them to relinquish their surface meaning. Sensation, then, for Mallarmé, is persistently patterned by the nebulous contours of poetic language which repeats itself incessantly in the suspension of meaning.

That is to say, Mallarmé's 'rhythmic sensation' is attained through strategies of verbal repetition (of a phoneme, of a rhyme ending, of the same word in a different poetic context, of speaking the same word or words to oneself, for example); it is within the interstices between the moments of repetition that the suspended vibration of a rhythmic sensation is patterned. The recurrent patternings are not, however, necessarily regular.[6] They create a rhythmic sensation that is a) dynamic (because it exploits the duration over time of the effect of a word, phoneme, or collection of words); b) palpable (because it has a corporeal potency, particularly if words are 'voiced'); and c) imamnent (because it is self-sufficient, created by the words themselves). The more oblique or hypothetical the meanings of a word ('la plus rare ou valant'), the more profound the rhythmic sensation, because surface meanings are more readily disregarded, which enables the uncovering or 'déchiffrage' of the fundamental patternings of existence that Mallarmé terms 'les purs motifs rythmiques de l'être' (II, p.294).

The process of 'déchiffrage' set in motion by Mallarmé's rhythmic sensation is all the while founded on the uncertainty of meaning. Mallarmé thwarts any possibility of regular, unproblematised meaning, just as much as he thwarts the possibility of regular, unproblematised rhythm, of both poetry and the human body. He exacerbates distances between possible meanings by emphasising the overriding importance of a rhythmic sensation, which suspends meanings indefinitely in a more profound exploration of human language. By now it will have become clear that for Mallarmé the 'sens' that can

6   As David Evans has shown, regularity is not a given constant of Mallarmé's notion of rhythm. See, for example, *Rhythm, Illusion and the Poetic Idea* (Amsterdam and New York: Rodopi, 2004), p.251.

be derived from a rhythmic sensation of language is both complicated and elusive, but profoundly revealing, as is clear from a letter to Leo d'Orfer dated 27 June 1884:

> La Poésie est l'expression, par le langage humain ramené à son rythme essentiel, du sens mystérieux des aspects de l'existence. (I, p.782)

Rhythm for Mallarmé cannot correlate with the hypothesis, such as that put forward by Henri Meschonnic in *Critique du rythme*, that 'le rythme est une organisation du sens'.[7] For Mallarmé, rhythm is a 'sensation du sens'. Any organisation of meaning goes against Mallarmé's poetics because it implies a regular order; the patternings of meaning in the suspended vibrations of a rhythmic sensation of poetic language take the form of irregular interstitial pulls that may be re-awakened or re-discovered on each re-reading of the texts of Mallarmé's poems.

If we return to the description of the 'winged sensation' expressed in 'Le Démon de l'analogie', and place this alongside four of Mallarmé's verse poems published in the November 1883 volume of *Lutèce* at Verlaine's behest, it becomes clear that the rhythmic sensation of poetic language arrives at a more profound meaning through a persistently suspended and irregular vibration which is established across junctures both within and between poetic texts. Whilst the same words describing the 'winged sensation' do not always recur exactly in each of the four poems published in *Lutèce*, the semantic resonances are clear, as the two following tables demonstrate:

---

7   Henri Meschonnic, *Critique du rythme* (Lagrasse: Verdier, 1982), p.71.

Poem title	Diction of 'sensation'
'Le Démon de l'analogie' (I, p.416)	la sensation propre d'une aile glissant sur les cordes d'un instrument
'Apparition' (I, pp.113–4)	Des séraphins en pleurs Rêvant, l'archet aux doigts, dans le calme des fleurs Vaporeuses, tiraient de mourantes violes De blancs sanglots glissant sur l'azur des corolles. (v.1–4)
'Sainte' (I, p.114)	sa viole (v.3) Que frôle une harpe par l'Ange Formée (v.10–11) le plumage instrumental (v.15)
'Don du poème' (I, pp.115–6)	l'aile saignante et pâle, déplumée (v.2) la lampe angélique (v.5) rappelant viole et clavecin (v.11)
'Cette nuit' (I, p.115)	Il a ployé son aile indubitable en moi (v.4)

'Le Démon de l'analogie'	Lutèce poems
Aile	Aile, plumage, déplumée, ange, angélique, séraphins
Glissant	frôle, tiraient
Instrument	harpe, viole, clavecin, archet, instrumental

What, however, does the repetition of similar words reveal? It eluci-
dates the notion of rhythmic sensation on both a large scale (between
poems) and on a smaller scale (within an individual poetic unit). This
is due, in part, to the implied rhythmicity of the imagery of the wing
which is so closely allied, as a number of critics have demonstrated,
with Mallarmé's predilection for the imagery of the fan; both wings
and fans imply a patterned movement which is not necessarily regular
but which emphasises the potential for reciprocity. In her analysis of
the 'plis' of the Mallarméan 'éventail', Elizabeth McCombie has
shown that 'the intervening space pulsates in rhythms of mobile stasis,
resistant affinity, and open closure'.[8] The recurrences of diction per-
taining to the same verbalised description of a sensation are by no
means regular recurrences, precisely because of the intervening space
established between the individual poems themselves.

The strongest recurrence of the 'winged sensation' is found in
'Apparition' (I, pp.113–4), where the angels are playing stringed
instruments. The 'sanglots' extracted from the angels' viols figura-
tively thematise the anguished irregular suspense inherent to the
notion of rhythmic sensation. Mallarmé establishes a sense of irregular interstitial relationships through the *enjambement* of the first four
lines of the poem. After the initial sentence unit of the first hemistich
of the first line, the remainder of the quatrain takes the form of one
long sentence of which the syntax flows over the verse line-ends:

> La lune s'attristait. Des séraphins en pleurs,[9]
> Rêvant, l'archet aux doigts, dans le calme des fleurs
> Vaporeuses, tiraient de mourantes violes
> De blancs sanglots glissant sur l'azur des corolles. (v.1–4)

The disruptive interstices established by the *rejets* of 'Rêvant' and
'Vaporeuses' linger throughout the rest of the poem, even where the
alexandrine line is employed regularly, because the interstice of
the verse line-end is problematised from the very outset of the poem.

8   Elizabeth McCombie, *Mallarmé and Debussy: Unheard Music, Unseen Text*
     (Oxford: Clarendon, 2003), p.197.
9   In the Deman edition of 1899, there is no comma at the end of the first line. The
     version referred to here is the *Lutèce* version of 1883.

The disruptive metrical patternings, coupled with small-scale repetitive devices within this poem (in particular the extensive use of the [ã] sound throughout), show Mallarmé's poetic language in a state which endeavours to capture the rhythmic sensation of the interstices established between irregular recurrent patternings.

The anguish of the irregularity of the rhythmic sensation established in the 'sanglots' extracted by the angels' string-playing persists throughout. The poem is one of romantic torment, as is signalled not only by diction such as 'martyriser' or 'tristesse' which come at the ends of lines 6 and 7 respectively, but also by the metrical angst of further sense units that continue to run on beyond the line-end:

> Ma songerie aimant à me martyriser
> S'enivrait savamment du parfum de tristesse
> Que même sans regret et sans déboire laisse
> La cueillaison d'un Rêve au coeur qui l'a cueilli. (v.6–9)

The piling-up of alliterative patterns, particularly on 'm' and 's' sounds in lines 6, 7 and 8, and on the accentual 'c' sounds in line 9, intensifies the irregularity of the patternings inherent to this poem. The insertion of traces of anaphora (the repeated 'sans' in line 8) and of hints of a mirrored structure in line 9 (with the 'cueillaison' at the beginning reflecting the 'cueilli' at the end of the line) create the impression of a rhythmic coherence. Yet this is undermined by the actual appearance of anaphora on the 'Et' at the beginning of lines 12 and 13, coupled with the culmination of the narrative drama with the arrival of the apparition, 'tu m'es en riant apparue' (v.12), which has been prepared by the pivotal 'Quand' at the beginning of line 11:

> J'errai donc, l'œil rivé sur le pavé vieilli,
> Quand, avec du soleil aux cheveux, dans la rue
> Et dans le soir, tu m'es en riant apparue
> Et j'ai cru voir la fée au chapeau de clarté
> Qui jadis sur mes beaux sommeils d'enfant gâté
> Passait, laissant toujours de ses mains mal fermées
> Neiger de blancs bouquets d'étoiles parfumées. (v.10–16)

The evocation of the poetic voice's childhood in line 14 establishes an even wider gap between the words of the poem and a suspended vibration of meaning which recalls what Pearson describes as being able to 'remember' the past of words. The relationship between what passes and what remains is played out significantly at the beginning of the penultimate line of the poem through the juxtaposition of the verbs 'Passait, laissant'. That between 'Passait' and 'laissant' there is nothing more than a comma (and that the two words not only look but also sound similar in the reflected patterns of the [e] vowel and the double 's') establishes a tight rapport which is simultaneously challenged by the syntactic pull of each of the words. The interstice between what is past and what remains is one of both proximity and distance: the proximity is textual, the distance is semantic. The interstice between the memory of a word which has been murmured aloud and its presence on the page exploits both textual proximity and semantic distance, and this interstitial relationship is fundamental to Mallarmé's rhythmic sensation which suspends meaning and effaces words.

Poetic regularity is no longer able to validate human existence in Mallarmé's aesthetic. Being able to 'déchiffrer' what Mallarmé calls 'les purs motifs rythmiques de l'être' (II, p.294) offers a way of exploring the uncertainties, or suspensions, set in motion by the dissolution of regularity. A new sensation of language is elicited, providing a more profound validation for existence which is no longer governed by a spurious model of direct, regular language, but which instead thrives on the interstitial rhythmic pulls between the possibilities set in motion by a most irregular meaning.

Suggested Reading

Bowie, Malcolm, *Mallarmé and the Art of Being Difficult* (Cambridge: Cambridge University Press, 1978).

Evans, David, *Rhythm, Illusion and the Poetic Idea: Baudelaire, Rimbaud, Mallarmé* (Amsterdam and New York: Rodopi, 2004).

Marchal, Bertrand, *La Religion de Mallarmé* (Paris: Corti, 1988).

McCombie, Elizabeth, *Mallarmé and Debussy: Unheard Music, Unseen Text* (Oxford: Clarendon, 2003).
Meschonnic, Henri, *Critique du rythme* (Lagrasse: Verdier, 1982).
Pearson, Roger, *Mallarmé and Circumstance: The Translation of Silence* (Oxford: Oxford University Press, 2004).
—— *Unfolding Mallarmé* (Oxford: Clarendon, 1996).

MATTHIAS ZACH

Rhythms in Poetic Translation:
Bonnefoy and Shakespeare

Yves Bonnefoy is one of the most important French poets of the twentieth century (*Du mouvement et de l'immobilité de Douve* (1953), *Dans le leurre du seuil* (1975)[1] and the prose text *L'Arrière-pays* (1972)[2] are among his primary literary works). At the same time, Bonnefoy has written extensively on questions of poetry and poetics as well as the history of art; he has published a volume of Mallarmé's prose texts and has edited a dictionary on mythology. But most importantly, for present purposes, Bonnefoy is one of the most prolific translators of Shakespeare into French, a pursuit that goes back to the 1950s when he translated *Hamlet* as well as several other dramas and narrative poems for the new edition of Shakespeare's *Collected Works* in the *Club Français du livre*. Since then, the translation of Shakespeare has been a constant preoccupation for Bonnefoy. To date, he has translated all of Shakespeare's tragedies, several other plays and a selection of the *Sonnets*, which I will focus on at the end of this article.

Bonnefoy's poetics lends itself extremely well to an examination of the importance of rhythms in poetic translation. After having sketched Bonnefoy's poetics in its broad outlines, I will elaborate the notion of rhythm as presented by Henri Meschonnic and relate it to Bonnefoy's own approach to translation. This analysis of Bonnefoy's translation of Shakespeare's Sonnet 17 will then look at a particular example of how rhythms play a central role in poetic translation.

---

1   Along with other volumes of his poetry, *Du mouvement et de l'immobilité de Douve* and *Dans le leurre du seuil* are collected in Yves Bonnefoy's *Poèmes* (Paris: Gallimard, 1982).

2   Bonnefoy, *L'Arrière-pays* (Genève: Skira, 1972); republished in 2003 by Gallimard.

Aspects of Bonnefoy's poetics

Bonnefoy's poetry, and the concomitant developments in his prose
works and essays, attempt to transcend the limitations of ordinary
language (in this respect, he is firmly rooted in the Mallarméan tradition).[3] For Bonnefoy, language has an inevitable tendency to estrange
us from what he calls 'presence', that is from a complete appreciation
of our place in the world. According to Bonnefoy, the awareness of
'presence' would make us sensitive to our own 'finitude' but also to a
fundamental unity which links us to the world and the people around
us and which is responsible for our own unity as subjects. Ordinarily,
however, we are oblivious to this unity: for Bonnefoy, the reason for
this lack of awareness is language's capacity for conceptualisation and
abstraction. These features, he believes, make us overlook the individual, whether it is the individual person or object we encounter or
our own unique, finite existence.

Poetry, for Bonnefoy, is a means of resistance against abstraction
and conceptual thinking, but it is also at permanent risk of creating
mere images that only seem to bring us closer to reality whilst actually
estranging us from it. (As will become clear later on, this aspect of
Bonnefoy's poetics is particularly important in his translations of
Shakespeare's *Sonnets*). Conceived of and practised in the right way,
however, the poetic use of language helps us become newly aware of
the richness and the underlying unity of our existence. This is also
where rhythms come into play: the poetic use of language treats words
themselves as objects and pays precise attention to the material quali-

---

3   Bonnefoy develops his poetics in a great number of essays, which are collected
     in the following volumes, all published by Gallimard: *L'Improbable et autres
     essais* (1992), *Le Nuage rouge* (1999) and *La Vérité de parole* (1995). See also
     Bonnefoy, *Entretiens sur la poésie* (Paris: Mercure de France, 1990). For a
     critical introduction, see John E. Jackson, *Yves Bonnefoy* (Paris: Seghers, 2002).
     See also Jérôme Thélot, *Poétique d'Yves Bonnefoy* (Genève: Droz, 1983), and
     Michèle Finck, *Yves Bonnefoy: le simple et le sens* (Paris: Corti, 1989).

ties of words, such as sonorities and rhythms. Rhythms in a particular structure thereby perhaps validate our finite existence.[4]

In this article, I wish to read Bonnefoy's poetics together with Meschonnic's reflections on rhythm. Given Meschonnic's structuralist background and also the sometimes (characteristically) violent criticisms of Bonnefoy's translations in his *Poétique du traduire*,[5] it should be noted that there is not generally a close proximity between Meschonnic and Bonnefoy. However, Meschonnic's insistence on subjectivity and on the material qualities of language bear important analogies with Bonnefoy's poetics, and Meschonnic's approach provides useful methodological tools for the subsequent analysis of Bonnefoy's translation of Shakespeare's *Sonnets*.

Meschonnic: rhythm as individuality

Meschonnic's notion of rhythm is based on an article by the linguist Émile Benveniste, first published in 1951 and later included in his text *Problèmes de linguistique générale*. In the section entitled 'La notion de « rythme » dans son expression linguistique', Benveniste demonstrates how the original notion of rhythm goes back to pre-Socratic philosophy and how Plato has altered it profoundly. Having studied the use of the term 'rhythm' before Plato, Benveniste asserts:

---

4   'La poésie est recherche au cours de laquelle ce que les rythmes ont d'immédiat en nous, de spontané, nous aide à déchirer les représentations de nous-mêmes ou du monde que nos concepts nous proposaient, de façon toujours trop hâtive [...]' Bonnefoy, 'Traduire les sonnets de Shakespeare', in William Shakespeare, *Vingt-quatre sonnets*, trans. Yves Bonnefoy (Losne: T. Bouchard & Y. Prié, 1995), p.57.

5   Henri Meschonnic, *Poétique du traduire* (Lagrasse: Verdier, 1999). See pp.236–239 in particular.

> Il n'y a [...] aucune variation, aucune ambiguïté dans la signification que Démocrite assigne à ρυθμός,[6] et qui est toujours « forme », en entendant par là la forme distinctive, l'arrangement caractéristique des parties dans un tout.[7]

Taken in the sense of 'distinctive form', the notion of rhythm is closely linked to that of individuality. Importantly, the distinctive form of which Benveniste writes, is understood not in the sense of a stable essence, but as the shape of a given instant. It becomes the momentary form of an entity that is in constant change and movement:

> ρυθμός, d'après les contextes où il est donné, désigne la forme dans l'instant qu'elle est assumée par ce qui est mouvant, mobile, fluide, la forme de ce qui n'a pas de consistance organique [...]. C'est la forme improvisée, momentanée, modifiable.[8]

This notion of rhythm as something individual, momentary and unstable is taken up by Meschonnic. Again however, according to Benveniste, the notion of rhythm has already been altered profoundly by Plato, a transformation that has been of great importance for the later history of the concept. Benveniste argues that, in Platonic philosophy, the notion of rhythm is confounded with that of *metre*:

> Platon emploie encore ρυθμός au sens de « forme distinctive, disposition, proportion ». Il innove en l'appliquant à la *forme du mouvement* que le corps humain accomplit dans la danse, et à la disposition des figures en lesquelles ce mouvement se résout. La circonstance décisive est là, dans la notion d'un ρυθμός corporel associé au μέτρον et soumis à la loi des nombres: *cette « forme » est désormais déterminée par une « mesure » et assujettie à un ordre.* [...] *La notion de rythme est fixée.*[9]

In other words, beginning with Plato, the notion of rhythm moves away from that of an individual form towards an objective, pre-established order that is imposed upon the individual. If we were to translate this into Bonnefoy's terms, we could say that the Platonic

6   Rhythm.
7   Émile Benveniste, 'La notion de « rythme » dans son expression linguistique', in *Problèmes de linguistique générale*, 2 vols (Paris: Gallimard, 1969–74), Vol 1, pp.327–335 (p.330).
8   Ibid., p.333.
9   Ibid., p.334; emphases added.

notion of rhythm as a fixed order is analogous to the tendency toward abstraction inherent in language, whereas the original notion of rhythm as an individual form is very close to what Bonnefoy seeks in genuine poetic expression.

The analogy becomes even more striking when we take into account the further development of this notion in several of Meschonnic's writings, since Meschonnic defines rhythm as the inscription of the subject in discourse. Meschonnic, translator of the Bible and author of several works on the theory of translation, has also written extensively on questions of rhythm.[10] Meschonnic's reflections are summarised in *Traité du rythme*, published in 1998 and written in cooperation with his colleague Gérard Dessons. Referring to the definition of rhythm before Plato, the authors argue this notion:

> convient spécifiquement au langage, envisagé comme *discours*, non comme *langue*. Discours, c'est-à-dire inscription de celui et de celle qui s'énonce, en parlant ou en écrivant. Car le discours est l'organisation de ce qui est en mouvement dans le langage. On peut alors redéfinir *le rythme dans le langage comme l'organisation du mouvement de la parole*, « parole » au sens de Saussure, d'activité individuelle, écrite autant qu'orale.[11]

From this double reference to Saussure and Benveniste, Meschonnic and Dessons derive the close link between rhythm and subject:

> Le rythme est l'organisation du mouvement de la parole par un sujet [...][12]

> le rythme [...] apparaît comme une organisation, spécifique à chaque art et particulière au langage, du sujet tout entier comme historicité: une forme sujet.[13]

---

10   See in particular Meschonnic, *Critique du rythme: anthropologie historique du langage* (Lagrasse: Verdier, 1982) and *Politique du rythme: politique du sujet* (Lagrasse: Verdier, 1995).

11   Gérard Dessons and Henri Meschonnic, *Traité du rythme: des vers et des proses* (Paris: Dunod, 1998), p.26; original emphasis.

12   Ibid., p.28.

13   Ibid., p.56.

Hence, far from being synonymous, metre and rhythm here become opposites: metre is an external restriction, whereas rhythm is the individual, subjective design of an utterance. In a metric text, then, rhythm is to be understood as the modification of metre through individual accentuations and through the use of the words' material qualities (of sound repetitions in particular) as a structural device. Rhythm thus creates individual arrangements that run counter to the rigidity of the metric pattern.

The idea of rhythm as the inscription of the subject in discourse is then applied to literary translation, which, for Meschonnic, becomes the art of responding to the original rhythm in the translated text. Meschonnic both sums up his definition of rhythm and states its application to literary translation in his *Poétique du traduire*:

> Je ne prends plus le rythme comme une alternance formelle du même et du différent, des temps forts et des temps faibles. À la suite de Benveniste, qui [...] a montré [...] que le rythme était [...] l'organisation du mouvant, je prends le rythme comme l'organisation et la démarche même du sens dans le discours. *C'est-à-dire l'organisation (de la prosodie à l'intonation) de la subjectivité et de la spécificité d'un discours: son historicité.* Non plus un opposé du sens, mais la signifiance généralisée d'un discours. Ce qui s'impose immédiatement comme l'objectif de la traduction. *L'objectif de la traduction n'est plus le sens, mais bien plus que le sens, et qui l'inclut: le mode de signifier.*[14]

For Meschonnic, translation has to try and recreate what he calls *signifiance* or the *mode de signifier*. Rhythm thus constitutes the very centre of the translator's enterprise, while the creation of the translator's own rhythm represents the aim of poetic translation. If translation is the 're-énonciation spécifique d'un sujet historique', as Meschonnic had already argued in *Pour la poétique II*,[15] it is in the translator's rhythm that this 're-énonciation' takes place.

---

14 Meschonnic, *Poétique du traduire*, p.99; emphases added.
15 Meschonnic, *Pour la poétique II* (Paris: Gallimard, 1973), p.307.

Bonnefoy on translation: a dialogue between authors

In various ways, Bonnefoy's approach to literary translation generally complements Meschonnic's ideas on rhythm and on the role of rhythms in translation in particular. One important aspect of Bonnefoy's poetics that may be linked to Meschonnic's idea of rhythm as an inscription of the subject in discourse is that Bonnefoy always conceives of translation as a dialogue with another author, and with another poet in particular (for even when he translates Shakespeare's dramatic texts, he regards the author first and foremost as a poet). In the foreword of *La Communauté des traducteurs*, Bonnefoy refers to 'les traducteurs authentiques' and asserts:

> Ceux-là, et parmi eux les poètes, quel sera, en pratique, leur rapport aux textes qu'ils admirent, ou disons plutôt qu'ils aiment, *car c'est alors dans ces pages la présence d'un être qu'ils perçoivent*, une présence comme éveillée, à nouveau active, et appréhendée par eux d'une façon parfois même plus délicate et profonde que l'idée que cet écrivain avait eue de soi?[16]

Translating poetry constitutes a dialogue with another author, whose subjectivity has been inscribed in the original text and which can therefore be adopted by the translator, especially by a poet-translator like Bonnefoy. For the translator, this is a way of enriching and transforming himself, a transformation that finds its expression in the rhythms he himself uses both in his translation and in his own poetry. In his afterword to the translation of Shakespeare's *Sonnets*, Bonnefoy speaks of his own 'parole qui veut en revivre une autre – en revivre le sens, mais aussi la naissance libre.'[17] The translator 'relives' the rhythm of the original and, by transforming the initial rhythm into his own, gives it a different expression. At the same time, the original rhythm also transforms the distinctive form of the *poète-traducteur*.[18]

---

16   Bonnefoy, 'Avant-propos', *La Communauté des traducteurs* (Strasbourg: Presses Universitaires de Strasbourg, 2000), p. 9 ; emphasis added.
17   Bonnefoy, 'Traduire les sonnets de Shakespeare', p.59.
18   Although here I can only focus on a particular example from Bonnefoy's translation of Shakespeare's *Sonnets*, it is clear that a more complete examination of

In addition, Bonnefoy also frequently reflects upon the difference between the languages involved in translation, especially the difference between French and English. In particular, Bonnefoy often speaks about the supposed concreteness of English in opposition to the supposed abstractness of French – a point that is of course related to Bonnefoy's general view of poetry as a permanent struggle against abstraction. Also, Bonnefoy comments on the well-known prosodic differences between French and English: English poetry, based on stressed and unstressed syllables, is in contrast to French poetry, which is based on the number of syllables in a line.[19] For Bonnefoy, the difference in prosody between the two languages, and the role of word accents in English in particular, make for the fact that English is much better suited to express the passage of time as well as human finitude (a fundamental notion in Bonnefoy's poetics, as indicated above).[20]

Bonnefoy's dialogue with Shakespeare's *Sonnets*

It is with this idea of the passage of time as a central feature of Bonnefoy's interest in Shakespeare that I now want to turn to his translations of Shakespeare's *Sonnets*. Through the creation of rhythms, poetry structures the passage of time and, in accordance with his

the role of rhythms in poetic translation would also take into account the literary work of the poet-translator himself. Bonnefoy often points out the role of Shakespeare translation for his own work: for example, he asserts that 'l'expérience du pentamètre anglais [l]'a certainement aidé à [s]e déplacer dans [s]a propre pratique prosodique.' See Bonnefoy, 'Shakespeare sur scène', *La communauté des traducteurs*, p.114.

19   Because of the group accent in French, Meschonnic refers to French prosody as 'une prosodie syllabo-accentuelle'. See Meschonnic, *Traité du rythme*, p.24.

20   In a recent interview, Bonnefoy states: 'It's in the current that passes from the lure of timelessness to the experience of finitude that I want to follow Shakespeare.' John Naughton, 'Interview with Yves Bonnefoy', in Bonnefoy, *Shakespeare & the French poet*, ed. and trans. John Naughton (Chicago: University of Chicago, 2004), pp.257–269 (p.264).

interest for this theme in Shakespeare, Bonnefoy's translations often highlight this link between the passage of time and the creation of poetry. One of the ways in which Bonnefoy enhances the reflexive nature of these sonnets is by introducing references to poetry even in places where these references are not necessarily present in the original, or only at an implicit level. Take, for example, the following lines from Sonnet 5:

> For never-resting time leads summer on
> To hideous winter and confounds him there.[21]

Bonnefoy both stays quite close to the original and introduces an allusion to poetry by using the preposition 'vers' in his translation. Through homophony, Bonnefoy also refers to poetry which is highlighted, as in the original, by the enjambement and its position at the beginning of a line:

> Car sans repos le temps mène l'été
> Vers l'hiver haïssable et là le tue.[22]

The same use of homophony can be noted at the end of Sonnet 6:

> Be not self-willed for thou art much too fair
> To be death's conquest and make worms thine heir.[23]

This is translated as:

> Ne sois pas obstiné, tu es trop beau
> Pour être la conquête de la mort
> Et n'avoir d'héritier que le ver immonde.[24]

21   Shakespeare, *Vingt-quatre sonnets*, p.16.
22   Ibid., p.17.
23   Ibid., p.18.
24   Ibid., p.19.

Through his translation, and through the homophony, in which 'ver immonde' may be heard as talking either about worms or about verse or poetry, Bonnefoy renders more explicit than the original the close link between the passage of time and the decay of created being on the one hand and the creation of poetry on the other. The expression 'ver immonde' (and the association with 'vers immonde') also points to Bonnefoy's belief that poetry is always in danger of becoming disconnected from reality, of becoming a mere image. However, these features of Bonnefoy's translation are situated more at the level of meaning than at the level of rhythm (or, in Meschonnic's terminology, at the level of *sens* and not the level of *signifiance*). It is therefore important to examine a translation of an entire sonnet and analyse what Bonnefoy's translation attempts to do on a rhythmic level.

In the original, the most important texts highlighting the link between time and poetry are sonnets 17 to 19. Here, the request to produce offspring and the role of the poet's creations in preserving youth are both addressed explicitly, with varying emphasis either on the destructive action of time or on the potential remedy constituted by poetry. In this final section, I want to look briefly at Sonnet 17, the conclusion of which would seem to be more pessimistic than those of the following two sonnets and which therefore corresponds well to the precarious situation of poetry as Bonnefoy understands it. In the version printed in Bonnefoy's *Vingt-quatre sonnets*, Shakespeare's Sonnet 17 reads as follows:

> Who will believe my verse in time to come
> If it were filled with your most high deserts?
> Though yet heaven knows it is but as a tomb
> Which hides your life, and shows not half your parts;
> If I could write the beauty of your eyes,
> And in fresh numbers number all your graces,
> The age to come would say this poet lies,
> Such heavenly touches ne'er touched earthly faces.
> So should my papers (yellowed with their age)
> Be scorned, like old men of less truth than tongue,
> And your true rights be termed a poet's rage,
> And stretched metre of an antique song.

But were some child of yours alive that time,
You should live twice[:]^{25} in it, and in my rhyme.[26]

According to Meschonnic's approach developed above, the sonnet's distinctive form, and thus its rhythm, is constituted by the
specific way in which the iambic pentameter is modified, rendering an
individual sequence of stressed and unstressed syllables. But the
sonnet's form is also created by the interplay of alliterations and
assonances, by the rhymes, by the punctuation and, of course, by the
semantic factors (although those cannot be clearly separated from the
other aspects – the point of Meschonnic's notion of *signifiance* is
precisely to transcend the traditional distinction between meaning and
form). The combination of all these features produces places of higher
and lower rhythmic density (that is, passages with particularly many,
or few, accentuated syllables and sound repetitions). These features
constitute the translator's starting point.

In Sonnet 17, there are passages of particular rhythmic intensity:
in lines 5 to 8, 10 to 11 and also in the final line. Lines 5 to 8 are
highlighted first through metric irregularities – lines 5 and 6 both
comprise three successive unstressed syllables ('beau<u>ty of your</u>' and,
in the following line, 'num<u>ber all your</u>'), whereas there are three
successive stressed syllables in the two following lines ('<u>say this</u>
<u>po</u>et', '<u>ne'er touched earth</u>ly'). There are also alliterations on [n] (in –
numbers number), [t] (to – poet – touches touched) and [th] (The –
this). There is an assonance in 'heaven' and 'earthly' and, perhaps
most importantly, the etymological figures which combine a noun and
a verb form that share the same root: 'in fresh numbers number' and
'touches ne'er touched'. Lines 10 and 11 also display a heightened
rhythmic intensity. In line 10, there is twice the succession of two
stressed syllables, in 'old men' and in 'less truth'. Line 11 displays
three successive stresses ('your true rights') as well as a number of
alliterations, on [d], [l], [n], [t], and [th]. Finally, the last line is
emphasised by the fact that there are three stresses in the first four

25   Modern critical editions have a colon at this point, unlike the text printed in the
     bilingual edition of Bonnefoy's translations. Bonnefoy's translation indicates,
     however, that he reads this passage as if there were a colon.
26   William Shakespeare, *Vingt-quatre sonnets*, p.40.

syllables: 'You should live twice,' is marked by the assonances on [u], [i] and [ai].

As noted above, these passages of particular rhythmic interest are a starting point for appreciating Bonnefoy's translation of Sonnet 17. The question that may be asked from a Meschonnician point of view is how Bonnefoy responds to the rhythm of the original sonnet and how his dialogue with Shakespeare features in the creation of his own rhythm. Let us now examine Bonnefoy's translation.

> Qui croirait mes poèmes, dans l'avenir,
> Si je les emplissais de ta valeur?
> Et pourtant le ciel sait qu'ils ne sont que la tombe
> Qui cèle avec ta vie tes plus grands mérites.
>
> Eussé-je su montrer la splendeur de tes yeux
> Et en des nombres neufs dénombrer tes grâces,
> Les siècles à venir: « Ce poète ment »,
> S'écrieraient-ils, « tant de ciel n'a jamais
> Touché de doigts si clairs face terrestre ».
>
> Et mes écrits, tout jaunis par le temps,
> En seraient méprisés: des vieillards, du verbiage,
> Mais pas de vérité! Ton portrait le plus juste,
> On le tiendrait pour rêve de poète
> Dans le boursouflement des vieilles rhétoriques.
>
> Mais que ta descendance vive encore
> Et tu vivrais deux fois: en elle et dans mes vers.[27]

An immediately obvious aspect of Bonnefoy's translation is that, in a way, he has given up on the sonnet form: his translation of Sonnet 17 has sixteen lines. His translations of the sonnets never possess fourteen lines, but are always between sixteen and eighteen lines. As a consequence, there is a clear discrepancy between the original and the translation in terms of 'visual rhythm': Bonnefoy keeps the overall form of the original only in the broadest sense and reshapes it within the general framework. This is a clear example of how he gives his own distinctive form to his translation and thus expresses his individuality in his dialogue with Shakespeare. As the sonnet form

27   Ibid., p.41.

appears to impose fourteen lines upon the translator, Bonnefoy asserts his own vision in a translation which has sixteen lines.[28]

As for the translation itself, in lines 3 and 4, Bonnefoy intensifies the original statement concerning the link between time and poetry by omitting the original comparison again. Shakespeare writes that the poet's verse 'is but *as* a tomb / Which hides your life, and shows not half your parts', whereas, in Bonnefoy's translation, the 'poèmes', in the plural, 'ne sont que la tombe / Qui cèle avec ta vie tes plus grands mérites'. Poetry is not *like* the tomb, it actually *becomes* or *is* the tomb. Thus, the danger of a kind of poetry devoid of reality and truth is expressed with even more urgency.

Bonnefoy's translation reproduces certain passages of heightened rhythmic intensity in the original, but, as with the 'visual rhythm' referred to above, there are paramount transformations. The second stanza is marked through versification: while the first quatrain consists of two regular 'decasyllables' and two regular 'alexandrine' lines, the second stanza contains the first line in this text with an uneven number of syllables, since line 6 in the translation is an eleven-syllable line, corresponding precisely to the passage in the original (which refers to 'fresh numbers' and which Bonnefoy translates as 'en des nombres neufs dénombrer'). There are two more eleven-syllable lines in this stanza. This acts, perhaps, as a self-conscious reference both to the history of French versification, in which uneven lines constitute a deviation from the norm of the 'alexandrine' line in particular, and to Bonnefoy's own poetry, which is, for the most part, in free verse. In line 6, in contrast with his translation of line 8, he also keeps the etymological figure present in the original ('nombres – dénombrer'), and he intensifies the original alliteration by translating the adjective 'fresh' by 'neufs'. Bonnefoy's translation of the second quatrain is further characterised by a number of changes in punctuation, since he introduces a colon as well as quotation marks so as to render explicit the direct speech that is implicit in the original.

---

28 This raises the question of how well the translation 'works' from a poetic point of view: it might be argued, for example, that by giving up on fourteen lines, Bonnefoy also loses some of the density of the Shakespearean text.

Bonnefoy also puts great emphasis on his translation of the original poem's 'like old men of less truth than tongue'. Again, he changes the punctuation and introduces a colon. He then emphasises the original by distributing this phrase over two lines and by drawing the parallel between 'des vieillards, du verbiage' and 'pas de vérité'. This parallel is underlined by a number of alliterations and assonances, all the more so as another assonance is superimposed on them, namely the assonance on [é] and [i] that links, in lines 10, 11 and 12, 'Et mes écrits', 'méprisés' and 'vérité' (the assonance also echoes the phrase 'tes plus grands mérites' from line 4). Whilst reproducing the rhythmic intensity of the original, Bonnefoy also makes several adjustments of his own. For example, the change of punctuation that has just been evoked or the translation of the expression 'poet's rage', the traditional *furor poeticus*, by 'rêve de poète', where the term 'rêve' points to the great importance that dreams have within Bonnefoy's own poetics.[29]

In Bonnefoy's translation, the third stanza is the passage of greatest rhythmic intensity. Compared to this rhythmic and semantic knot, his insistence on the final line is less strong than in the original, even if the marks of rhythm are apparent – in particular the alliterations on [d] and [v] and the introduction of a colon.[30] Nonetheless, the last line of his translation, a regular alexandrine, is less marked than Shakespeare's final line with its succession of a whole number of stressed syllables. In doing so, Bonnefoy displaces the rhythmic centre of the text and underscores a part of the sonnet which represents most immediately his own poetic concerns – namely, the danger of poetry becoming a mere image and rhetoric wordplay, another issue which constitutes a central feature of Bonnefoy's own poetics. Significantly, and in confirmation of Meschonnic's approach to rhythm in poetic translation developed above, this expression of the poet-translator's

---

29   Cf. Bonnefoy, *Récits en rêve: L'Arrière-pays; Rue Traversière; Remarques sur la couleur; L'Origine de la parole* (Paris: Mercure de France, 1987), and John E. Jackson, *La Souche obscure des rêves: la dialectique de l'écriture chez Yves Bonnefoy* (Paris: Mercure de France, 1993).

30   This colon is present in some editions of the original sonnet as well, but absent from the edition Bonnefoy worked with for his translation.

own individuality is situated not at the level of meaning but at the level of rhythm.

In conclusion, Bonnefoy thus reproduces the rhythm of the original in the majority of places, but he also carries out a significant number of rhythmic transformations, both at the level of the sonnet's overall form and at the micro-level of the text's rhythmic features. These transformations should not be viewed as the inevitable result of a supposed difference between the English and the French languages, nor should they be regarded as flaws in Bonnefoy's translation. On the contrary, it is precisely in these transformations that the inscription of Bonnefoy's own rhythm, and thus of his own poetic project, takes place. For Bonnefoy, poetry and poetic translation are consequently two aspects of the same activity. In general, rhythm in poetic translation is simultaneously a dialogue and a creative process. It is because of the inventive and transformative quality inherent in rhythm that poetic translation must be considered as poetry in its own right.

Suggested Reading

Benveniste, Émile, 'La notion de « rythme » dans son expression linguistique', in *Problèmes de linguistique générale*, 2 vols (Paris: Gallimard, 1969–74), Vol 1, pp.327–335.

Bonnefoy, Yves, *La Communauté des traducteurs* (Strasbourg: Presses Universitaires de Strasbourg, 2000).

—— *Théâtre et poésie: Shakespeare et Yeats* (Paris: Mercure de France, 1998).

Dessons, Gérard and Henri Meschonnic, *Traité du rythme: des vers et des proses* (Paris: Dunod, 1998).

Meschonnic, Henri, *Critique du rythme: anthropologie historique du langage* (Paris: Verdier, 1982).

—— *Poétique du traduire* (Paris: Verdier, 1999).

—— *Politique du rythme, politique du sujet* (Paris: Verdier, 1995).

—— *Pour la poétique II* (Paris: Gallimard, 1973).

Shakespeare, William, *Vingt-quatre sonnets*, trans. Yves Bonnefoy (Losne: Bouchard & Prié, 1995).

ARIANE KOSSACK

Between Poetry and Philology: Rhythms of the Orphic Myth in Mallarmé's Aesthetics

Rhythm stems from the Greek word *rhythmos*, which is derived from the verb *rheein*, 'to flow'. Indeed, in its pre-Socratic origins, rhythm is the spontaneous, modifiable materialisation of a shape out of a flow, a pattern of improvisation accomplished by all living organisms; it is an organic, unbridled and continuously flowing manifestation of the natural world. Plato's essentialist approach, however, seeks to order this fluid notion of rhythm by exploring continuous activities, such as walking, which can be mechanically broken down into elementary units, beats or steps that are subject to physical laws and ordered according to a strict timing or metre, as in a military march. Still, the fundamentally vague and flexible nature of rhythm raises the overarching problem of its definition. How do we truly identify the different forms of rhythm in music, dance, poetry or any other mode of (non-)artistic expression without falling into lengthy analyses of musical tempo, kinetic intensity or poetic feet?

Ancient thinkers tended to distinguish between rhythm and metre: rhythm was musical and applied to the motion of bodies, whereas metre belonged to the domain of words and was consequently found in poetry. Today, however, we readily accept that rhythm is intrinsic to the life of poetry. It is responsible for infusing poetic writing with a particular current that bears the unmistakable quality of music, giving it a sense of regularity, flow and movement. This essay will not attempt to write a historico-philosophical analysis of the concept of rhythm, nor will it directly explore the rich, exciting and innovative nuances of rhythm in particular developments of nineteenth-century French poetry.[1] Instead, we address the relations between the time-based arts of music and poetry in the work of Stéphane Mallarmé (1842–1898), relations as fertile and fascinating, as they are complex and elusive.[2]

One way of understanding the relationship between the sister arts of poetry and music, at least on a symbolic level, is to trace how Mallarmé makes recourse to Orpheus, the ancient mythical bard and quasi-patron saint of song and music. The Orphic journey to the purgatorio-space of the netherworld becomes, for him, a mythopoetic screen onto which to expose the mechanisms, processes and rhythms of the creative act. Mallarmé is, of course, not alone: a host of poets, writers, composers, visual artists and filmmakers have reached to the theme of Orpheus as a powerful instrument of the imagination for accessing valuable insights concerning the creative self as well as the artistic encounter. Orpheus' search for, and recovery of, lost song enacts the non-militaristic rite of passage of the poetic hero. In other words, a poet is not a poet if he does not brave the catabatic mission to the dystopic arena of Hades. The rhythmic vertical movement of 'descent and return'[3] intrinsic to the *katabasis* is a prototypical pattern of epic convention dictated by key literary visits to the underworld in the *Odyssey*, the *Aeneid* or the *Divine Comedy*, as well as in popular accounts of archetypal journeys into the bowels of the Earth by Jules Verne or even J.R.R. Tolkien. After briefly introducing the theme of Orpheus and highlighting its key hallmarks, I will turn directly to an analysis of two different rhythms or guises borne by the Orphic motif in Mallarmé's aesthetic thought – the one strictly poetological and the other more philological.

1   On rhythm in nineteenth-century French poetry, see David Evans, *Rhythm, Illusion and the Poetic Idea: Baudelaire, Rimbaud, Mallarmé* (Amsterdam and New York: Rodopi, 2004).

2   An excellent recent publication in the field of French word and music studies is Peter Dayan's *Music Writing Literature, from Sand via Debussy to Derrida* (Aldershot: Ashgate, 2006).

3   Walter A. Strauss views the Orphic theme as a simple vertical movement of 'descent and return'. Cf. Walter A. Strauss, *Descent and Return: The Orphic Theme in Modern Literature* (Cambridge, Mass.: Harvard University Press, 1971).

Orpheus introduced

The myth of Orpheus, best known through Latin accounts by Ovid (*Metamorphoses* X, XI) or Virgil (*Georgics* IV), is the foundational myth of the artist, narrating his suffering as well as his success. The Orphic theme concerns the drama of creativity, the enabling and disabling consequences of the artistic task, so that Orpheus himself is the predecessor of the modern self-conscious poet who, aware of classical tradition, must find his own distinctive voice through the stress and pain of his personal trajectory. Orpheus' role as the magical creator of a potent, all-transforming music enables him to defy the laws of nature and to overcome death by venturing where mortals cannot tread. The exquisite harmonies of his lyre charm the guardians of the underworld, softening the hearts of Hades and Persephone and lulling the three-headed Cerberus to sleep; in the Argonautic expedition, Orpheus' lyre drowns the fatal song of the Sirens. By controlling nature, both animate and inanimate, Orpheus is able to enchant, transform and civilise the world anew. He tames wild beasts, entices the stones, trees, plants and mountains into dance and arrests the rivers in their course. Orpheus, indeed, embodies art and all creative activity, encouraging harmony and order in the world.

However, as the Orphic mission shows, the possibility of true, triumphant music is the product of an urgent crisis, a limit-situation and a catastrophic confrontation with the absolute and the extreme. The premise of Orpheus' descent is that of the loss and bereavement of his poetic ideal, Eurydice, the muse and *raison d'être* of his song. This generates a calamity or a horrific confrontation with the absolute in the form of Death, both the death of his bride and the 'death' or breakdown of his artistic work. In 'Le Regard d'Orphée', Maurice Blanchot writes:

> c'est vers Eurydice qu'Orphée est descendu: Eurydice est, pour lui, l'extrême que l'art puisse atteindre, elle est, sous un nom qui la dissimule et sous un voile

qui la couvre, le point profondément obscur vers lequel l'art, le désir, la mort, la nuit semblent tendre.[4]

Hades may represent an absolute area of the extreme but, for Orpheus, the passing mortal intruder, it is a liminal site of ambiguity, a grey area where hesitation, negotiation, impatience and aporia prevail. It is a shady casino where he is prone to win or lose everything he has, if he does not strike a balance between control and desire, between self-awareness and loss of self. The Orpheus motif is, then, emblematic of the risk-filled creative process, as the poet's descent into the under-world (of his subconscious) represents the quest to bring back what is most important to him, lending it new life through art. The point of the story, however, is that this process should be driven by emotion and instinct, and should not be rational. If the artist looks too closely or obsessively at the object of his pursuit, if he submits it to excessive analysis and critical scrutiny, then he will lose precisely what he is searching for. Of course, near the rim of Hades, Orpheus tragically requires visual proof of the object of his love and must forfeit all that he desires.

The second part of the Orphic mission is the sublimation of the poet's loss, which can only be granted by further creative action, reha-bilitating the full potential and economy of Orphic song. For this, the artist must embark on the ascent, alone, back to the upper world where, as the myth recounts, he remains true to his poetic ideal (Eury-dice), singing endless laments on his rambles through the Thracian countryside. Orpheus continues to enchant the world by spreading his sublime music even beyond his brutal death, the *sparagmos* or dis-memberment, at the hands of the raging Maenads in their Dionysian orgies. His head and lyre, thrown down the river Hebros, refuse to subside in their plaintive song, finally moving the Muses to place his instrument amongst the stars where it can be seen today, at the outer edge of the Milky Way, as the harp-shaped constellation Lyra.

The Orpheus theme is a way of addressing key issues of con-sciousness, identity and self-knowledge (both on behalf of the poet and of the poetic enterprise at large), so that Orphic *Weltanschauung*

4   Maurice Blanchot, *L'Espace littéraire* (Paris: Gallimard, 1955), p.179.

becomes a form of quasi-Narcissistic *Selbstanschauung*. At the outset of his mission, as noted above, the poet is in search of lost inspiration and song – in search of Eurydice. On the one hand, she represents the precarious source and wellspring, within the poet, of inspiration and creativity, of that which activates and edifies his artistic production. Blanchot reads Orpheus' prohibited glance at Eurydice, the moment in which desire betrays or violates lawfulness, as the stroke of inspiration itself: 'Regarder Eurydice, sans souci du chant, dans l'impatience et l'imprudence du désir qui oublie la loi, c'est cela même, l'*inspiration*'.[5] On the other hand, Eurydice, abstracted, is the other half of the poetic self. She corresponds to the poet's creative feminine side, incessantly wound up in a self-perpetuating process of doubt and certainty, dying and reviving, loss and triumph. If fluid identity boundaries allow for moments of transcendence, then Eurydice may be, in Jungian terms, the image of his 'anima' (that is, the female aspect present in the male psyche). As a result, the impatient look back at Eurydice is simultaneously a solipsistic move *into* the creative self so that the glance stands for the self-reflexive act of artistic consciousness itself.

Finally, the myth of Orpheus and Eurydice demonstrates the rhythm of what Julia Kristeva, in *La Révolution du langage poétique*, calls the 'thetic break' or the moment when the separation between self and other gives rise to symbolic as opposed to semiotic language.[6] The semiotic drive, associated with rhythm and tone, is the element of meaning in signification that does not signify, whereas the symbolic, preconditioned by the semiotic yet associated with syntax, grammar and the assumption of an enunciatory position, does signify. In artistic practices, as Kristeva argues, the semiotic is effectively that which destroys symbolic discourse, but the relationship between the two is a dialectic oscillation which produces the speaking subject and leads to the thetic break, a limit point at which the subject receives an identification and a perspective. The splitting of the subject and the object,

5   Blanchot, *L'Espace littéraire*, p.182; original emphasis.
6   Julia Kristeva, *La Révolution du langage poétique: l'avant-garde à la fin du XIXe siècle, Lautréamont et Mallarmé* (Paris: Seuil, 1974).

of Orpheus and Eurydice, is, then, the moment that brings about language, enunciation and narrative.

In view of the crisis and catastrophe of the netherworld, the Orpheus theme thus enacts how artistic language is produced – produced, one might add, 'in dürftiger Zeit'. It seems to answer Hölderlin's enquiry in the affirmative,[7] relating how and why the modern poet is compelled to narrate and sing his painful story, moving onwards and upwards after his traumatic sojourn in Hades. He must start his poetic trajectory anew after the ultimately solipsistic act of encountering and overcoming the crisis at the heart of his artistic medium and, at the same time, within himself. Indeed, Orpheus stands as a mythical reminder that the artist should not relinquish his craft, even in the face of darkness, crisis and despair.

'Creuser le vers'

On 16 November 1885, Mallarmé pens a now famous letter to Paul Verlaine, friend and fellow poet, in which he articulates his ambitious vision of writing the book of all books, a literary utopia addressed as 'le Livre' or 'le Grand Œuvre'. Just after defining this meticulously planned *magnum opus*, 'un livre, architectural et prémédité',[8] Mallarmé's epistolary account gives what is perhaps the poet's most significant allusion to the Orpheus myth, testifying that the Orphic theme is *in nuce* that which informs his poetic project: 'L'explication orphique de la Terre [...] est le seul devoir du poëte et le jeu littéraire par excellence [...]' (*OC*, p.663). Mallarmé uses the adjective 'orphique' to refer to the aesthetic enterprise as well as to the social duty of the poet; for him, it is only the Symbolist work of literature that can

---

7   Cf. 'und wozu Dichter in dürftiger Zeit?' in Friedrich Hölderlin's elegy, 'Brod und Wein' (1800/01).

8   Stéphane Mallarmé, *Œuvres complètes*, ed. H. Mondor and G. Jean-Aubry (Paris: Gallimard, Bibliothèque de la Pléiade, 1945), p.663. Henceforth abbreviated in the text as *OC*.

decipher the manifold transcendental mysteries of the universe. Orpheus was, of course, also closely connected with religious or (spi)-ritual life, founding important cults (those of Apollo *and* Dionysus) and instituting mystic rites and rituals of initiation and purification. Thus, Mallarmé's Orphic reference not only bears poetological but also mystical implications. Aesthetic and spiritual concerns easily marry in his famous definition of Poetry as the human expression of a primal or 'essential rhythm':

> La Poésie est l'expression, par le langage humain ramené à son rythme essentiel, du sens mystérieux des aspects de l'existence: elle doue ainsi d'authenticité notre séjour et constitue la seule tâche spirituelle.[9]

These confident statements stem from the mid-1880s, a time when the poet had, as we know, finally established himself aesthetically. However, to understand the full implications of the above quotations, we are compelled, like Orpheus, to retrace our steps and to consider Mallarmé's aesthetic musing during his 'Crise de Tournon', a meta-physical-spiritual crisis experienced most profoundly during 1866–67, traumatic months of existential stress, agony, exhaustion and insomnia (aggravated, perhaps, by an exposure to Hegelian thought), in which the troubled poet apprehended a possible onset of spiritual and literary sterility. Feeling as if he were losing touch with the phenomenological world, he still, however, adhered to the idea of poetry as a means of clinging onto a fading reality.

It is not gratuitous that Mallarmé articulates his crisis as a so-called 'descente aux enfers', both as the catabatic descent into the deepest recesses of the psyche and as the plunge into a linguistic inferno. Doubts were harboured as to the capacity of language, in its denotative nature, to penetrate beyond reality and express the world of Platonic Ideas. As testified in the letter below, written to Henri Cazalis on 28 April 1866 at the acme of his aesthetic depression, Mallarmé describes his poietic assignment using the phrase 'creuser le vers'. Authentic literary practice implies a preoccupation with the matter and

---

9 Stéphane Mallarmé, *Correspondance* vol. II, 1871–1885, ed. H. Mondor and L.J. Austin (Paris: Gallimard, 1965), p.266.

meaning of language, a process of digging, drilling, ploughing and obsessively mining its site in search of the adequate expression of the Ideal. And what are the fruits of his excruciating search? A sort of *horror vacui*:

> Malheureusement, en creusant le vers à ce point, j'ai rencontré deux abîmes, qui me désespèrent. L'un est le Néant, auquel je suis arrivé sans connaître le Bouddhisme, et je suis encore trop désolé pour pouvoir croire même à ma poésie et me remettre au travail, que cette pensée écrasante m'a fait abandonner.[10]

In July 1866, three months after this letter, Mallarmé is able to write to Cazalis again, intimating more optimistically that the worst perhaps now lies behind him. In this letter, the poet reports his findings post-Nothingness, namely, Beauty:

> En vérité, je voyage, mais dans des pays inconnus et si, pour fuir la réalité torride, je me plais à évoquer des images froides, je te dirai que je suis depuis un mois dans les plus purs glaciers de l'Esthétique – qu'après avoir trouvé le *Néant*, j'ai trouvé le *Beau* – et que tu ne peux t'imaginer dans quelles altitudes lucides je m'aventure.[11]

Throughout his Tournon-turmoil, Mallarmé uses a wintry, icy and glacial terminology to illustrate his cerebral aesthetic ventures, solitary forays conceived as an ascent or expedition into luminous, pure and lucid 'altitudinal' regions. However, the dictum 'après avoir trouvé le *Néant*, j'ai trouvé le *Beau*' mirrors the traditional vertical pattern of Orpheus' catabatic descent – only, the lofty aesthetic altitudes are *mutatis mutandis* inverted or negated. The Orphic singer travels to a counter-world (Hades) where he is confronted with fears of the absolute (death or Nothingness) and where he must heroically recapture the purpose of his song (Eurydice or Beauty). Mallarmé's confession reveals the way in which the poet, in a doubt-filled moment of critical reflection, looks deep into the heart or essence of poetry, sensing there an absurd, irrevocable nothingness requiring

10   Stéphane Mallarmé, *Correspondance* vol. I, 1862–1871, ed. H. Mondor and J.-
      P. Richard (Paris: Gallimard, 1959), p.207.
11   Ibid., p.220f.

aesthetic transformation. This does not imply that Mallarmé is a poet of nothingness or a nihilist who places the real world in parentheses. Quite the reverse, he is hopeful and has an extreme, unshakeable faith in the purity of the artistic ideal, which only intensifies his spleen. Indeed, from the 'Crise de Tournon' onwards, it is to the absolute idea or enlightening Orphic *knowledge* of Beauty that Mallarmé understands he must devote his work. As an idealist, he sets his literary goals high and quasi-inaccessible so that disillusionment becomes inexorable, necessarily inducing a fundamental crisis in poetry. Even if many of his texts are precariously poised or built around a conceptual void or nullity, with a profusion of terms such as 'blanc', 'absence', 'vide', 'silence', 'rien', 'aboli' or 'nul', this does not empty Mallarmé's poetry of meaning and render it nihilistic. On the contrary, his Symbolist awareness of the void implies a positive metaphysical absence of circumstantial matter. The ascetic Mallarméan quest is therefore not for nothingness, but rather for pure transcendental matter.

As I have suggested here, the Orphic statement 'après avoir trouvé le *Néant*, j'ai trouvé le *Beau*' contains the implication *in extremis* that poetry concerns a traumatic process of self-examination, potentially even self-destruction, but finally and necessarily of triumphant creation. We now turn to a different, less known allusion to Orpheus, a short piece entitled 'Orphée, mythe grec et latin' found in *Les Dieux antiques* (1880), Mallarmé's 'textbook' on mythology. With its picturesque abundance of mythological symbolism, this text acts as a counterpart to enliven the abstract poetological use of the Orpheus motif during the time of Mallarmé's 'Crise de Tournon'. Orpheus' catabatic trajectory is, in the following work, dictated by the cyclical nature or recurrent rhythms of a 'solar drama' preoccupying Mallarméan thought at the time.

'Orphée' in *Les Dieux antiques*

Mallarmé's pronounced democratic, social or egalitarian artistic conscience led him to complement his poetry and aesthetic texts with
manifold pieces of non-fictional, journalistic or pedagogical writing.
Les Dieux antiques, 'une nouvelle mythologie illustrée', is Mallarmé's
translation-*cum*-adaptation of *A Manual of Mythology* (1867) by
George W. Cox who, through a series of textbooks, sought to popu-
larise Friedrich Max Müller's ideas of a linguistic comparative mythology. Mallarmé's discovery of the philological theories of Cox and
Müller was a revelation for him, and, as we shall see, he is particularly
keen to appropriate the idea of the Orphic myth as primarily solar,
thus transforming Orpheus into a solar hero.[12] Mallarmé does not hide
his attraction to the myth of the singer-poet – '[s]on histoire est des
plus belles' (*OC*, p.1239) – yet what he draws out of Orpheus' stock
narrative, distilling it into two paragraphs, concerns us here.

Orphic song is understood dialectically. First, the author wishes
to call attention to the darkness and the void threatening the tragic
heroes of mythological narratives. Not the wondrous omnipotence of
Orpheus' song, but rather its *silencing* is an issue early in the text, a
listless silence resulting from the singer's bereavement: 'Orphée, mal-
heureux de cette perte, n'eut plus le cœur d'éveiller sur sa lyre d'or la
musique qui faisait que bêtes, arbres et hommes le suivaient avec
délices' (*OC*, p.1239). In this version, then, Orpheus does not ascend
to the upper world as a wandering bard after his lover's departure.
Silence accompanies him from Eurydice's death until his own: 'La
douleur d'Orphée imposa de nouveau silence à sa musique, cela
jusqu'aux temps où il mourut sur les bords de l'Hèbre' (*OC*, pp.1239–
40). Thus, instead of asserting the correlation between Eurydice and
the generous source of Orphic music, Mallarmé rather seems to be
strengthening the relationship between *melos* (or song) and melan-

---

12   F. Max Müller interprets ancient myths as 'diseased' versions of an original
     solar myth, a narrative about the death and rebirth of the sun which, as an
     illustration of the rhythmic cycle of mortality, offers a reassuring structure to
     human life.

choly, as the former is the aesthetic product of anguish, loss, sorrow and lament.

However, the idea of Orphic sterility is quickly inverted in the second part of the essay's dialectic in which music, likened to the wind, is regarded as a kind of primal or natural energy, wild and unbridled. Orpheus is correlated with the breath, sigh or moan of the storm winds on their path through the forest: 'Orphée représente, dans l'opinion de quelques-uns, les vents qui arrachent les arbres dans leur course prolongée, en chantant une sauvage musique' (*OC*, p.1240). Indeed, most ancient mythological accounts of music associate the unpredictable power of wind with the natural birth of music: the Aeolian harp was crafted to make the wind sing, and Pan, the fabricator of the syrinx, was enchanted by the sweet sound of wind he found blowing through marsh reeds, just as Hermes, the inventor of the lyre, let the wind blow over dried sinews strung across a hollow tortoiseshell. It is the natural, spontaneous energy of wind that these mythological protagonists skilfully transform and manufacture into a product of pleasurable value.

In accordance with the intellectual source material of *Les Dieux antiques*, as provided by Max Müller's thesis of an original solar myth, Mallarmé proceeds to interpret the meanings and connotations of the names Orpheus and Eurydice:

> Son nom est le même, Orpheus, que l'indien Ribhu, appellation qui paraît avoir été, à une époque très primitive, donnée au soleil. [...] Le nom d'Eurydice vient du mot qui a donné leur forme aux noms Europe, Eurytos, Euryphassa, et beaucoup d'autres: tous dénotant le vaste jaillissement de l'aurore dans le ciel. (*OC*, p.1240)

Orpheus' solar attributes allow the singer to be located in an auroral or matutinal light and to be related to a décor of fleetingness and transience. Erroneously claiming that the Greek name *Eurydike* (or 'wide justice') signifies the bursting forth of dawn, the entry envisages the triumphant union of Orpheus and Eurydice as the bounteous spreading of dawn in the morning sky. Such a vision seems to stem from Müller's proposal that the earliest language possessed a kind of mythopoetic energy; man sought to understand the original meaning of words (for example, night and day) by conceiving of them, with the help of the fertility or death-rebirth cycle, as beings of a particular sexual nature. The article progresses with an interpretation of Eurydice's death by the bite of the serpent whereupon she is instantly pulled into the obscurity of the underworld, which allows the author to suggest that Orpheus' mission or 'pilgrimage' to Hades is a manifestation of the cyclical, nocturnal travel of the sun. Like a ritual, the sun sets in the west every twelve hours only to rise again gloriously twelve hours later in the east. The predictably recurrent rhythm of the sun's nocturnal trajectory must, of course, be accomplished so that its resplendent diurnal journey, vital for life on earth, can take place:

> Le pèlerinage d'Orphée enfin représente le voyage que, pendant les heures de la nuit, le Soleil passait pour accomplir afin de ramener, au matin, l'Aurore, dont il cause la disparition par sa splendeur éblouissante. (*OC*, p.1240)

Therefore, co-dependent like the Apollonian and the Dionysian and precariously poised between the rhythmic poles of creation and destruction, the lovers Orpheus and Eurydice relentlessly perform a symbiotic, evanescent and eternally repetitive dance, a ritual (of fertility and/or sexuality) in which the triumphant emergence of the one requires the turbulent disappearance of the other.

This highly visual, symbolic reading of the Orphic myth in terms of a rhythmic solar drama allows Mallarmé not only to foreground the vital natural energies of Orphic song (in terms of wind or solar power), but also to make a case for the omnipotent, productive or life-enhancing aspect of music. At the same time, the interaction between Orpheus and Eurydice offers an imaginative vision of the Orphic *katabasis* in line with Walter A. Strauss's view of the Orpheus theme as a schematic vertical paradigm. As discussed earlier, traumatic moments of Mallarmé's own poetological crisis (recounted by the poet himself) show that the Orphic theme takes shape in his thought as a simple and starkly effective dialectic of images – as a rhythm, in other words, of descent and return, night and day, darkness and light, sunset and sunrise as well as of death and rebirth, loss and regain and silence and sound.

Mythmaking, to conclude, is a fictional, non-rational means of figuring the phenomenal world using a culturally-codified form of symbolic, allegorical speech. The tropes and messages of myth, both personal and universal, seek to fathom the unfathomable whilst, at the same time, serving a purpose that resists justification. Nineteenth-century European writers and thinkers were particularly keen to deepen their mythological consciousness, believing that the 'primitive' cultural authenticity of myth had a continuing relevance and could lend valuable creative power to a scientific, secularised and enlightened modern world.

However, for a music-conscious poet such as Mallarmé, as well as his nineteenth-century Symbolist colleagues, the allusion to the Orphic myth is also a symbolic means of communicating the poet's primordial function and the intimate relations between music and poetry. It is worth remembering that Orpheus' narrative stems from a mythical time when poetry and music were easily united under the same cultural auspices of *mousike*. Modern recourse to his myth, then, encourages a weighing out and negotiation of the sibling arts, inciting a self-referential quest for the roots, nature and purpose of the musico-poetic enterprise as well as the creative self that is responsible for it. By looking at two different appraisals of the myth in Mallarmé's work, one strictly poetological and the other philological or peda-gogical in its symbolism, we hope to have shed some light on the rhythms of the Orphic enterprise in his aesthetic thought.

Suggested Reading

Blanchot, Maurice, 'Le Regard d'Orphée', in *L'Espace littéraire* (Paris: Gallimard, 1955), pp.179–184.

Dayan, Peter, *Music Writing Literature, from Sand via Debussy to Derrida* (Aldershot: Ashgate, 2006).

Evans, David, *Rhythm, Illusion and the Poetic Idea: Baudelaire, Rimbaud, Mallarmé* (Amsterdam and New York: Rodopi, 2004).

Strauss, Walter A., *Descent and Return: The Orphic Theme in Modern Literature* (Cambridge, Mass.: Harvard University Press, 1971).

II   Narrative Rhythms

BRENDA GARVEY

Rhythms, Repetitions and Rewritings in *Passion Simple* by Annie Ernaux

A trajectory can be drawn across the works of Annie Ernaux which traces the gradual striptease of her texts as she pulls away the clutter of fiction to reveal an evermore minimalist and frank prose. The patterns that have developed in her work over time have allowed critics to pair or group texts according to subject and genre. Her first three novels for example, *Les Armoires vides* (1974), *Ce qu'ils disent ou rien* (1977) and *La Femme gelée* (1981), stand a little apart from the rest of her corpus which becomes increasingly autobiographical, and which can be categorised into diaries or ethnographic observations, into accounts of her parents or her childhood or her own personal traumas.[1] However, we can also detect a more global rhythm which directs her work and which, beyond generic or thematic divisions, follows a conscious path through an exposition of the workings of fiction and literature. This journey sees the author narrowing the gap between action and narration, striving towards a certain simultaneity of experience and representation, and attempting to capture and freeze the passage of time. We can immediately identify a progression in Ernaux's work from her first novels to her most recent publication, *L'Usage de la photo* (2005), which marries text and image. Her formal experimentation has become more pronounced as the autobiographical voice grows stronger, emerging from the blurred beginnings of her early trilogy and gradually divesting itself of apparent artifice, until it speaks allegedly unedited in her journals. Within this itinerary, *Passion simple* (1992) marks something of a turning point, and the repeated rhythms in this text, as well as the rewritings

---

1   For further examples of possible groupings see Siobhán McIlvanney, *Annie Ernaux: The Return to Origins* (Liverpool: Liverpool University Press, 2001).

within and around it, expose the temporal concerns that shape Ernaux's prose.

Passion simple is Ernaux's barest, sparest text, as well as being one of her most intimate pieces, and it incorporates extreme examples of her typographical and formal experiments. The *écriture plate* developed since *La Place* (1983) is at times reduced to barely punctuated lists, and the frequent references to popular music, magazines and television suggest a rejection of canonical literature in favour of more mainstream media. Extending the biographical mode of *La Place* and *Une Femme* (1987), the author focuses on herself as subject and writes about events in her recent adult past. It is an unusual book. The provocative title and the front cover of the Folio edition, with its seductive red illustration of crumpled bed sheets, appear to promise drama and eroticism but, turn to the back and a single sentence quotation sums up the narrative: 'À partir du mois de septembre l'année dernière, je n'ai plus rien fait d'autre qu'attendre un homme: qu'il me téléphone et qu'il vienne chez moi'.[2] In *Passion simple* nothing much happens, a woman waits, and in this waiting we begin to perceive certain rhythms: biological rhythms of breathing and heartbeat, daily rhythms of mundane chores and habits, and cyclical rhythms of arrivals and departures. Each rhythm marks out presence and absence, sound and silence, stasis and action, but it is the moments of emptiness, the voids and gaps and spaces, that allow a closer examination of the movements and pulses of life.

The story of *Passion simple* can be easily summarised: the narrator, over a period of time, conducts an illicit affair with a married man who is visiting France and who must eventually return to his own country. The man is referred to only as the initial A., an absence. So the novel apparently hinges on a simple, traditional structure with a beginning, a middle and an end. The opening and closing events, however, are not included in the text; we are never told how the couple met and we are given no farewell scene. Instead, the focus is on the less dramatic duration of the affair. Since her earliest works, Ernaux has rejected traditional chapter enumeration and played with

2   Annie Ernaux, *Passion simple* (Paris: Gallimard, 1992), back cover citation.
      Page references will be given in the text.

spacing as a means of demarcating shifts in narrative and perspective. The story opens, after a short prologue, by directing the reader back to a recent past, locating a precise moment in time and suggesting duration: 'À partir du mois de septembre l'année dernière [...]' (p.13). It also indicates that the novel is intrinsically about the passage of time and warns us that at its centre is a void: 'je n'ai plus rien fait d'autre qu'attendre un homme' (p.13). *Passion simple*, then, is a story of absence, the absence of action surrounding the absence of the lover. This enables the author and reader to concentrate on the movements of the narrative and the subtleties of the language. Everything passes in a haze of impatience and the story's chronology is of little importance. Time is measured only in accordance with the lover's telephone calls and visits which mark phases in a cyclic pattern.[3] The waiting is interrupted by a telephone call arranging a meeting which sets in motion a series of habitual reactionary emotions: anticipation of the visit, euphoria during the visit itself, exhaustion following the lover's departure, a dreamlike state of reminiscence and then the gathering of doubts and the recommencement of waiting for that call. The author-narrator tells us herself:

> Je ne fais pas le récit d'une liaison, je ne raconte pas une histoire (qui m'échappe pour la moitié) avec une chronologie précise, « il vint le 11 novembre », ou approximative, « des semaines passèrent ». Il n'y en avait pas pour moi dans cette relation, je ne connaissais que la présence ou l'absence. (p.31)

The rhythm is already established in this binary motion. For the reader, however, this oscillation between presence and absence is reversed because the moments when the narrator is with her lover are invisible, while the text is filled with the periods when he is gone. We learn later that the affair spans a time of historic change and unrest, of riots in Algeria and of the fall of the Berlin wall, and yet these events go unnoticed and unspoken, as if anything that does not pertain to the affair has ceased to exist. Without an alternative, external timeline against which to judge progress, the reader must

3   See passages pp.16–22.

accept the indefinable duration of the affair and concentrate instead on its internal mechanisms.

Passion simple is made up of blocks of text, which follow each other often apparently arbitrarily, separated by stretches of blank page. These blocks, though sometimes linked by a common theme, are often completely interchangeable and, at times, do not even begin with capital letters so that they lose any distinction or authority. Frequently the text disintegrates until we are left with nothing more than a list.[4] Let us look closely at a passage in which the author employs several of these textual styles:

> Les contraintes que m'imposait sa situation d'homme marié – ne pas lui téléphoner – ne pas lui envoyer de lettres – ne pas lui faire des cadeaux qu'il justifierait difficilement – dépendre constamment de ses possibilités de se libérer – ne me révoltaient pas.
>
> je lui remettais les lettres que je lui écrivais au moment où il partait de chez moi. Soupçonner, qu'une fois lues, il les jetait peut-être en petits morceaux sur l'autoroute ne m'empêchait pas de continuer de lui écrire.
>
> je prenais garde à ne laisser aucun signe de moi sur ses vêtements et je ne lui faisais pas de marques sur la peau. (p.37)

In keeping with the theme of absence in the novel, the language here is stripped bare. We are given a parade of verbs but they are powerless, having been prohibited. The dashes horizontally connect what is essentially a list, and a rhythm is set up in the repeated negatives. The catalogue is continued in the next two paragraphs which begin without capitalisation. The line indentation, the lower case *j*, and the repeated first person pronoun encourage the reader to move down the page. In fact the shape of this extract on the page looks more like a poem than a piece of prose, but the language lacks any poetic ornamentation, striving instead to be as clear and 'simple' as possible. This passage is typical of *Passion simple* and demonstrates how the first sense of shape or direction we get in the text is from typographical manipulations. In a story without sequential action, progress is enforced through internal rhythms of the visual leaps from one block of text to

---

4   See in particular p.14 and pp.27–30.

the next, through the horizontal dashes and vertical lists, and through the surprising use of footnotes. Unusual in a narrative discourse, these footnotes further fragment the text, causing the reader's eye to jump from one space on the page to another and back again. Ernaux thereby disrupts the traditional novelistic flow and eschews the linear model we so often associate with fiction. The shape that is developing here so far is somewhat disjointed and does not appear to follow a coherent pattern. We have discovered a tension between the forward momentum necessary to drive the text and the rejection of chronology in order to express the impotence and impatience of the narrator. We have a text that insists on spatial progression while trying to freeze time. There is a forced movement between the textual blocks, but the scenes described within them are often static.

As the title suggests, *Passion simple* is the story of a love affair and little else. Consumed by her desire, the narrator is almost paralysed by her anticipation of her lover's next visit, and she limits her actions to the very minimum in order to avoid leaving the house in case she misses his call. She stills herself to a state of bare existence in which she can experience as acutely as possible the sweet agony of waiting. All action, therefore, is framed and limited, and time is measured in relation to the absent lover, A. The narrative is embodied in the narrator, and everything is translated through her. In minimising external factors and retreating into a reflective meditation, Ernaux focuses on the passage of time through the perpetually moving, growing and ageing space of the body. While the body has physical boundaries, it is not detached or divorced from its surroundings and is never in a state of pure rest or isolation. The body becomes another model for the measurement and experience of time and an example of the inter-permeation of movements through time and space. The narrator's life is reduced to a routine of daily chores, expressed in the text by the imperfect tense:

> J'allais au supermarché, au cinéma, je portais des vêtements au pressing, je lisais, je corrigeais des copies, j'agissais exactement comme avant, mais sans une longue accoutumance de ces actes, cela m'aurait été impossible, sauf au prix d'un effort effrayant. (p.13)

The choice of tense reflects the sense of habitual action, the repeated verbs drum home the monotony, while the dragging vowel sound of the imperfect tense 'ais' reinforces the sense of duration without progress, a churning motion, heavy and slow like a tired heartbeat.

So far we have two structuring devices which shape the text: the imposed blocks and jumps of the typography, and the waiting *je* which strives to be as still as possible. The first person narrative imposes direction on a text and here, as well as expressing the claustrophobic, repetitive nature of the experience, it heightens the intensity and intimacy of the narrative. A careful reading of the main section of *Passion simple* reveals however that the narrative *je* is in fact double, and it is the second *je* – the authorial, commentating *je* – that more directly orients and shapes the novel.

Within *Passion simple*, and apparently alongside the non-action of the affair, the author intrudes and explains the process of writing the text. Most of the footnotes, for example, function as additional commentaries and differ little from the authorial asides included in the text itself. In fact they sometimes comment on these too and therefore suggest a further degree of revision and edition. The presence of this second *je*, the author as opposed to the mistress, imposes another layer on the text and forces a second or repeated reading. Clearly we have two important narratives in *Passion simple*: the story of the affair, which occupies the central section of the text and which, written in retrospect, allows for authorial intervention – this second voice which intrudes on the tale. Again we have a binary motion, a narrative which swings between a past and present first person. The author footnotes page 66 with the following observation: 'je passe de l'imparfait, ce qui était – mais jusqu'à quand? – au présent – mais depuis quand? – faute d'une meilleure solution.' This leaves us with the impression that language cannot sufficiently express the narrator's experience, that she is bound by tenses that are insensitive to the gradual move-ments of time and which too eagerly mark boundaries between the past, present and future. Just as the story ends, we find ourselves back at the beginning: 'J'ai commencé de raconter « à partir du mois de septembre je n'ai plus rien fait qu'attendre un homme », etc., deux mois environ après le départ de A., je ne sais plus quel jour' (p.60). The sentence illustrates well the oscillation between the two time periods set up if we plot the movement between the repeated first person pronoun. We have three beginnings here: 'J'ai commencé', which refers to a time still measured relative to A., with all the approximation and blurred memory we now associate with it; and in '« à partir du [...] »', we have a double backward motion towards the beginning of the affair and to the beginning of the text. The story is over and yet the narrative does not end. The author has become her own reader and brings us back to that one line which summarises the story and underlines the absence of action. And so, in a *mise en abîme*, the text thickens and acquires another commentary and another copy. In this way, the novel continues, repeatedly adding brief sections, each of which marks a possible conclusion and yet none of which succeeds in closing the text. The story renews itself time and again until the narrator admits: 'Je n'arrive pas pourtant à le quitter, pas plus que je n'ai pu quitter A' (p.69).

We become aware, when reading *Passion simple*, of the pile of copies and versions building up behind it as well as the repeated readings and revisions within it. There is the diary lying open on the desk, the loose leaves of barely legible handwritten drafts, typed sheets, the commented text, the expanding novel with subsequent sections being added on, this bound copy and thousands more like it. The text now exists, finite and complete, but the story continues to turn and be retold with each new reading. Ernaux suggests that a certain delay and distance is necessary in order to allow the private text to become public; perhaps with each retelling, each draft and copy, the story stretches its connection to her memory. The text does not stand alone but forms part of a cycle, part of a rhythm built of recurring versions of a single story. This pattern continues, eternally returning, throughout Ernaux's literary life.

Published in 2001, *Se perdre* is the largest of Ernaux's works, running to almost 300 pages. It is the diary of her affair with a married Russian man and is, she tells us, unedited. This is the author at her most autobiographical and most vulnerable as she exposes her innermost thoughts, insecurities and surprising dependencies. The text is frequently repetitive, often monotonous, and the seasoned Ernaux reader is even robbed of the voyeuristic intrigue one might enjoy when reading someone else's diary because the story of *Se perdre* has already been told. One might think that to publish the original notes or the first draft of a story after the polished, reworked literary piece is a backward step but, for Ernaux, it is an attempt to get closer to the reality of the event, to approach the truth she is constantly pursuing.[5] We have already seen these excavations in her work as she strips away the artifice and throws off her fictional voice in favour of strikingly sparse, unadorned narratives. *Se perdre* is a fuller version of *Passion simple*. Free of metacommentary, apart from the introduction, the author removes herself as editor and critic and allows her journal entries to tell the story. Perhaps this is a sign of increased confidence, her fear of judgement diluted by her literary success. She is ready now to expose herself by publishing the private diaries she kept during her relationship with A. and up until she began writing *Passion simple*.[6] She is trying to shorten the gap between the public and private texts and hopes that her journal entries, written close to the events and occupying a different literary space, will reveal another version of the tale. *Se perdre* does not replace *Passion simple*; it adds another telling. Referring us to her earlier novel, Ernaux says in the introduction:

> En janvier ou février 2000, j'ai commencé de relire les cahiers de mon journal correspondant à l'année de ma passion pour S., que je n'avais pas ouverts depuis cinq ans. (Pour des motifs qu'il n'est pas nécessaire d'évoquer ici, ils avaient été resserrés dans un endroit qui me les rendait indisponibles.) Je me suis aperçue qu'il y avait dans ces pages une « vérité » autre que celle contenue dans *Passion simple*. Quelque chose de cru et de noir, sans salut, quelque chose de l'oblation. J'ai pensé que cela aussi devait être porté au jour.[7]

We find ourselves questioning this rewriting, however, and wondering whether something important lies in the events retold or in the act of retelling. All of Ernaux's works have a strong autobiographical strain, and the incidents to which she returns are pivotal moments in her life.

5   At the beginning of *Une Femme*, Ernaux explains: 'Mon projet est de nature littéraire, puisqu'il s'agit de chercher une vérité sur ma mère qui ne peut être atteinte que par des mots. (C'est-à-dire que ni les photos, ni mes souvenirs, ni les témoignages de ma famille ne peuvent me donner cette vérité).' Ernaux, *Une Femme* (Paris: Gallimard, 1987), p.23.
6   In *Se perdre*, A., still mostly absent, is referred to as S.
7   Ernaux, *Se perdre* (Paris: Gallimard, 2001), p.14.

Recurrent themes include the trauma of an illegal abortion, the complexities of her affairs, her Yvetot origins and the shock of her father's violence towards her mother. It cannot be denied that these events were important but, while this might explain the desire to write, the desire to rewrite is a different thing. It suggests that the importance is in the telling and not in the tale.

In Ernaux's best known and most widely acclaimed work, *La Place*, the narrator, explicitly identified as the author for the first time, describes her father and her relationship with him. In so doing, she recounts her own childhood and adolescence, her experience of growing up in a *café-épicerie* in the Normandy town of Yvetot, and her education which distances her from her father and her roots. The text is innovative and inventive, employing a flat, neutral language, and playing with the (auto)biographical genre, but the story itself is not new to readers of Ernaux. In her debut novel, *Les Armoires vides*, the narrator, a university student called Denise, recalls her experience of growing up in a *café-épicerie* in a Normandy town and how her education has separated her from this past. Denise, alone and afraid in a university bedroom after seeking an illegal abortion, is also an early twin of the author-narrator of *L'Événement* (2000), Ernaux's account of her own abortion. And so the pattern continues: the *café-épicerie* returning like a beat, a constant reminder of origin, each text duplicating another, with situations and stories reappearing and overlapping. Usually the subsequent tellings of an initial tale strip it gradually of its fiction, drawing it closer to autobiography. It appears that each book fulfils a specific function in Ernaux's discovery of herself as writer, that a familiar framework allows for freer literary experimentation, and that she will repeat the same story until she finds the form and voice that suits it best.

The proliferation of versions of the tale at once distances us from the event, by planting copies and layers between the reader and the event, and clarifies the scene by providing multiple viewpoints. Distance, however, is what Ernaux wishes to avoid; she endeavours to close the gap between the event and its recording and to preserve, as

purely as possible, the present moment.[8] Repetition takes on a ritual-
istic feel, a mantra recalling a past event, willing it back into existence. Equally, there is a tug between movement and stasis that we
have identified in the rigidity of the scenes and the dynamic textual
layout, as well as in the almost paralysed *je* of the affair and the
energetic authorial voice. Linear and circular forms clash both within
and beyond this text. Internal repetitions oppose the enforced linearity
of reading, and the growing corpus of Ernaux's texts cannot break free
from the constant return to the familiar.

   This desire to return is, in fact, an obsession with the memory of
the present. Ernaux tells us clearly towards the end of *Passion simple*
that, 'quand je me suis mise à écrire, c'était pour rester dans ce temps-
là' (p. 61). The statement suggests that the desire was not simply to
remember the past but to somehow relive it. We see the narrator at
times practising her own rituals in the desperate hope that she will
experience not a renewed time but 'un temps réversible'. Ernaux
explores the possibility of regaining times past first through sheer
force of will and imagination:

> Je revoyais des moments de cette époque, qui n'avaient rien de particulier – je
> suis dans la salle des fichiers de la Sorbonne, je marche boulevard Voltaire,
> j'essaie une jupe dans un magasin Benetton – avec une telle sensation d'y être
> encore que je me demandais pourquoi il était impossible de *passer* dans ce jour-
> là, ce moment-là de la même façon qu'on passe d'une chambre à une autre.
> (p.58)

However, this effort of the imagination is not enough, and as anniver-
saries approach, she dresses in the same clothes as before and retraces
her steps, visiting the monuments to her past she has created, hoping
that this faithful pilgrimage will allow her to relive that same happy
day: 'Durant cette période, toutes mes pensées, tous mes actes étaient
de la répétition d'avant. Je voulais forcer le présent à redevenir du
passé ouvert sur le bonheur' (p.58). When this too fails, Ernaux turns

---

8   Ernaux's most recent publication, *L'Usage de la photo*, experiments with this
    preoccupation further by photographing the scene after love-making in an effort
    to capture the memory. However, once again, the action is curiously absent and
    only an emptiness, represented by the abandoned clothes, remains.

to writing, where she tries to force the resurgence of emotion through the concentrated reconstruction of events.

We can identify, therefore, two inter-related rhythms in the works of Annie Ernaux, and in *Passion simple* in particular: a fugue-like progression with recurrent motifs throughout the texts, and a stronger, louder beat regrouping everything to a single point of departure. The internal and inter-textual repetitions and rewritings appear to perform a dual function, that of revealing the truth which Ernaux believes to be captured in a quasi-simultaneous recording of the event and its action, and the immortalisation of the present. Perhaps this is one and the same thing since, for Ernaux, the truth lies in the present, and any departure from the present moment leads inevitably to fiction.

Suggested Reading

Ernaux, Annie, *Passion simple* (Paris: Gallimard, 1992).

—— *La Place* (Paris: Gallimard, 1983).

—— *Se perdre* (Paris: Gallimard, 2001).

—— *L'Usage de la photo* (Paris: Gallimard, 2005).

Ernaux, Annie and Jeannet, Frédéric-Yves, *L'Écriture comme un couteau* (Paris: Stock, 2003).

Fallaize, Elizabeth, 'Love Stories: Annie Ernaux's *Passion Simple*', in *French Fiction in the Mitterrand Years: Memory, Narrative, Desire*, ed. Colin Davis and Elizabeth Fallaize (Oxford: Oxford University Press, 2000), pp.123–143.

McIlvanney, Siobhán, *Annie Ernaux: The Return to Origins* (Liverpool: Liverpool University Press, 2001).

Thumerel, Fabrice, *Annie Ernaux, une oeuvre de l'entre-deux* (Arras: Artois Presses Université, 2004).

LUKE SUNDERLAND

The (Future) Perfect Knight:
Repetition in the *Cycle de Guillaume d'Orange*

This essay is about a particularly medieval narrative form: the 'cycle'. Cycles were vast compilations of texts produced from the thirteenth century onwards. They were often built around a core of twelfth-century narrative which was later reworked to a varying extent, and to which were added prequels and sequels. Cycles thus grew in both directions at once, with the ultimate aim being the provision of the complete story about one particular character, lineage or empire. They normally ended up as single, bound codices. Their sheer length is what first strikes the modern reader; this length responded to a specific desire for narrative to be definitive. The cycle under consideration here, the *Cycle de Guillaume d'Orange*, thus aimed to offer not just *an* account of Guillaume's life, but rather *the* account.[1] This required two kinds of completeness: one linear (whereby we have the narrative of the character's entire life, from birth to death) and one cyclical (whereby we see every episode in the character's life, through many repetitions of similar episodes).

The first poems about Guillaume appeared in the early twelfth century; the core of the cycle is the three texts known as *Le Couronnement de Louis* (composed c. 1130), *Le Charroi de Nîmes* (1130–40)

---

1   The cycle is considered here in its shorter version, which works as a biography of Guillaume, rather than its longer version, which includes prologue texts about Guillaume's ancestors in order to give a history of the entire lineage. Even in its shorter version, texts where Vivien and Rainouart rather than Guillaume are the main characters also appear, but the *raison d'être* of the cycle remains the biography of Guillaume. Space does not permit consideration of the range of different manuscript versions here.

and *La Prise d'Orange* (1140s).[2] To this core were added later in
the twelfth century two sequels: *Aliscans* (1185–90)[3] and *Le Moniage
Guillaume* (c. 1170).[4] Finally, the prequel *Les Enfances Guillaume*
was added early in the thirteenth century to complete the cycle.[5]
Surviving cyclical manuscripts date from the mid-thirteenth century
onwards.

These latter two texts – the *Enfances*, which tells of Guillaume's
youth,[6] and the *Moniage*, which tells of his days of penance preceding
his death – will be our focus here. These poems ensure linear completeness at each end of the cycle by recounting the emergence and
demise of the main character respectively. And here, a tension between the two types of completeness – linear and cyclical – is brought
out. Linearity demands transformation, development and eventual
closure, whereas cyclicity requires the repetition of similar feats. The
cyclical drive is an impulse towards the maximum amount of narrative

---

2   *Les Rédactions en Vers du 'Couronnement de Louis'*, ed. Yvan G. Lepage,
     Textes Littéraires Français, 261 (Geneva: Droz, 1978), no date of composition
     given; *Le Charroi de Nîmes*, ed. Duncan MacMillan (Paris: Klincksieck, 1972)
     gives dates for both *Couronnement* and *Charroi*, pp.42–43; *La Prise d'Orange*
     ed. Claude Régnier, 7th edn (Paris: Klincksieck, 1967), date given pp.34–35.
     References to all texts are given as line numbers. Translations of Old French
     quotes are given in the footnotes.

3   *Aliscans*, ed. Claude Régnier, 2 vols, Textes Littéraires Français, 110 & 111
     (Paris: Champion, 1990), date given I, p.40. One should also note the existence
     of *La Chanson de Guillaume*, a poem composed between 1150 and 1175, which
     does not appear in any cyclical manuscript, ed. and trans. Philip E. Bennett
     (London: Grant & Cutler, 2000), date given p.9. *Aliscans* draws upon material
     found in the *Chanson*.

4   *Le Moniage Guillaume*, ed. Nelly Andrieux-Reix, Classiques Français du
     Moyen Age, 145 (Paris: Champion, 2003); no date given. The date of c. 1170 is
     provided by Philip Bennett, *Carnaval héroïque et écriture cyclique dans la
     geste de Guillaume d'Orange* (Paris: Champion, 2006), p.13.

5   *Les Enfances Guillaume*, ed. J.-L. Perrier (New York: Columbia UP, 1933);
     date given p.iii.

6   It should be noted that the meaning of the Old French 'enfances' does not
     correspond to the meaning of the word in modern French. Rather, it denotes a
     young man's time making his name, before he attains fief and wife. A man
     could be an 'enfes' well into his thirties.

about the character; it constantly demands more of the same, resisting change.

It is in thinking this tension within completeness that the concept of 'rhythm' is useful. The cycle is given integrity not just by its linear structure (and thus by its end points) but by repetition within it. It would of course be possible to give an account of rhythm at a micro level, in the repetition of phrases, rhymes and even of the very decasyllabic lines of the poems.[7] Here, however, I would like to focus on rhythm at a macro level, witnessed in the repetition of similar narrative material. Indeed this repetition is what creates links between the texts composing the cycle. Each text here makes itself an authentic Guillaume-text by showing Guillaume doing a particular thing: fighting Saracens. Though he does so in different guises at different stages of the cycle – as defender of the weak king Louis in the *Couronnement*, as hero conquering fiefs abroad in the *Charroi* and the *Prise*, as defender of these territories in *Aliscans* – he is constantly performing the same action. In these texts, repetition does not jar with linear development; the different guises of Guillaume allow him to re-enact the same feats. However, in the *Enfances* and the *Moniage*, we expect – but do not get – a different Guillaume. Thus the *Enfances* in fact do not simply tell of Guillaume's youth but rather anticipate his later triumphs; in the *Moniage*, Guillaume attempts to become a monk but ends up, yet again, in combat against Saracens. These two texts are thus evidence of an irresistible rhythm at the heart of the cycle.

It is because of this omnipresence of repetition that I would like to filter my account of rhythm in the cycle through the psychoanalytic concepts of non-chronological time offered by Jacques Lacan and subsequently Julia Kristeva. First, in one of the most radical aspects of his theory, Lacan develops a concept of non-linear time in relation to the workings of the psyche and of language. He argues that in the

---

7   On repetition in the *Cycle de Guillaume*, see Edward A. Heinemann, *L'Art métrique de la chanson de geste* (Geneva: Droz, 1993). The key work on structural repetition in the epic remains Jean Rychner's *La Chanson de geste: essai sur l'art épique des jongleurs* (Geneva: Droz, 1955). Roger Pensom's work on the prosody and structures of repetition with variation of the *Chanson de Roland* should also be noted: see his *Literary Technique in the 'Chanson de Roland'* (Geneva: Droz, 1982).

psyche, time can act in reverse, through the processes of 'retroaction' and 'anticipation'.[8] The former concept means that the significance of past events is constantly reworked in the present, with the past being given meaning retroactively (*nachträglich* or *après-coup*). In language too, the final word of a sentence confers meaning upon all the words that precede it. Anticipation is the other end of the same process, referring to the effect of the future on the present, represented grammatically by the future perfect tense.[9] Confirmation of meaning will come in the future, when we will learn what the present 'will have been'. The present thus awaits the certainty, security and unity of the future. Here too, we can make a comparison with language: the first word of a sentence lies in expectation of signification to come later. And finally, both concepts – retroaction and anticipation – show us how time as perceived in the psyche is based around repetition, defying linear chronology.

Kristeva's model of cyclical time is a significant departure from Lacan's. She relates non-linear time to the body, and, gendering the concept, to the female body in particular. In a famous paper, 'Le temps des femmes', Kristeva notes the association of the feminine with gestation, and suggests that women's time is not linear but cyclical, determined by the 'éternel retour d'un rythme biologique'.[10] Women are for Kristeva involved in this time rather than the (mascu-

8   For a summary of Lacan's ideas about time, see Dylan Evans, *An Introductory Dictionary of Lacanian Psychoanalysis* (London: Routledge, 1996), pp.205–7. For a summary of debates surrounding the concept of time, medieval and modern, see Jeffrey J. Cohen, *Medieval Identity Machines* (Minneapolis, MN: Minnesota University Press, 2003), pp.1–34.

9   Lacan's concept is a development of Freud's *Nachträglichkeit*, the idea that the present can affect and construct the past. See Lacan, 'Le temps logique et l'assertion de certitude anticipée', in *Écrits*, 2 vols (Paris: Seuil, 1999), I, pp.195–211. For a concise summary of the significance of the future perfect for Lacan, see Bruce Fink, *The Lacanian Subject: Between Language and Jouissance* (Princeton: Princeton University Press, 1995), pp.64–65. For a fascinating reading of the Vulgate Cycle that makes use of the concept of logical time, see Miranda Griffin, *The Object and the Cause in the Vulgate Cycle* (London: Legenda, 2005).

10   Julia Kristeva, 'Le temps des femmes', in *Les Nouvelles Maladies de l'âme* (Paris: Fayard, 1993), pp. 297–331 (p. 298).

line) linear or historical time of teleology and project. They are therefore associated with the need for reproduction to sustain social orders. Societies too are therefore linked with reproduction, and thus have intentionality towards the past, constantly rediscovering what is lost there, and attempting to recreate it. Renewal of the social order is thus dependent on reviving the past. In the contemporary European Union project, the construction of a social unit superior to that of the nation, Kristeva notes the presence of

> une temporalité paradoxale: une sorte de 'futur antérieur', où le passé le plus refoulé, transnational, confère un visage particulier à l'uniformité programmée. Car la mémoire dont il s'agit, le dénominateur symbolique commun, concerne la réponse que des groupes humains [...] ont donné, non pas aux problèmes de *production* de biens matériels [...] mais de *re-production*, de survie de l'espèce, de vie et de mort, de corps, de sexe, de symbole.[11]

Society's ideal future in fact lies in the past; the only way forwards is backwards.

Lacan thus provides us with a way of thinking about the link between cyclical time and (narrative) language; Kristeva in turn relates this to the body and to the social order. I hope, however, to show that Kristeva's gendering of cyclical time can be rethought through examination of the *chanson de geste*, where men too are involved in cycles of repetition defined by the body. In the *Moniage*, it is Guillaume's physicality that forces him into a repeat performance that is linked with (re)producing the social order. His heroic feats are associated with the continuity of lineage, community and Christendom on the one hand and with the genesis of narrative on the other. Through the physical performance of violence, Guillaume is the embodiment of an ideal: a French Christian polity united under a king and defended by a loyal fighter.

The *Enfances*, on the other hand, concentrates on a different ideal: a fantasy of Christian superiority abroad. Yet, in both cases, the ideal is in fact to be anticipated or recaptured. Only the past or future can be ideal; the present is never ideal. Thus in the prequel and sequel to the cycle, the present is evacuated; these texts work instead as an

11   Ibid., p.303.

anticipation of the future and a retroactive construction of the past respectively. The space of cyclicity therefore becomes a void between a past to be rediscovered in the future and a future prefigured in the past. There is a constant *va-et-vient* between the two. Indeed the *Enfances* was written after the rest of the cycle, and is thus literally a shaping of the past in anticipation of the future. Similarly, in the *Moniage*, we see a constant reinterpretation and re-enactment of the past, whilst we also anticipate the ultimate fulfilment of Guillaume's existence in posthumous sanctity.

Les Enfances Guillaume

The *Enfances* is ostensibly about setting the scene for the narrative that will occupy the main body of the cycle. Yet it does so by ignoring certain elements of the plot to anticipate the part it sees as the 'best bit'. It is thus less an innocent introduction than an attempt to set the agenda for how the entire cycle is read. It is a retroactive creation of the past that makes the past, in turn, an enactment of the future. Thus the prologue promises that we will hear how Guillaume conquered his fief, Orange, and won his bride, Orable (the Saracen princess and enemy leader's woman, who changes her name to Guibourc after marrying the hero). Yet these amatory and military conquests in fact belong to the *Prise*. Drawn towards identifying with this text as key, the *Enfances* makes itself, paradoxically, into a repeat of what is to come; it is an anticipation of the future perfect Guillaume.

Throughout the text, Guillaume himself seems driven towards the future, to such an extent that he neglects his present. For example, when Guillaume and his brothers are invited by Charlemagne to serve him at court, he alone refuses. He chastises his siblings, asking them if their 'anfance' ('youth', 78) will last forever, and swearing to undertake the conquest of Orange the next day. He then repeatedly states his intention to convert Orange to Christianity (572–73, 1036–37). Later, he is even pleased to be captured by the Saracens, as this means that they will take him to Orange as prisoner (1124–25). And the Saracens constantly mount other attacks on his family fief of Narbonne, delaying his journey to Paris where he is to be knighted. Guillaume's later narrative pursues him here, occasionally tempting him, but always preventing him from living in his present.

He is moreover already in (albeit remote) contact with Orable, sending her a sparrowhawk (574). She in turn sends him a message to warn him of an impending Saracen attack (768–80). Crucially, she preserves her virginity for Guillaume by deluding her husband Tiebaut with a series of spells and illusions known as the 'jeux d'Orange'. Yet the all-consuming importance of Orange and Orable here introduces inconsistencies with the plots of later texts. The first element of Guillaume's reputation in the *Couronnement* is his fierce loyalty to his king; he seeks peace at home and only later (from the *Charroi* onwards) conquest abroad. And it is not until the *Prise* that he hears of Orange and Orable for the first time from a messenger who has escaped from the city.

This incongruity is reflected in other characters' opinions about him. Thus the Saracen enemy is confused about Guillaume's status, with some characters terming him a 'diauble' ('devil', 630) and warning that he will mount a fierce attack on Orange (1659–62), whereas others insist upon his youth, citing the fact that he is not yet a knight (1443–44), and does not yet even have a beard (930–31) or a good sword (1685). The narrator highlights his prodigious prowess by referring to him as 'l'anfes Guillaumes' ('Guillaume the youth', 1003), even as he leads French troops into battle. A contrast is being set up here between Guillaume as a precocious 'enfes' and King Louis in the *Couronnement* (which directly follows the *Enfances*), who is also referred to as an 'enfes', but is portrayed as weak and cowardly. And after killing hordes of Saracens, Guillaume states that:

> Damoisiaus suix, meschins et bacheleirs;
> Onkes ancores ne fui jou adoubez,
> Espié ne lance ne hauberc n'ai porté[12]

---

12 'I am a young man, a knight-in-waiting; I have not yet been dubbed, nor have I carried a lance or spear or worn mail', 1052–54.

Finally, a baron at Charlemagne's court who insults Guillaume by dismissing him as a youth soon gets his come-uppance as Guillaume hurls him against a pillar. Throughout, Guillaume is thus a youth but, more importantly, also a prefiguration of his future self. The man clearly makes the boy here. And when Guillaume is finally knighted, there is the sense that nothing could be more fitting: 'Molt gentement bien li sisent ses arme'.[13]

The text that exists to tell the tale of Guillaume's youth thus actually tells the tale of his adulthood again, differently. The *Enfances* comes up with a beginning for the story of Guillaume that only makes sense after the middle of the story. If we take this text at face value, Guillaume was never really a youth. He was always associated with one particular act: the capture of Orange. This ideal moment, encapsulating Christian superiority over the Saracens, is reverberating backwards through time. This repetition of one gesture brings cyclicity into conflict with linearity, with the consistency of the plot harmed by the excessive consistency of character. The narrative thus gains a different kind of unity: one where the past is remodelled in the light of what is to come. Guillaume was always going to do what he did; things could never have been different. Repetition is played out retroactively, in an imaginary future perfect, with a great emphasis on later achievement, on what Guillaume 'will have done'. The text is tense about the present, as it seeks a perfect future.

Le Moniage Guillaume

The *Moniage* closes the cycle, and therefore aims for transformation. Guillaume's military triumphs involved the sin of violence and to compensate, Guillaume is to try to make peace with his maker by living a life of penance in a monastery. Thus Guillaume is trying to rewrite his past to reinvent himself as saint not sinner. He wishes retrospectively to confer sublimity on his entire existence. The text is

13   'His arms suit him marvellously well', 2734.

again anticipating a perfect future (Guillaume as saint) here, but cannot avoid the past. Guillaume's early days in fact haunt him in a way he does not expect. In order to present the change in his behaviour, then, the text resurrects and adapts a famous line from the *Couronnement*, where Guillaume told King Louis that he would dedicate the best part of his life to him: 'En ton servise vueil ma jovente user'.[14] Now, similarly, he declares his intention for his latter days: 'A Deu servir userai mon ëage'.[15] The parallelism of the formulations shows the later text's reworking of the past. Transformation means rethinking what has gone by. Again here, the perfect future lies in the past.

The shift from knight to monk is therefore a hard one to make, both for the character, and thereby for the text, which finds itself correspondingly obliged to switch from epic to hagiographic mode. To deal with character first, then, it is clear from the start that Guillaume has a *chanson de geste* physicality that makes him incompatible with monastic life. If, for Kristeva, it is the body of the woman that associates her with cyclical time (through biological rhythms), then Guillaume's body too associates him with another kind of repeat performance. He renounces all his goods, land and even his armour and horse; he prays diligently. In short, he performs the role of monk, but he nonetheless remains essentially different. Indeed, no one has ever seen such a big monk and he looks ridiculous in robes. The gatekeeper of the monastery is scared of his 'espaules...braz...et...bu' ('shoulders, arms and chest', 109).[16] Moreover, his body predisposes him to excess: he eats as much as four monks. His immense appetite ultimately threatens to endanger the fragile economy of the monas-

---

14   'I want to spend my youth in your service', *Couronnement*, rédaction AB, 2228.
15   'I will spend my old age in the service of God', *Les Deux Rédactions en vers du 'Moniage Guillaume'*, ed. Wilhelm Cloetta, 2 vols (Paris: Firmin-Didot, 1906–11), seconde rédaction, I, 5469. This parallelism in the formulations is picked up on by Sara Sturm-Maddox in her article 'From *Couronnement* to *Moniage*: the *"jovente"* and the *"ëage"* of Guillaume', in *VIII Congresso de la Société Rencesvals, Pamplona–Santiago de Compostela 15 a 25 de agosto de 1978* (Pamplona: Institución Príncipe de Viana, 1981), pp.491–95.
16   *Moniage*, ed. Andrieux-Reix. All subsequent references are to this edition.

tery. Guillaume simply does not fit in, remaining more hunk than monk.

Guillaume therefore needs another way to reinterpret his past in preparation for his holy future. Indeed, as an angel tells him:

> Sire Guillelmes, sez que Dex t'a mandé?
> Tu l'as servi de bone volanté
> Et sor paiens ton cors molt a grevé;
> Par moi te mande li rois de majesté
> Qu'en paradis a fet ton lit paré
> Quant la venra que tu devras finer;
> Mes encor, voir, te velt Dex esprover,
> Encor t'estuet granz paines endurer.
> En cest desert feras tu ton hostel,
> Serviras Deu et soir et avesprer;
> Et il te mande qu'il te dorra assez;
> Ton bien sera el ciel guerredoné[17]

The temporality of the passage is interesting: heaven awaits in the future, but God has *already* prepared Guillaume's place; the word 'encor' appears twice, highlighting the repetition of the past in the future; finally the text ends with an insistent sequence of four verbs in the future tense ('feras', 'serviras', dorra', 'sera'). Guillaume's previous bodily performance is explicitly cited as worthy (*'ton cors molt a grevé'*), but the salvation promised requires transformation as well as repetition. Yet, in his next incarnation as a hermit in the desert, Guillaume's immense frame just seems to attract trouble, always leading him back to violence. First, he is attacked by robbers, and then later a giant, before his old enemy finds him. Guillaume has spent his life fighting Saracens in repeated battles throughout the cycle, and they are not about to let him rest now. They want revenge against him for his previous feats against them, and see his retirement as a chance

---

17   'Lord Guillaume, do you know what message God sends you? You have served
     him willingly, and pained your body by fighting pagans; through me the great
     Lord tells you that he has prepared your place in heaven where you shall go
     when you die, but first, it is true, God wishes to test you more, you still have
     great trials to suffer. In this desert you will make your lodging, you will serve
     God in the evening and at night and he tells you that he will grant you that your
     goodness will be rewarded in heaven', 2580–91.

to defeat him and finally conquer France. Conversely, his body too seems timeless: it does not age and is always able to accomplish more feats of violence, thus perpetuating the narrative dynamic. The *Moniage*, which has the job of closing the cycle, is trying to install a different type of heroism, through a process of transformation. But it is instead getting caught in the cycle's mechanisms of repetition, forcing Guillaume back into performance of his old self. The text is striving towards the perfect future of closure, but is riddled with re-plays of the past.

Guillaume finds himself surrounded by unwanted enemies. And even after he wins this battle against the Saracens, we are told that his time for peace has not yet come: 'Or recommencent ses paines a venir'.[18] Again the present is a rerun of the past ('or *re*commencent'), stretching out to an implied future ('a venir') of more of the same. To guarantee transformation, then, to move from knighthood to saint-hood, the text first has to repeat knighthood, differently. This is done by making Guillaume a reluctant hero, an unwilling fighter, thereby returning to the dynamic at work in the *Couronnement*, where Guil-laume first takes on the thankless and endless task of defending Louis. He becomes Louis's reluctant saviour again here, as another horde of Saracens surrounds Paris. Louis sends for Guillaume, who pretends to be someone else, reporting Guillaume's death. This provides him with the anonymity necessary when he decides to save the day once again. The body and identity are thus finally separated: Guillaume fights, but not as 'Guillaume'.

After this feat, the text is free of its debt to the *chanson de geste* genre and is finally able to pursue transformation. Guillaume is there-fore finally given a new enemy: the devil. He sees a perilous ford and decides to build a bridge so that the pilgrims of the future will be able to cross more easily. But the devil comes each night to knock down whatever Guillaume has built during the day. After a month, there is a final confrontation in which Guillaume throws the devil into the water. He finishes the bridge, passes away and takes up his place in paradise. The future perfect point has been reached, and the cycle now closes.

18   'Now his troubles are starting again', 4923.

Transformation thus finally comes out of repetition. The initial failure to achieve change in identity produces the comic effect of Guillaume as a ridiculous monk, but as a hermit Guillaume straddles two identities, remaining epic hero whilst anticipating his saintly end. As Sara Sturm-Maddox puts it: 'the particular interest of the *Moniage* lies in its successful assimilation of the heroic pattern of epic to that of hagiographic narrative, while preserving the distinctive features of the legendary biography for which it serves as conclusion.'[19] He repeats previous feats with a difference, as in his final battle against the Saracens he is *incognito*. This loss of identity in turn prefigures the self-effacement of his thankless task of bridge-building. Similarly, his confrontations with Saracens foreshadow his encounter with the devil. The future can here only work as a reinvention of the past.

Neither the *Enfances* nor the *Moniage* is able to resist the rhythm that dominates and shapes the cycle. Thus the *Enfances* is warped by the purpose of anticipating the future; the *Moniage* struggles to achieve transformation because it is haunted by a past rooted in the body. The former fits closely the Lacanian concept of time, whereas the latter forces us to rethink productively Kristeva's idea of corporeal temporality. In both texts, the present moment is caught in a dialectic between past and future and is thereby evacuated. The point here is not to admonish these medieval texts for failing to achieve a smooth linear narrative. Rather, through use of the concept of rhythm, we have seen that the clash between linearity and repetition is symptomatic of the cycle's structure and model of time. Linearity does not have priority; preference is given to cyclical time, with repetition and rhythm as structuring factors. Rhythm here shapes the reading experience as much as development and closure, and is thus vital to appreciating the unique narrative and aesthetic system that constitutes medieval cycles. These intricate and apparently contradictory texts actually find their (cyclical) consistency in their (linear) inconsistency.

19   Sturm-Maddox, 'From *Couronnement*', p.494.

Suggested Reading

Bennett, Philip, *Carnaval héroïque et écriture cyclique dans la geste de Guillaume d'Orange* (Paris: Champion, 2006).

Besamusca, Bart, and others (eds), *Cyclification: The Development of Narrative Cycles in the Chansons de Geste and the Arthurian Romances* (Amsterdam: North-Holland, 1994).

Sturm-Maddox, Sara and Donald Maddox (eds), *Transtextualities: Of Cycles and Cyclicity in Medieval French Literature* (Binghamton, NY: SUNY, 1996).

III Disruptive Rhythms

DEE REYNOLDS

Kinesthetic Rhythms: Participation in Performance

I shall argue below that perception of rhythm in different art forms is grounded in kinesthesia, and that through kinesthetic experience the receiver can participate actively in performing the work. Also, innovative rhythms can alter familiar, habitual kinesthetic patterns. I shall discuss the receiver's engagement with rhythm in the poem 'Un coup de Dés jamais n'abolira le Hasard' by Stéphane Mallarmé, in Piet Mondrian's New York and Boogie-Woogie paintings, and in dances by Merce Cunningham.

The kinesthetic basis of rhythm

The etymology of the word 'kinesthesia' has two parts, both Greek: 'kinesis', meaning movement, and 'aesthesis', meaning sensation. So, most simply, kinesthesia refers to sensation of movement, though its definition also often includes sensation of position. Kinesthesia is not a single discrete sense, but can involve sense receptors located throughout the body: muscles, joints, tendons, vestibular;[1] eyes, ears, skin (exteroceptors); mouth, stomach, nose (interoceptors). As pointed out by Jeffrey Longstaff, the common distinction between proprioception, referring to internal stimuli from the body, and exteroception, referring to external stimuli from the environment, has been shown to be invalid, because these two types of stimuli are frequently linked. For instance, 'external stimuli such as visual-field motion or audio-field motion [...] can induce perceptions of self-motion even in the

1   The non-auditory part of the inner ear.

absence of joint, muscle, tendon and vestibular sensations.' Similarly 'receptors in the skin must also be classified as both exteroceptors and proprioceptors since they can receive stimulation from the environ- ment or from the body.'[2]

Kinesthesia, then, involves interaction between different senses, and gives us information about our position and movement in space and time. According to phenomenologist Algis Mikunas,

> the kinesthetic modality underlies all perceptual fields [...] it is possible to translate one field of experience into another in terms of a common denominator: the kinesthetic awareness [...] it is possible to speak of kines- thetic awareness as a basic process of knowing, which sub-tends all bodily actions, and synthesises them.[3]

On this account, kinesthetic awareness is foundational to all sensory experience and to consciousness itself.

My argument that rhythm is grounded in kinesthesia draws on the concept of effort analysis developed by the movement theorist Rudolf Laban (1879–1958). Effort analysis takes as its starting point the behaviour and experience of moving subjects. It can be applied to actions ranging from walking down the street, through physical tasks executed in the workplace, to dance performed on stage. Effort is both physical and mental, and consists both in motor impulse and an 'inner' attitude.[4]

Laban analysed effort attitudes according to the degree of active resistance or passive yielding on the part of the mover to what weight, space, time and flow. Resistance, or lack of it, can range from 'fight- ing against' to 'indulging in', correlating to differing degrees of effort intensity, which are experienced kinesthetically, in that they give rise

2   Jeffrey Longstaff, 'Cognitive Structures of Kinesthetic Space: Reevaluating Rudolf Laban's Choreutics in the Context of Spatial Cognition and Motor Control' (Unpublished D.Phil. thesis, City University, London and Laban Centre, London, 1996), pp.35–6.

3   Algis Mikunas, 'The Primacy of Movement', *Main Currents in Modern Thought*, 31.1 (September–October 1974), 8–12, (pp.8–9).

4   'The impulse given to our nerves and muscles which move the joints of our limbs originates in inner efforts.' Laban, *Modern Educational Dance*, ed. Lisa Ullmann, 3rd edition (London: Macdonald and Evans, 1975), p.26.

to movement sensations on the part of the mover.[5] To take just the time element, for instance, if I am walking slowly down the street (in Laban's terms, a 'sustained' use of time) and then break into a run (a 'sudden' use of time) to catch a piece of paper which has fallen from my pocket and blown away in the wind, I progress from an 'indulgence' in time to a 'fighting against' time, and from a less intensive to a more intensive effort quality. In terms of space, if the paper is blowing around the pavement and I have to keep running after it in different directions, my use of space is what Laban would call 'flexible' (as opposed to 'direct'). If I finally catch the paper by stamping it underfoot, this action is executed with strong use of weight.[6] In the action of stamping on the paper, the flow will be extremely free (on a scale from 'free' to 'bound'), because I know that the pavement will provide external resistance and therefore the movement does not need to be internally controlled, as in 'bound' flow.

Laban argued that modulations of effort produced 'effort rhythms',[7] which he described as 'an alternation of stresses or more intensive effort-qualities with less intensive ones.'[8] Effort rhythms cannot be equated with metrical measures. For instance, the action of 'pressing' involves strong use of weight, direct use of space, and sustained use of time. 'Gliding' is similar, but here the weight element is light, so progression from 'pressing' to 'gliding' involves modulation of the weight element. It would be possible to perform two repetitions of a pressing-gliding sequence, with no alteration in effort qualities, but where one sequence was of shorter duration than the other. Hence,

5   See Laban, *The Mastery of Movement*, 4th edition revised and enlarged by Lisa Ullmann (Plymouth: Northcote House, 1980), p.77.
6   Laban in fact refers to 'heavy' and 'light', but as argued by Cecily Dell: '"heavy" and "light" [...] describe the conditions of objects or people who are acted upon – lifted, carried etc., – while a person who actively changes his weight quality in movement can best be described in terms of strong or light.' Cecily Dell, *A Primer for Movement Description using Effort-Shape and Supplementary Concepts* (New York: Dance Notation Bureau, 1970), p.23.
7   Laban, *Modern Educational Dance*, p.75.
8   Laban, *Rudolf Laban Speaks about Education and Dance,* ed. Lisa Ulmann (Surrey: Laban Art of Movement Centre, 1971), p.28.

effort rhythms are distinct from metrical beat. Also, the former, unlike
the latter, cannot be expressed in quantitative terms.

Rhythm in dance and other art forms

Effort rhythms are experienced kinesthetically, through movement
sensations of weight, space, time and flow, and they are clearly
present in dance, as an art of movement. Not surprisingly, kinesthetic
sensitivity has often been cited as a crucial element of response to
dance. It came to the fore in early twentieth-century modern dance,
which moved away from the narrative-based forms of ballet towards
a more autonomous, movement-based art. The canonical modern
dance critic, John Martin, was influenced by the philosopher Theodor
Lipps (1851–1914), who developed the theory of kinesthetic empathy,
according to which the spectator could perceive objects in terms of the
dynamics of the act of perception itself, for example, a vertical line
seen as 'rising' or 'sinking'.[9] Martin argued in 1936 that:

> When we see a human body moving, we see movement which is potentially
> produced by any human body and therefore by our own; through kinesthetic
> sympathy [same meaning here as 'empathy'] we actually reproduce it
> vicariously in our present muscular experience and awaken such associational
> connotations as might have been ours if the movement had been of our own
> making. The irreducible minimum of equipment demanded of a spectator, then,
> is a kinesthetic sense in working condition.[10]

Although Martin has been accused of essentialism in treating kinesthetic empathy as a universal given, kinesthesia remains central to
dance theory and criticism. In 1992, Ann Daly, writing on Isadora
Duncan, argued that the kinesthetic appeal of Duncan's dance, which

9   Theodor Lipps, *Ästhetik, Psychologie des Schönen und der Kunst*, 2 vols
      (Hamburg: Leopold Voss, 1923 [1903] and 1920 [1906]), I, p.226.
10   John Martin, *America Dancing: The Background and Personalities of the
      Modern Dance* (New York: Dance Horizons, 1968), p.117.

involved the response of the whole body, and not just the eye, enabled spectators to feel that they were participating in the performance, by 'moving with' Duncan, rather than objectifying her by their gaze.[11] Susan Foster has criticised Martin's account of 'empathetic exchange' as justifying 'his conception of choreography as an essentialised or distilled version of feelings which, via inner mimicry, transfer into the viewer's body and psyche.' However, she asserts her belief that 'feeling another body's feelings is a highly significant (and under-valued) aspect of daily and artistic experience.'[12]

Kinesthetic empathy mobilises boundaries between subjects. The subject position becomes intersubjective in the act of looking, where the spectator imaginatively participates in the perceived action, with physiological effects. In the case of seeing another human performing an action, there is evidence to indicate that a system of 'mirror neurons' comes into play, where the spectator encodes the perceived action in terms of their own motor repertoire. The degree to which this takes place is influenced by whether or not the spectator has acquired the motor skills necessary to perform the observed action. It may also be influenced by the extent to which other factors (e.g. gender) link the spectator with the subject who is performing the action.[13] Neural pathways can be 'excited' (primed for action by the transmission of electrical impulses to muscles) simply as a result of observing movement, without any contraction of the muscles taking place. An area of the brain which has been identified as a locus of mirror neuron

11   Ann Daly, 'Isadora Duncan and the Male Gaze', in *Gender and Performance: The Presentation of Difference in the Performing Arts*, ed. Laurence Senelick (Hanover, NH: University Press of New England, 1992), pp.239–59 (p.255).

12   Susan Leigh Foster, 'Choreographing History', in Susan Leigh Foster, *Choreographing History* (Bloomington: Indiana University Press, 1995), pp.3–24 (p.20).

13   B. Calvo-Merino, D. E. Glaser, J. Grèzes, R. E. Passingham and P. Haggard, 'Action Observation and Acquired Motor Skills: An fMRI Study with Expert Dancers', *Cerebral Cortex*, 15:8 (2005), 1243–1249.

activity is the lateral premotor cortex,[14] which is activated before
movement is actually performed.

Movement does not need to be actually executed in order for
neural and muscular activity to take place: observation of and/or
preparation for movement can suffice. Merleau-Ponty characterised
preparation for movement as 'a certain *potential for action* in the
framework of the anatomical apparatus.'[15] Both empathetic identification with structures perceived as dynamic (imitation) and projected extension of established patterns (anticipation) are key elements
of processes where movement is imagined rather than actually executed, and where physiological effects are produced in the spectator's
body. They are also key elements of response to rhythm. Regular
structure encourages the receiver to actively prepare for the next
movement (or beat, or rhyme), and thereby to participate in the
'performance' of the work. This participation can be virtual or actual;
for example, while listening to music with a strong beat, one might
begin striking the next beat with one's foot before it has actually taken
place.[16] Traditionally, the temporal arts (notably music and poetry)
have used conventional rhythmic forms which encouraged receivers to
participate through anticipating the next stage of regular patterns.
However, receivers can also participate in the performance of the
work through kinesthetic empathy with spatiotemporal structures
which disrupt expectations. Where the dynamics of formal structures

14   Sophie Manthy, Ricarda I. Schubotz, and D. Yves von Cramon, 'Premotor
       cortex in observing erroneous action: an fMRI study', *Cognitive Brain
       Research*, 15 (2003), 296–307.
15   Maurice Merleau-Ponty, *Phenomenology of Perception*, trans. C. Smith
       (London: Routledge and Kegan Paul, 1962), p.109, my emphasis. I have altered
       this translation slightly, from 'power of action' to 'potential for action', to
       translate 'puissance d'action'. See *Phénoménologie de la perception* (Paris:
       Gallimard, 1945), p.126.
16   Paul Valéry defined rhythm in terms of the receiver's participation, rather than
       as an objective, quantifiable structure, arguing that it is impossible to reduce
       rhythm to objective observation, because it is constructed by what the receiver
       adds to the sequence of what he can perceive. 'Il est impossible à mon avis de
       réduire le rythme à l'observation objective [...] C'est ce que J'ajoute à la suite
       des perceptions enregistrables qui construit le rythme [sic]'. Valéry, *Cahiers*,
       ed. J. Robinson-Valéry, 2 vols (Paris: Gallimard, 1973–1974), I, p.1351.

are closely related to the content which the work evokes, this provides a strong trigger for kinesthetic empathy.

Because movement sensations bring into play both time (progression) and space (position), rhythm in a spatial art, such as painting, involves experience of time, and rhythm in a temporal art, such as poetry, involves experience of space. Additionally, because kinesthetic receptors are located in different senses and parts of the body, activation of kinesthetic sensation may stimulate senses which are not directly involved in perception of the work (for example, the visual sense when listening to music). In watching dance, there can be an intersubjective, corporeal engagement which does not have a direct parallel in a poem or a painting, where the artwork does not take the form of another's body. However, effort rhythms of weight, space, time and flow can operate in the formal structures of art forms other than dance, where we also engage with rhythm as embodied, kinesthetically sentient subjects.

Stéphane Mallarmé, 'Un coup de Dés'

Mallarmé's poem, 'Un coup de Dés jamais n'abolira le Hasard' (1897) is a striking example of kinesthetic rhythms. The poem revolves around the question of whether the dice will fall and if so, whether this event will produce any significant difference. It disrupts expectations of regular verse structure, and also of conventional prose layout. The words are scattered all over the page, often with enormous blank spaces between them, and there are eleven different types and sizes of typefaces. It was not until the edition published by Ronat and Papp in 1980 that the poem appeared in an authentic form.[17] Mallarmé used the visual spread of the double folio page, which is very large (57 x 38cm), and which is treated as a visual field, where the 'blancs' create the rhythm, 'scanning' the movement of reading. Here, both the

---

17 Stéphane Mallarmé, *Un coup de Dés jamais n'abolira le Hasard*, ed. Mitsou Ronat and Tibor Papp (Paris: Change errant/ d'atelier, 1980).

physical act of reading the text and the poetic images foreground kinesthetic experience, centring on contrasts between rising and falling and between balance and instability.

The use of the double page already exemplifies this. The margin down the centre forms a vertical line, which is highlighted by the use of a wide central margin, where no words are placed. Normally, this vertical axis (the text's 'spine') would be balanced by symmetrical horizontal lines of text on both sides of the page. Here, however, although the text is printed in horizontal lines, the left and right side of the page are unbalanced, creating a sense of instability and potential for movement. There is frequently a greater volume of text on the right than on the left, and this text tends to appear lower down on the page. In the context of the direction of reading from left to right, and from top to bottom, this emphasises a downward vector. The use of large letters in heavy type (as in the title phrase) produces a marked movement sensation of weight, where the text 'strikes' the page (as in the action of 'un *coup* de Dés'). By contrast, small letters in italics create movement sensations of lightness and speed, and these letters are used when evoking the image of a 'plume', which flutters around the central abyss. In this sequence (double pages 6–8) the reader can experience the kinesthetic effects associated by Laban with 'indirect' use of space, as well as lightness and suddenness. A large number of words appear singly in separate lines, emphasising the lack of linear progression through space, which has been replaced by a flexible, multidirectional movement, as the feather is buffeted about. At the same time, the tension is heightened here around the contrast between rising and falling (will the fall take place?), as the central double page holds an unprecedented (and unrepeated) balance between right and left sides, staving off for a brief moment the inevitable descent, which recommences on the next page: the image 'par avance retombée' (double pages 2–3) prefigures the later 'choit la plume' (double page 10).

In this poem, even the reader's action of turning the page has kinesthetic significance. This action produces its own rhythm of rising and falling. The shape, appearance and movement of the double page itself are analogous to the image of the whitened 'Abîme' on double page 3, which forms first the wings of a bird, then the sails, and finally the hull of a boat. The opening and turning of the pages, as one reads, form the 'v' shape of the wings of the 'Abîme' and also suggest the rocking movement of the ship and the rising and falling movement of the waves. It is as if the reader holds in their hands the kinesthetic drama of the poem, which is played out in the rhythmic movement of the 'voile alternative' (double page 3), and the spacing and weighting of the text on the page. Here, the reader, as an embodied spectator, 'performs' the text by enacting, both imaginatively and physically, its 'effort rhythms' of weight, space, time and flow.

Piet Mondrian's New York and Boogie-Woogie paintings

From early on in his career, Mondrian regarded jazz and the city as important influences on his painting. When he began painting with rectangles and primary colours in the 1920s, the compositions were spare, and by the end of the 1920s his pictures evoked an ascetic, contemplative quality. In the early 1930s, for the first time, he introduced double lines, and many of his 1930s paintings have a grid-like structure, with only small planes of colour. In 1940, Mondrian moved to New York, and there he reworked some of his earlier canvases, for example, 'Rhythm of Black Lines' (1935–42) and 'Composition II with Red, Yellow and Blue' (1939–42). Here, the complexity of the patterns formed by the lines makes focusing difficult: if one does maintain a fixed focus, the lines themselves appear to expand and dilate, and optical flickers appear at the intersections.

In the 1930s, Mondrian had maintained a clear distinction between black lines and coloured rectangles. In New York, however, he began adding small strips of free-standing colour, and even introduced coloured lines alongside black ones. In 'New York City I' (1942), the black lines have completely disappeared and have been replaced by coloured ones. The impossibility of a fixed focus means that the spectator has to experience the picture kinesthetically, involving movement in both space and time. The dynamics of perception are transferred onto the lines themselves, which appear to move as the spectator perceives them in different configurations. The uneven spacing of the lines makes it difficult to focus and creates a 'swinging' rhythm as one's gaze shifts from one chromatic framework to another, while a 'staccato' effect is created by the irregular intersections. The varying distances between intersections on both vertical and horizontal lines encourage different speeds of perception. The eye can move at leisure (in Laban's terms, a 'sustained' use of time) and with free flow along unbroken vertical and horizontal stretches of line, but the flow becomes more bound (marked by a readiness to stop) in sections where lines are frequently intersected by other lines running at right angles, which shift attention to different 'frames'. Through this device, despite the predominance of linear structures, use of space is flexible (indirect), as the spectator's gaze is constantly being led in different directions.

These effects are accentuated in Mondrian's final pictures, 'Broadway Boogie-Woogie' (1942–3) and 'Victory Boogie-Woogie' (1943–44, unfinished). As their titles suggest, these paintings were inspired by the edgy, restless rhythms of jazz and urban life. The titles in fact cue the spectator for a kinesthetic response. Here, all the lines are fragmented into cubes, to the point that – especially in 'Victory Boogie-Woogie' – there is no clear distinction between lines and rectangles. Juxtaposition of large and small areas of primary colours produces contrasts between greater and lesser intensity. The viewer's attempts to find a 'pathway' through the painting are constantly defeated: the entire surface appears to vibrate as the eye is drawn at varying speeds and in continuously changing directions. Kinesthetic rhythms are strongly synesthesic, with dominant movement sensations of shortness (speed) and bound flow being linked with complex explorations of linearity and multidirectionality. Here, too, the spectator 'performs' the painting by experiencing a kinesthetic rather than a purely visual equivalent of the urban soundscapes and visual stimuli of 'Broadway' and the pulsating rhythms of 'Boogie-Woogie'.

Kinesthetic rhythms in dance: Merce Cunningham

Innovative rhythms have the potential to impact on receivers' familiar, habitual kinesthetic patterns, and this has particular significance in dance, which is directly related to experience of movement and in-culturated habits. As mentioned above, Isadora Duncan was cited by dance critic Ann Daly as an example of how dance could appeal to spectators kinesthetically, involving the whole body rather than just the eye. Duncan's dancing style highlighted the unity of the body moving as an organic whole and integrated movements derived from everyday life, such as walking, skipping, running and jumping. Laban was a great admirer of Duncan, whom he regarded as having

> reawakened a form of dance expression which could be called dance lyrics, in contrast to the mainly dramatic dance forms of the ballet [...] she reawakened the sense of the poetry of movement in modern man [...] this dancer had the courage to demonstrate successfully that there exists in the flow of man's movement some ordering principle which cannot be explained in the usual rationalistic manner.[18]

Duncan's work presented kinesthetic qualities which were both sufficiently familiar to her spectators that they could relate to them spontaneously, but were also transformed and idealised so to provide them with experiences which expanded and raised their familiar kinesthetic horizons.

The dance critic John Martin was guided by principles similar to the Russian Formalists' concept of 'defamiliarisation', where the habitual is 'made strange'.[19] Martin argued that through a dual process of using patterns which spectators recognise through their muscular memory, while at the same time incorporating innovative material which conflicted with this experience, dancers could set up a tension between what he called 'internal' and 'external' rhythms.[20] The

---

18   Laban, *Modern Educational Dance*, pp.5–6.
19   See Victor Erlich, *Russian Formalism: History, Doctrine* (New Haven: Yale University Press, 1981), p.76.
20   Martin, *The Modern Dance* (New York: A. S. Barnes, 1933), p.78.

dancer's movements 'retain enough of the stuff of common experience to establish an emotional association in the mind of the spectator, but [...] he sets up, along with the familiar patterns, such departures from them as to give them a new cast, a new meaning.'[21] Here, kinesthetic empathy concerns difference as well as sameness, and can lead to a decentring of the self through participation in the kinesthetic experience of an other.

There is a wide divergence between dance styles which remain in the area of the familiar and those which challenge habitual modes of perception. Both through our own habitual, everyday behaviour, as well as through our experience of dance, particular effort patterns and their associated experiences of weight, space, time and flow, become familiar. This familiarity is in part normative, as it involves conformity to cultural norms. Dance which radically challenges kinesthetic habits, like Cunningham's, can challenge such habitual patterns of embodied, spatiotemporal experience. From early on in his career, Cunningham, who was interested in expanding movement possibilities rather than in expressing subjective emotions or preferences, looked to sources of inspiration beyond the human, including the animal world[22] and new technologies. His *RainForest* (1968) presents an extraordinary world of movement behaviour, which has recognisably human but also non-human (mainly animal-like) qualities, as indeed the title suggests.

There are six dancers in *RainForest*, three men and three women. The dance lasts for twenty minutes, and has five sections. The dancers wore flesh-coloured leotards and tights, which Jasper Johns had cut and ripped with a razor blade. David Tudor's music ('RainForest') is strangely evocative of animal noises in a rainforest. The dance opens on a striking set, where helium-filled balloons, designed by Andy Warhol, float around and above the stage. The use of the floor for sliding, crawling and rolling movements produces strongly animalistic connotations, as does the sight of Cunningham, near the beginning of the dance, crouched on his hunkers, rather like a four-legged creature

21   Martin, *America Dancing*, pp.114–5.
22   See his remarkable book, *Other Animals: Drawings and Journals* (New York: Aperture, 2002).

on its hind legs. Also near the beginning, in the background, we see another male dancer (Albert Reid) standing, intermittently performing curious twitching movements with his hands and fingers, and moving his arms in a robot-like fashion. The nervous quality of this movement has associations which are at once animal-like and technological. Marcia Siegel comments that the dancers in *RainForest*, seem 'poised between their humanness and some nonhuman existence that could be either animalistic or artificial.'[23] There is a wide variety of travelling steps and positions which are atypical of human movement and postures. Some movements are similar to actions such as walking, running and skipping, but with unfamiliar elements, for example, off-balance use of weight, abnormally fast execution, extreme stiffness and strange, awkward angles.

The movement is performed with great intensity and sense of purpose, and is mostly tense, light, fast, and seamless, but it is sometimes punctuated by 'slashing' actions, where speed and flexibility are combined with strong use of weight.[24] The tempo alternates very dramatically between extreme rapidity and very slow motion, replacing modulation with rhythmic dislocations and concentration of energy. The execution of small, rapid, darting, tightly controlled movements in quick succession figures prominently in the female role in a duet near the end. The predominant movement qualities here are light, indirect, fast and bound, involving a high degree of energy expenditure on resistance to weight, time and flow. At the end, the energy is picked up and further amplified in an extraordinary solo by Cunningham, where his whole body is saturated by tiny, jabbing gestures, as if animated by a series of electrical currents which move his body in different ways all at once, while at the same time he projects a strong sense of intensity and controlled concentration. This movement juxtaposes direct effort attitudes to space (individual 'jabbing' movements) with indirect attitudes (movement into different directions in space), a combination which produces rhythmic dislocation.

---

23   Marcia Siegel, *At the Vanishing Point: A Critic Looks at Dance* (New York: Saturday Review Press, 1972), p.239.
24   See Laban, *Modern Educational Dance*, p.71.

In describing Cunningham dances, where, since the early 1990s, computer technology has been employed as a choreographical tool, critics often use images drawn both from the natural world and IT. *Pond Way* (1998) can be seen as a companion piece to *Beach Birds* (1991) and other nature pieces. *Pond Way* has been described as looking like 'nature run through a computer',[25] and the dancers are often compared with insects or waterbugs. In *Beach Birds*, the quirky fragmentations of the body, the oddly angled limbs and, at times, a quasi-robotic rigidity and stiffness, show the influence of 'Life-Forms',[26] which encouraged Cunningham to choreograph separately for different parts of the body (arms, legs, torso), thereby making rhythms less organic and increasing their complexity.[27] At the same time, *Beach Birds* famously captures a range of bird-like but also human movements. Leslie Kendall speaks of 'a whole vocabulary of familiar, angular motions: twitching, jerking, hopping, leg shaking, wing stretching, head cocking, group immobility, encroaching on one another's territory for territory or pairing.'[28]

The destabilisation of the category of the 'human' can be reinforced by elements of décor and sound as well as movement. Jack Anderson comments on *Beach Birds*:

---

25   Tresca Weinstein, 'Cunningham's work is full of beauty', *Times Union*, 30 July 1998. Archives of Cunningham Dance Foundation.

26   'LifeForms' is a special computer program designed for creating choreographic elements by simulating choreographic work processes. The user can animate a figure by entering it on the timeline in pre-defined positions/ single images. The computer then calculates the intermediate transitions (interpolation) and generates the finished animated figure, or choreography. Alternatively, the user can also model positions/ single images on a basic figure first and then insert this figure into the timeline. See Glossary, in *Dance and Technology: Moving Towards Media Productions*, ed. Söke Dinkla and Martina Leeker (Berlin: Alexander Verlag, 2002), p.430. 'LifeForms' has been renamed 'DanceForms'.

27   This can also be seen as an extension of the 'chance' principle of juxtaposing unconnected events.

28   Leslie Kendall, 'Cunningham dancers focus on pure movement at the Pillow', *The Daily Gazette*, 8 July 1983. Archives of Cunningham Dance Foundation.

the impression of avian fluttering is reinforced not only by passages of quivering and flapping, but also by the fact that the arms and shoulders of the costumes designed by Marsha Skinner are black, whereas the rest of the outfits are white. The arms therefore become especially winglike in appearance.[29]

They appear elongated because the hands are gloved in black. Moreover, the costumes have a direct effect on how the movements are perceived: 'These costumes and the amazingly odd arm movements that Cunningham has invented conspire to make the dancers' upper bodies seem cut off from the lower ones.'[30] Cunningham would later go on to explore further ways of opening up human kinesthetic patterns, notably through the technique of motion capture. In *Fluid Canvas* (2002), the backdrop involved a projection where motion-captured data from Cunningham's hands was combined with movement data drawn from animals, producing a new rhythmic 'hybrid'.[31]

Clearly kinesthetic response is engaged more directly in the experience of watching dance than in art forms which do not involve watching other people moving. In Cunningham's work, kinesthetic response is directly linked with what Mikunas refers to as 'a basic process of knowing'. His radical approach to rhythm allows spectators to engage kinesthetically with recognisably human effort rhythms, while also decentring them through interactions with different patterns which disrupt expectations and even experiential parameters of what constitutes the kinesthetically 'human'. However, receivers of art forms other than dance are also people who move, and who experience movement sensations of weight, space, time and flow. By activating these sensations and making them central to content, rhythmic structures can extend the parameters of the medium and enable readers and spectators to participate directly in producing the work as a kinesthetic 'performance'.

29   Jack Anderson, 'Hints of Sea and Sky Amid Stillness', *The New York Times*, March 15 1994. Archives of Cunningham Dance Foundation.

30   Nancy Goldner, 'The Cunningham spirit in leaps and bounds', *The Philadelphia Inquirer*, March 19 1992. Archives of Cunningham Dance Foundation.

31   For further discussion of motion capture, see my *Rhythmic Subjects: Uses of Energy in the Dances of Mary Wigman, Martha Graham and Merce Cunningham* (Alton: Dance Books, 2007), pp.203–4.

Suggested Reading

Daly, Ann, 'Isadora Duncan and the Male Gaze', in *Gender and Performance: The Presentation of Difference in the Performing Arts*, ed. Laurence Senelick (Hanover, NH: University Press of New England, 1992), pp.239–59.

Laban, Rudolf, *The Mastery of Movement*, 4th edition revised and enlarged by Lisa Ullmann (Plymouth: Northcote House, 1980). First published as *The Mastery of Movement on Stage* (London: Macdonald and Evans, 1950).

—— *Modern Educational Dance*, ed. Lisa Ullmann, 3rd edition (London: Macdonald and Evans, 1975 [1948]).

Longstaff, Jeffrey, 'Cognitive Structures of Kinesthetic Space: Reevaluating Rudolf Laban's Choreutics in the Context of Spatial Cognition and Motor Control' (Unpublished D.Phil. thesis, City University, London and Laban Centre, London, 1996).

Martin, John, *America Dancing: The Background and Personalities of the Modern Dance* (New York: Dance Horizons, 1968 [1936]).

Mikunas, Algis, 'The Primacy of Movement', *Main Currents in Modern Thought*, 31.1 (September–October 1974), 8–12.

Reynolds, Dee, Rhythmic Subjects: Uses of Energy in the Dances of Mary Wigman, Martha Graham and Merce Cunningham (Alton: Dance Books, 2007).

Louise Hardwick

Dancing the Unspeakable: Rhythms of Communication in 'Laghia de la mort' by Joseph Zobel

The Caribbean is renowned for musical invention, yet representations of rhythmic practices in Francophone Caribbean literature remain scarce. Few authors attempt to capture the vibrancy of a satirical carnival song or the intensity of a dance on the printed page. Joseph Zobel's eponymous short story 'Laghia de la mort' is remarkable both for its depiction of Antillean music and dance, and its terse, rhythmic narrative.[1] Zobel (1915–2006) is seldom known beyond the novel *La Rue Cases-Nègres* and its subsequent film adaptation.[2] His literary achievements, however, are significantly more substantial: between 1946 and 2002 he published four novels, four collections of short stories, two volumes of poetry and one *livre d'art*. Originally printed in 1946, *Laghia de la mort*, a series of tableaux of Martinican life, has a valid claim to being Zobel's most dynamic and compelling literary creation. Zobel's affection for the work is evident: 'Gertal', the first story of his final publication *Gertal et autres nouvelles* (2002), gives its name to the collection and revisits the main characters of 'Laghia de la mort' created fifty years earlier, bringing his career full circle.[3]

Music and rhythms pervade *Laghia de la mort*. Opening *nouvelles* 'Laghia de la mort' and 'Défense de danser' are structured around dances, 'Coup de nuit' is dominated by the menacing nocturnal rhythms of the tambour, whilst music forms a backdrop in both

---

1   Joseph Zobel, 'Laghia de la mort', in *Laghia de la mort* (Paris/Dakar: Présence Africaine, 1978 [1946]), pp.9–20. All subsequent page references are given in brackets in the text.

2   Zobel, *La Rue Cases-Nègres* (Paris/Dakar: Présence Africaine, 1974 [1950]).

3   Zobel, *Gertal et autres nouvelles* (Martinique: Ibis Rouge, 2002).

'Le premier convoi' through the blare of the military bugles, and 'Il était une fois', a *rêverie* set against a neighbour's saxophone practice (indeed, the two stories in which music is absent consider schooling, themes to be later developed in *La Rue Cases-Nègres*).[4] This article will examine Zobel's exploitation of the tension between audible, danced rhythms and the written word in 'Laghia de la mort', exploring the boundaries between public expression and private, non-verbal communication. A close reading enables analysis of the structural and narrative techniques employed to convey rhythm and create the internal dynamics of this tense, atmospheric text. The implications of Zobel's decision to focus upon the dance are also explored in the Antillean literary context; 'Laghia de la mort' is considered as exemplifying Zobel's approach to social realism and Negritude, whilst foreshadowing several preoccupations of the Creolists in the 1990s.

Music and dance in Zobel: beyond *doudouisme*?

The West Indies is a musical infusion of African, European and American influences, and in 'Laghia de la mort', Zobel depicts these elements without straying into hollow cliché. *Doudouisme*, prevalent in the early twentieth century, refers to descriptions of Antillean culture which fail to go beyond the reaffirmation of the 'exoticism' of the islands, perpetuating colonial stereotypes. In Zobel's work, passages describing music and dance, rather than confirming clichés of primitive African musicality and catering to an external audience, both enliven the narrative and provide a footnote of cultural authen-

---

4   Music and dance are leitmotifs in Zobel's œuvre; see for example 'La Rue Blomet ou Paris by Night' in *Le Soleil Partagé* (Paris/Dakar: Présence Africaine, 1964), which depicts the influence of Antillean music in Europe, especially the beguine craze that led to the establishment of fashionable Parisian venues such as *Le Bal Nègre* in the Rue Blomet. In this story, native Parisians are introduced to Antillean culture at the dancehall, and roles between newly arrived Antilleans and Parisians are reversed, as the metropolitans become visitors to their own capital.

ticity. Whereas Césaire's canonical poem *Cahier d'un retour au pays natal* is structured on the premise of a Martinican returning to view the Antilles, Zobel's gaze is unwaveringly internal and rooted in plantation society. And while Césaire famously chose not to write in Creole, Zobel, his contemporary, includes snippets of Creole songs to portray a society rich in Creole tradition; the laghia is one such example.

The first obstacle any reader encounters is the title itself: even an Antillean reader may be unfamiliar with the term 'laghia'.[5] The laghia is a dance depicting a mock combat, similar to the Brazilian *capoeira*, and is believed to have its origins in a transplanted African tradition. When Zobel wrote, this Creole term had no standardised spelling: Glissant writes 'laggia' while the Creolists term it 'ladja', using their method of phonetic spelling (a written Creole which avoids French calques).[6] Jacqueline Rosemain explores the unknown origins of the name of the dance:

> Faut-il y avoir la traduction créole de 'la guerre': 'laguèa', devenu quand les esclaves le prononçaient avec tout l'agressivité dont ils le chargeaient, 'laguía'? Toujours est-il que le laguía est une danse belliqueuse. Il mime une lutte et se termine par la mort du plus faible ou du moins habile des deux adversaires.[7]

A likely cause of the laghia's evolution is that because fighting amongst slaves was banned on plantations, dance became a permitted method of settling disputes. Although Rosemain emphasises its violent function in slave society, Zobel and Glissant, writing almost a century after abolition in 1848, depict it as a simulated combat, not necessarily entailing actual physical violence. Referring to Glissant's first novel, *La Lézarde*, Michael Dash defines the laghia as 'a traditional Martinican dance in which two partners go through the motions of a fight without touching each other.'[8] This suggests the dance has

5   The dance is also known as the 'damier', as in Confiant's *Le Meurtre du Samedi-Gloria* (Paris: Gallimard, 1999).
6   For clarity, the dance is henceforth referred to as the laghia.
7   Jacqueline Rosemain, *La Musique dans la société antillaise 1635–1902* (Paris: L'Harmattan, 1986), p.21.
8   J. Michael Dash, *Edouard Glissant* (Cambridge: Cambridge University Press, 1995), p.188.

evolved over time, and indeed for Glissant and Zobel the laghia is connected with the carnival tradition and jubilant celebration. In *La Rue Cases-Nègres*, José speaks with awe of the prowess of one dancer, 'quand il [M.Asselin] danse le laghia, le samedi soir, on souhaiterait que la nuit ne finisse pas et que les flambeaux ne s'éteignent jamais' (p.51), briefly depicted in Euzhan Palcy's film adaptation *Rue Cases-Nègres* in a scene of joyous but measured exuberance.[9] Another instance of the laghia as an outpouring of fraternity occurs towards the close of Glissant's *La Lézarde,* as the revolutionaries celebrate their success:

> Alphonse n'avait pas été le dernier à entrer dans la ronde où sa pratique du laggia [sic] se révéla complète; il dansa un combat avec Lomé, après quoi ils trinquèrent.[10]

In 'Laghia de la mort', Gertal commences 'sa danse d'amour et de joie' (p.11) and the sung reference to *chouval bois* suggests a link with carnival festivities:

> A celebratory music, chouval bwa's origins are associated with carnivals and fairs when this galloping rhythm accompanied the *manege* [sic] or merry-go-round (chouval bwa is Creole for *cheval bois,* referring to the wooden horses of the merry-go-round).[11]

The snatch of song, *Angèle en chouval bois/ Bas chemise li ka voltiger* (p.12), is unidentifiable with European rhythm due to its Creole structures and lack of metre or rhyme. Creole monosyllables interrupt the reader's flow (and comprehension) by introducing the metonymic gap. These staccato Creole terms also increase tempo and lead to the voluptuous *voltiger*, a suggestion of sexuality mirrored by *bas chemise* and *Angèle* (anticipating the name at the climax of the story).

9   *Rue Cases Nègres*. Dir. Euzhan Palcy. 1983. 103 min [distributed with English subtitles as *Black Shack Alley*].
10   Edouard Glissant, *La Lézarde* (Paris: Seuil, 1958), pp.229–30.
11   Simon Broughton and Mark Ellingham, *The Rough Guide to World Music Vol. 2: Latin and North American, Caribbean, India, Asia and Pacific*, ed. Richard Trillo (London: Rough Guide, 2000), p.291.

The laghia, however, is not always synonymous with joyful celebration. Zobel alludes to a more sinister version in *La Rue Cases-Nègres*: 'il y avait aussi des jeux de dés et de cartes en plein air, autour d'un tray et d'une torche, qui tournait souvent en combats épouvantables: laghias de la mort' (p.83). The adjective 'épouvantables' neither glorifies nor condones such violence, suggesting the author does not seek to sensationalise this darker form of the dance.

Articulating the inarticulate

'Laghia de la mort' depicts a dramatic conflict between dancers Gertal and Valère. Zobel creates an intriguingly tense dynamic between the two men, explained at the story's climax: Valère is Gertal's unacknowledged son. The narrative is a sequence of short paragraphs, with interspersed fragments of speech and song ensuring a rapid pace and edgy tone. The setting of the laghia suggests aggression by contrasting the darkness of the crowd with the intense light of the circle in which Gertal and Valère dance. The boundary between audience and dancers is in flux; the audience participates, calling out, singing and forming a raucous backdrop to the main action. Through constant switching of focus from the protagonists to the crowd, Zobel maintains the rapid internal rhythm of the story, heightening tension. This technique allows him to create three moments of climax: Valère's initial challenge to Gertal, the revelation of the dance's subtext of unacknowledged paternity and, finally, the emotive ending.

Valère's decision to dance with his father is a challenge, an act of warfare, and he is portrayed with the appropriate vivacity and rigour of a young and emotionally wounded man. The nature of the secret shared by Gertal and Valère is such that it has been impossible for them to express themselves in words. Valère's inability to voice his feelings towards Gertal is focused upon by the narrator:

> Ses lèvres trahissaient une sorte d'incapacité d'exprimer la méchanceté, et ses yeux donnaient tout au plus au visage assez de dureté pour faire sentir la colère qu'il y eût voulu mettre. (p.13)

Anger and emotion fail to be articulated as physical expression supersedes verbal communication.

Remarkable for its range of poetic imagery, the story describes the effects of music on mood and atmosphere: 'et voilà que toutes les voix chantaient au bord de la lumière et dans l'ombre. On sentait la nuit reculer très loin en arrière et continuer de s'ouvrir' (p.11–12); 'les voix se mirent à chanter avec des reflets d'eau étale' (p.14); 'Une batterie sourde et légère comme des pulsations que la douceur de l'air imprime au cœur' (p.15). Music becomes a form of expression for an altered state of consciousness and for sensations that transcend ordinary perception and articulation. Animal imagery within the story supports the narrative themes, exemplified by the depiction of Valère:

> L'immobilité de Valère contenait l'élan du tigre, le bond que va faire le lion qui a traqué le gnou, la détente du serpent jaune, ou la chute du torrent. Tous les élans, les bonds et les sauts qui donnent la mort. (p.18)

The image of stillness steeped in violent potential movement is original and portentous. Animal imagery, rather than reaffirming the stereotype of primitive African musicality, is a subtle nod to the dance's African origins in the tradition of Negritude. Gertal's characterisation is far less aggressive: '[Gertal semblait] jouer à la manière des fauves qui aguerrissent leurs petits' (p.13–14). This imagery is a precursor to the private conflict lying behind the public encounter and Gertal's behaviour is subtly indicated as paternal, although the filial bond has not yet been revealed.[12]

---

12   A parallel can be drawn with 'Défense de danser': Denise's dance has a cyclical structure, beginning out of defiance to an ex-lover, becoming totally independent in its middle stage and, only at the end, resuming seductive qualities. Her forced dancing at the nouvelle's opening, 'Elle dansait par bouderie, sans plaisir, mal' (p.26), contrasts with her grace once she dances alone. This dance is also a power struggle, demonstrating she is free of the influence of her former lover. As in 'Laghia de la mort', dance becomes a process of self-affirmation, assuming responsibility for sexual actions.

Valère's dance is an act of self-assertion, instigating the father–son confrontation: 'Lui, il n'obéissait pas à la musique. Il commandait son sang; il voulait se battre' (p.14). Frequent references to blood reinforce the blood-tie uniting the two men whilst suggesting the dance's volatile nature, an outpouring of emotion that could rapidly escalate into bloodshed, as the crowd hope and expect. Gertal resists violence for as long as possible. Although he recognises that the laghia has turned into a *laghia de la mort*, he remains cynical, suggesting the triumph of physical victory that Valère hopes for would not resolve his inner conflicts and emotional turmoil. Even when preparing to attack each other, the two men cannot help but be reminded of their common humanity:

> Leurs visages se touchaient presque; leurs souffles se gênaient l'un à l'autre, le souffle de l'un disant: « Tu sens le coupeur de canne » et le souffle de l'autre: « Et toi, l'enfant qui a joué avec les bêtes ». (p. 18)

Relating these actions in short phrases, heavy with reciprocity and repetition, the tone remains urgent, culminating in simple direct speech which contrasts two opposing descriptions.

Subversion of the laghia

Rosemain emphasises the laghia as 'l'affaire des initiés' (p.21), and undoubtedly the most important voice in 'Laghia de la mort' is the rhythmical beating of the tambour, as heard and interpreted by the protagonists. This voice is established through frequent personification, a technique used throughout the African diaspora which gives rise to the drum's epithet: *le tam-tam parleur*. We find 'la foule cria. Le tambour bafouilla' (p.13); 'le tambour, dans son langage, dit un mot qui demandait attention' (p.14); 'Et le tambour ponctua les gestes de Gertal, répétant les mêmes paroles' (p.15).[13] From the opening, the importance of the drum is underlined, as upon Gertal's appearance 'la surprise alla jusqu'au débit du tambour, qui bondit, tel un cheval qui bute et change d'allure', an attitude reflected in Gertal who 's'était cabré' (p.9). Passages describing the tambour's dictation of the dance are rendered in a cumulative, anaphoric structure, evoking dance moves and a euphoric, semi-hypnotic state:

> Il s'abandonnait au tam-tam.
> Le tam-tam l'impulsait comme un moteur.
> Le tam-tam désarticulait ses jambes, ses bras.
> Le tam-tam drainait et refoulait son sang dans son torse nu, dans l'épaisseur de ses lèvres, les palpitations de ses narines, le dur de son front, le feu de ses yeux. (p.11) [14]

As the story develops, we become privy to Gertal and Valère's individual interpretations of the tambour. The dialogue between Valère and Gertal, presented by Zobel in coherent prose, is an interpretation of danced gestures; although the development of the exchange suggests spoken conversation, the emphasis is on physical actions: 'Gertal esquissa une danse toute simple et débonnaire. Et il alla devant Valère, faisant de ses mains largement ouvertes: "Non, non. Amour et joie. Ecoute la nuit qui chante […]"' (p.14–15). Structural techniques contribute to this sense of intuitive understanding, whilst the lack of narrator leaves the narrative free to focus upon rhythmic action, emphasising the musicality of the situation. The tension between the two dancers remains unexplained until, in the first moment of climax in the text, the tambour spells out the unspoken secret:

> Le langage du tambour se fit encore plus grave, mais plus net.
> Soudain, tous semblèrent avoir compris. Et Gertal comprit que Valère savait ce que disait le tambour; et Valère sut que Gertal avait compris tout ce qu'il

13   In 'Coup de nuit', the tambour also speaks, reflecting the fears of the protagonist making his way home late at night after winning at cards: 'Un homme descend vers Bon Œil; barrez-le. Il est bourré d'argent' (p.59).
14   Anaphora is similarly used to convey the euphoria of the climactic end to Césaire's *Cahier d'un retour au pays natal* (Newcastle upon Tyne: Bloodaxe, 1995 [1939]).

> portait en lui de colère et de dépit [...] Et seuls Gertal et Valère entendaient
> « Angélina », au lieu des quatre coups modulés avec la paume et le pouce sur la
> peau tendue du tambour. (p.16)

Repeated wordy structures at the start of this climactic paragraph slow the tempo of the passage, as the two characters finally share a moment of agonised harmony and perspicacity. The alliteration of the 'p' and 't' sounds builds rhythm, as this sonorous quality of the prose enables the reader to also hear the four vital beats: An-gé-li-na.

After revealing the theme of unacknowledged paternity, the narrative switches back to the crowd's impatience, their clamour brought into sharp relief to heighten drama. Paradoxically, the more heated the dance becomes and the more the audience strains to see, the less they understand of the highly personal communication between Gertal and Valère, another device used by Zobel to modulate the speed and intensity of the story as he builds tension to the final (anti-)climax. The laghia, unbeknownst to the crowd, has been subverted from a public forum into an intensely private conversation. The tension between father and son is mirrored in the tension between the dancers and the crowd, who are slow to sense the subversion of the dance and attempt to provoke violence:

> La danse tirait en longueur. Quelques-uns ronchonnèrent dans la foule: un
> laghia, ce n'est pas ainsi; on danse, on fait ça et ça des jambes et des bras, et on
> frappe, l'un cherchant à assommer l'autre d'un coup de talon, ou à le prendre à
> bras-le-corps pour le soulever et...
> Est-ce un laghia, ça?
> Pourquoi Gertal refuse-t-il de prendre?
> Pourquoi Valère ne le charge-t-il pas?
> Laghia de la mort!
> La foule hurlait: 'Laghia de la mort!'
> Les échos répondaient partout à la ronde, terrorisés. (p.17)

The crowd goads the dancers, a bloodthirsty whole represented by aggressive individual voices whose invectives punctuate the narrative. Only tambour-beater Edmond comprehends the internalised conflict between Gertal and Valère. The crowd remains insensitive, believing that they are witnessing a traditional laghia, and their disappointment at the lack of physical contact is evident in their aggressive treatment of Edmond:

> Et pourquoi fais-tu des bêtises comme ça? Tu sais très bien qu'ils ne pouvaient pas s'empoigner, puisque tu n'as pas donné les deux coups qui commandent la prise. (p.19)

In contrast to the unreceptive crowd, Edmond is aware the conflict has resonances beyond those of the traditional laghia. He becomes the third point in a triangular relationship between the dancers and the tambour, and it is he who brings the events to a non-violent close. His drumming assumes a quasi-spiritual gravity, struggling to avert bloodshed: 'le tambour psalmodiait; et celui qui en jouait avait le cou dressé et les mâchoires serrées comme si les sons s'arrachaient de sa poitrine' (p.18). Whereas the thematic gravity and changes in tempo within the story suggest the final violent climax is swelling, Edmond breaks the hypnotic spell of the drum and the crowd by ceasing to play, wrenching Gertal and Valère back to reality. The story's close reaffirms the dance as non-violent, as the public revelation of the filial bond provokes tears, not blood.

Rhythms of Negritude, rhythms of *Créolité*?

The dignified portrayal of humble plantation life and the concentration upon authentic detail such as the laghia exemplifies Zobel's social realism. Zobel was born into plantation society and, following academic success, became a teacher at the prestigious *Lycée Schœlcher*, where he was encouraged to write by colleague Aimé Césaire. Despite close ties with leading thinkers of Negritude,[15] Zobel did not publish any theoretical works himself, and his best-known observation of the movement may be summarised in a single comment: 'Je n'ai pas

---

15   These ties are evident in his dedications. See *Le soleil partagé* for 'Rue Blomet ou Paris by Night', dedicated to Césaire, and for 'Joséphine', dedicated to Senghor.

le sentiment que ma négritude est un uniforme ou une fonction aux-
quels je dois sacrifier mon individualité'.[16] His actions, however,
testify to his commitment: Zobel's daughter remembers her father
as being greatly influenced by the ideas of Negritude, moving his
family to Senegal where he lived between 1957 and 1974, working
as a teacher.[17] Keith Q. Warner observes that the link to Africa, no
matter how vague, endures as a source of hope in *La Rue Cases-
Nègres*:

> Even Africa is a distant dream and not a reality except for the dances and other
> cultural vestiges that have survived. It is noticeable that the only time that the
> blacks are openly happy and carefree [...] is when they dance the *laghia* on
> weekends.[18]

Writing about the laghia is clear evidence of a desire to depict a
heritage denied and systematically obfuscated by colonial rule, a sub-
altern, parallel history. In this respect, it is interesting to consider
Zobel's work with reference to the Creolists Jean Bernabé, Patrick
Chamoiseau and Raphaël Confiant, who in 1989 jointly wrote and
published the manifesto *Éloge de la Créolité*.[19] As well as champion-
ing Creole language, the authors urge an inclusive reconsideration of
Creole culture:

> Les rituels liés aux 'milan', aux phénomènes du 'majò', aux joutes de 'ladja'
> [...] Ecouter notre musique et goûter à notre cuisine. Chercher comment nous
> vivons l'amour, la haine, la mort... Il ne s'agit point de décrire ces réalités sous
> le mode ethnographique... mais bien de *montrer ce qui, au travers d'elles,
> témoigne à la fois de la Créolité et de l'humaine condition.* (p. 41)

---

16   R. Hezekiah, 'Joseph Zobel: The Mechanics of Liberation', *Black Images*, 4.3–
      4 (1975), 44–55 (p.44). Hezekiah is citing an interview by Raymond Relouzat
      in *Joseph Zobel: La Rue Cases-Nègres* (Fort-de-France: Librairie Relouzat,
      year unknown).
17   My thanks to Jenny Zobel for this information.
18   K. Q. Warner, *Black Shack Alley* (Boulder and London: Lynne Riemer Publica-
      tions, 1997), p.xvii.
19   Jean Bernabé, Patrick Chamoiseau and Raphaël Confiant, *En Éloge de la
      Créolité/In Praise of Creoleness*, trans. M. B. Taleb-Khyar (Paris: Gallimard,
      1993).

Zobel's depiction of the laghia runs no danger of becoming a mere ethnographic exercise, skilfully mirroring the volatility of the dance in the tense dynamic between the protagonists. Whereas the manifesto has encountered criticism, especially for its perceived pre-scriptive and exclusive nature, several years after its appearance Raphaël Confiant agrees that Zobel's work displays affinities with the Creolists, suggesting a broader, more inclusive approach to *Creolité*:

> [La collection *Laghia de la mort* est] très peu connue et très belle – je trouve que *Laghia de la mort* est un texte magnifique. On a fait beaucoup de cinéma autour de *La Rue Cases-Nègres* parce que c'est l'histoire d'une enfance, un thème universel, mais je trouve que *La Rue Cases-Nègres* n'est pas très bien écrit, alors que *Laghia de la mort* est un petit chef-d'œuvre [...] Dans l'histoire littéraire, il y a des gens qui étaient déjà dans la Créolité, mais sans en avoir conscience. Et Zobel, dans *Laghia de la mort*, c'est de la Créolité.[20]

Zobel's comments on his decision to start writing are a simple echo of the Creolists:

> Je regrettais de ne pas trouver à l'époque quand j'étais à l'école [...] des situations, des paysages et des gens qui ressemblaient à ceux qui m'avaient entournés.[21]

Whilst setting his works in a specific Antillean context, no con-cessions are made to the non-Antillean reader in the form of footnotes or glossaries.[22] The story is written in an evocative, urgent style, thus providing enough detail on setting and atmosphere for the non-initiated reader to visualise the scene. Even if certain nuances prove elusive, Zobel's depictions prove reminders of the text's dignified cul-tural exoticism.

20 Louise Hardwick, 'Du français-banane au créole-dragon: entretien avec Raphaël Confiant', *International Journal of Francophone Studies*, 9:2 (2006), 257–276 (p.261).

21 Dominique Gallet and Mona Makki, *Joseph Zobel, Le soleil d'ébène*, documentary film, *Espace francophone* (AIF/France 3/CNC, 2002) [my own transcript].

22 Just two lines in the text are immediately translated from Creole into French when they occur on p.12.

Conclusion

The potency of 'Laghia de la mort' lies in Zobel's skilful fusing of elements of Creole society with a tense individual situation, producing – in line with the Creolists' aspirations – a text which *'témoigne à la fois de la Créolité et de l'humaine condition'* (p.41). He explores the musicality and rhythmic physicality of the laghia, focusing on protagonists, crowd and, more unexpectedly for the European reader, the *tam-tam parleur*. Moreover, the story gains integrity from his avoidance of the stereotypes that characterise *doudouisme*. Zobel's portrayal of an Antillean dance interwoven with the universal vibrations of a personal story, and his deftness in creating rhythmic suspense and intrigue, makes 'Laghia de la mort' a fundamental text in his repertoire and an example of early Antillean literature worthy of revisiting.

Suggested Reading

Zobel, Joseph, 'Laghia de la mort', in *Laghia de la mort* (Paris/ Dakar: Présence Africaine, 1978 [1946]).
—— *La Rue Cases-Nègres* (Paris/Dakar: Présence Africaine, 1974 [1950]).

GERALD MOORE

Clockwork Politics:
Rhythm and the Production of Time
in Mauss, Benjamin and Lefebvre

I

Placing two clocks adjacent to one another on a wall, the Dutch
scientist Christiaan Huygens discovered that after a time, and irres-
pective of their initial rhythms of oscillation, the pendulums of these
clocks would begin to harmonise with one another and, *ceteris pari-
bus*, eventually oscillate simultaneously. The wall acts as a medium
through which pendular rhythms are transmitted and ultimately
brought into alignment. We can extrapolate from this to suggest that
change is conveyed through the transmission of a rhythm, or more
precisely through the disruption of a particular rhythm by means of
another rhythm that serves to alter and overcode it. This claim is supported by an analysis of the archaic gift-economy, where gift-
exchange, it will be suggested, is ultimately about the production of
rhythm, understood as a technique for bringing about social solidarity
and collective subjectivity. This production of rhythm takes priority
over material forms of production.

A connection thus presents itself between rhythm and the production of subjectivity. It would be wrong to infer from this that all
forms of subjectivity might simply be related to the presence of different types of rhythmicity. Walter Benjamin can be read as endorsing
an understanding of Mauss that emphasises rhythm and gift as the key
components of an intersubjectivity that transcends the present. Yet
crucially, his diagnosis of modernity alludes to the absence of rhythm,
hence the absence of integrated time-consciousness, in modern subjectivity. The modern subject, for Benjamin, is one whose experience

translates as no more than a sustained series of 'shocks' that would once have been absorbed and cushioned by a (even unconscious) sense of historical identity. Drawing on Henri Lefebvre's *Éléments de rythmanalyse*, we might characterise this experience of shock as one of *arrhythmia*, in which the rhythms of transmission and exchange underlying pre-modern and archaic modes of experience are broken, leaving behind a subject abandoned by history, adrift and entrapped in the pure interiority of the present. In contrast to the *eurhythmia*, or harmonious functioning, of the archaic community, we find modernity as the pathological state of alienation just prior to cardiac arrest.

II

Even if Huygens (1608–47) did not make his discovery until the seventeenth century, the principle of transmission that he identified had been used to political effect since long before then. Marcel Mauss does not himself, in his famous study, 'L'Essai sur le don', pay explicit attention to the precise rhythms of exchange in archaic gift-economies, but it is not difficult to discern their presence in his descriptions of gift-economic practices. For example, of Malinowski's analysis of the Western Pacific culture of *kula*, which loosely translates as circle or circuit, Mauss writes:

> en effet, c'est comme si toutes ces tribus, ces expéditions maritimes, ces choses précieuses et ces objets d'usage, ces nourritures et ces fêtes, ces services de toutes sortes, rituels et sexuels, ces hommes et ces femmes étaient pris dans un cercle et suivaient autour de ce cercle, et dans le temps et dans l'éspace, un mouvement régulier.[1]

The circulation of items at regular intervals in time is indicative of a rhythm, the presence of which is corroborated by further descriptions

---

1   Marcel Mauss, 'Essai sur le don: forme et raison d'échange dans les sociétés archaïques' and 'Les techniques du corps', in *Sociologie et Anthropologie* (Paris: PUF/Quadrige, 1950), p.176.

of the precision of the demands placed on those participating in exchange:

> En principe, la circulation de ces signes de richesse est incessante et infaillible. Ni on ne doit les garder trop longtemps, ni il ne faut être lent, ni il ne faut être dur à s'en défaire, ni on ne doit en gratifier personne d'autre que des partenaires déterminés dans un sens determiné.[2]

To the extent that the structures and ceremonies of giving constitute a 'système des prestations totales',[3] a phenomenon that implicates all aspects of communal life, from economics to religion to diplomatic relations with neighbouring tribes, this rhythm can be seen to encompass the whole of society. Social order is rendered contingent upon the maintenance of the rhythms of exchange. The point, therefore, is that it is not the use-value of the gifts given that functions as the underlying motive for exchange. What is at stake in the circulation of gifts is nothing less than the production of rhythm to encode and regulate the behaviour of tribal members. *Contra* Lévi-Strauss's reading of Mauss, there is no suggestion of structuralism here, that is, of objective, (quasi-)transcendental social categories structuring an intersubjective experience of time. Rhythm becomes a technique of 'discipline', in the Foucauldian sense of 'une anatomie politique du détail',[4] a co-ordination of bodies in space and time; likewise of 'codage' in the sense employed by Deleuze and Guattari in their interpretation of Mauss in *L'Anti-Œdipe*. The three-fold obligation to give, to receive and to reciprocate serves *inscriptively* to ensure that the individual is subordinate to the place allotted to him or her in the circuit of exchange.[5] By emphasising the necessity of maintaining the rhythm of circulation, the laws of exchange iterate the subordination of the individual to the community and the rhythms that hold it together. Rhythm is what binds the community, inscribing its members as but particular instances of a unified, collective subjectivity. What is given,

---

2   Ibid., p.180.
3   Ibid., p.151.
4   Michel Foucault, *Surveiller et punir* (Paris: Gallimard, 1975), p.163.
5   Gilles Deleuze and Félix Guattari, *Capitalisme et Schizophrénie I: L'Anti-Œdipe* (Paris: Minuit, 1972), pp. 219–226.

as a result, is of little importance. Gifts are quite often useless in practical terms, purely ceremonial or symbolic. Nor are they necessarily
retained long enough to be put to any effect:

> il ne semble pas que l'échange soit réellement libre. Même, en général, ce
> qu'on reçoit, et dont on a ainsi obtenu la possession – de n'importe quelle façon
> – on ne le garde pas pour soi, sauf si on ne peut s'en passer; d'ordinaire, on le
> transmet à quelqu'un d'autre, à un beau-frère, par exemple. Il arrive que des
> choses qu'on a acquises et données vous reviennent dans la même journée,
> identiques.[6]

It is by connecting rhythm with the concepts of 'discipline' and
'codage' that we can most fully appreciate the Maori notion of *hau*,
the myth of 'l'esprit des choses', according to which each gift is
impregnated with part of the soul of the giver. For the Maoris, the gift
has no intrinsic value. It is animated by a spirit that causes it to
circulate in accordance with a rhythm. Through the rhythm of the *hau*,
one's soul is irreversibly woven into the fabric of the community,
bound up with the souls of others, which are sedimented in objects
as they circulate. With the passing of a gift from one member of
the community to another, its recipients come to understand their
own identity as being distributed across the group, as opposed to
distinct from a collective identity. Gift-exchange thus symbolises 'une
mélange des âmes', an 'esprit collectif'.[7] Gift-exchange:

> mêle les âmes dans les choses [et] les choses dans les âmes. On mêle les vies et
> voilà comment les personnes et les choses mêlées sortent chacune de sa sphère
> et se mêlent: ce qui est précisément le contrat et l'échange.[8]

Fundamental to this rhythm are the myths and cultural symbolisms
through which the rules of exchange are articulated. At the heart of
these myths is the assertion of an ancestral presence that continues to
make itself felt in the present. Stories are told about how the failure
to uphold the traditions of giving will incur the rage of forefathers
who will not hesitate to exact revenge on the younger generations.

6   Mauss, 'Essai sur le don', p.189f.
7   Ibid., p.260.
8   Ibid., p.173.

The *esprit collectif* of the archaic tribe is thus not confined to the tribe; the identity of the individual is indissociable from that of his ancestors:

> les esprits des morts et les dieux [...] qui sont les véritables propriétaires de ss choses et des biens du monde. C'est avec eux qu'il était le plus nécessaire d'échanger et le plus dangereux de ne pas échanger.[9]

The rhythms of exchange in the present are thus indistinguishable from the rhythms of exchanges between the past and present. These rhythms emerge as the expression of the relationality between past and present, their repetition reinscribing the former within the latter.

The encompassing nature of the structures of gift-exchange prohibits an overly restrictive definition of gifts in terms of tangible objects. Mauss's privileging of the myths underlying exchange suggests that gift-exchange is ultimately about the exchange of experience. The actual objects exchanged are merely placeholders that give substance to, and thereby facilitate, the repetition and transmission of cultural heritage.

III

The oral tradition of song and storytelling features heavily across all the cultures analysed by Mauss as the medium through which the rules of exchange are transmitted. It is interesting to compare the rhythms of the songs that convey the rules of exchange with the rhythms of exchange that they generate. We can at least acknowledge the possibility that the rhythms associated with the oral tradition feed not only into the rhythm of gift-circulation, but also into the notion of macro-rhythms between past and present, of the past being interwoven with, and hence indistinguishable from, the present.

---

9   Ibid., p.167.

Reading the archaic gift-economy in this way, in terms of rhythm, enables us to discern a certain continuity between the work of Mauss and that of another prominent thinker of the age, who likely came into contact with Mauss's theory of gift-exchange through Georges Bataille's Collège de sociologie.[10] According to Walter Benjamin:

> storytelling is always the art of repeating stories, and this art is lost when the stories are no longer retained. It is lost because there is no more weaving and spinning to go on while they are being listened to. The more self-forgetful the listener is, the more deeply is what he listens to impressed upon his memory. When the rhythm of work has seized him, he listens to the tales in such a way that the gift of retelling them comes to him all by itself.[11]

For Benjamin, the rhythm of a particular story or song induces the state of forgetfulness in which the listener is most receptive to permeation by the broader rhythms of history, which is to say the rhythms of time that weave between past and present, bringing the past into the present. It is because he has been permeated by the 'rhythm of the work' that the archaic subject is able to communicate the necessity of maintaining the rhythm (of exchange) to others. Benjamin's point is both more complex and more substantial than it seems. Drawing on the Freudian claim that 'consciousness comes into being at the site of a memory trace', and is as such 'incompatible within the same system',[12] he suggests that the experience of history and tradition conveyed through the oral tradition is sedimented in the subject. This sedimentation of history in the body serves to endow the subject with the sense of being embedded in tradition that protects it from destabilisation and the uncertainties of the future. The rhythms that regulate the gift-economy and the exchanges of experience in storytelling are thus not only techniques of disciplining subjects. The ongoing exchange between past and present creates an additional

---

10   See, for example, Pierre Klossowski's claim that Benjamin 'fut un auditeur assidu' of the Collège, in Denis Hollier, *Le Collège de sociologie* (Paris: Gallimard, 1979), p. 586.
11   Walter Benjamin, 'The Storyteller', in *Illuminations*, ed. Hannah Arendt, trans. Harry Zohn (London: Pimlico, 1999), pp. 83–107 (p.91).
12   Freud, cited in Benjamin, *Illuminations*, p.157.

stability, lending the certainty of the repetition of rhythm to the future. The experience of rhythm structures the experience of the passing of time (be it consciously or unconsciously). Moreover, it does so from the standpoint of finitude and man's Being-in-the-world.

In *On the Phenomenology of the Consciousness of Internal Time*, where he outlines how the stability of expectation might be related to the experience of rhythm, Edmund Husserl notes:

> In the case of a given experience – in the case of familiar melodies, for example, or of melodies that are perhaps repeated – we frequently have *intuitive expectations* as well. Each new tone of a melody then fulfils this forwards-directed intention.[13]

This clearly comes close to the claim that belief in the stability of the future is related to the repetition of rhythm. However, in Husserl, this expectation is made possible by subjective structures for the cognition of time. In neither Mauss nor Benjamin is there reference to such a conceptual horizon, that is, an ideal notion of time imposed on the world by the subject. In the absence of such structures of temporality, our projected behaviour is conditioned by the disciplining presence of rhythm. The expectation of its continuation mitigates the threat of a revolutionary future, that is, a decisive break with the established order of tradition. Directly reminiscent of Mauss, Benjamin describes the oral tradition of storytelling in terms of the 'exchange' of experiences, where the audience's gift of receptivity to the storyteller is met with the receipt of a gift of experience embedded in history (*Erfahrung*).[14] In fact, as one commentator has noted, this notion of exchange would seem to underlie the whole Benjaminian notion of historically-grounded experience, or *Erfahrung*, including notably the experience of the 'auratic' work of art:

> Inherent in the gaze <of the subject looking at art> is *the expectation to receive a response from that to which it gives itself* [*dem er sich schenkt*]. Where this expectation [...] is answered, the experience of the aura is given in its plenitude [...]. The one who is looked at or thinks that he is looked at opens his gaze. To

---

13 Edmund Husserl, *On the Phenomenology of the Consciousness of Internal Time (1893–1917)*, trans. John Barnett Brough (Dordrecht: Kluwer, 1991), p.172.

14 Benjamin, 'The Storyteller', p.83.

experience the aura of a phenomenon means to invest it with the faculty to open its gaze.[15]

According to Nägele, 'the gift [of the gaze] produces the expectation of a corresponding gift and where the exchange works the plenitude of the gift is given' in the experience of the aura.[16] Benjamin talks of a certain 'distance', a distance between subject and object that opens up in this act of exchange. The receipt of the auratic gaze creates a time (a temporal space?) through which the rhythms of the past (the 'rhythm of the work', in which we might include the rhythms of the artist's brush on the canvas; also the rate of a work's passage through time) enter into the present. This exchange enfolds the present in a time in excess of itself, a circular time interweaving past and present, which cannot as such be reduced to a time of self-presence.

Benjamin diagnoses modernity as the collapse of the aura, in other words the disappearance of the rhythms of history that reinscribe the past within the present. These rhythms had unconsciously permeated the subject in a way that safeguarded against collapse into the oppressive interiority of pure self-presence. With modern techniques of reproduction, there is no perceptible difference between the original work and the copy. Although the two appear identical, they correspond to fundamentally different experiences. The unconscious rhythm of the aura is intrinsically impossible to reproduce. The reproduction cannot return the onlooker's gaze in an exchange that would give rise to the experience of the past within the present, because it tears the work from the rootedness in tradition that originally made it accessible to the onlooker; because it is itself purely of the present.

In modernity, the experience of art becomes not so much an experience of intimate exchange as of isolation. Giving himself over to a work of art, the onlooker is met only by the *absence* of the rhythms that interweave past and present. No experience of time as

15   Rainer Nägele, 'The Poetic Ground Laid Bare (Benjamin Reading Baudelaire)', in *Walter Benjamin: Theoretical Questions*, ed. David S. Ferris (Stanford: Stanford University Press, 1996), pp.118–38 (p.130). This passage cites Benjamin, ''On Some Motifs in Baudelaire',', in *Illuminations*, pp.152–196 (p.184); retranslation and incerpts by Nägele; emphasis mine.

16   Ibid., p.130.

rhythm is forthcoming. In the absence of dissymmetry, of the difference between the presence of the on-looking subject and the historicity of the object, there is only equivalence, which renders exchange meaningless, no more than substitution (what Baudrillard would call the 'nihilism' of modernity). There can be no rhythm here, since rhythm is made possible by the repetition of difference, namely the repetition of the past within the present. In place of the rhythms that re-present the past, the modern subject is assailed by 'shocks' of pure-presence, fleeting moments of consciousness unmediated by the protective barrier of cultural or historical memory. Shock arises because technology denies the present its inheritance. The gift of the gaze is rejected, leaving the subject to dwell on the emptiness of a present cut off from its past.

The rise of mechanical reproduction means that rhythmic experience is replaced by the pure self-identity of mechanised repetition. In denying that mechanical reproduction can reproduce the non-self-identical rhythms of gift-exchange, Benjamin is in implicit agreement with Henri Lefebvre, for whom:

> Seul donc un mouvement non-mécanique peut avoir un rythme [...] le rythme, en comportant une mesure, implique une certaine mémoire. Alors que la répétition mécanique s'exécute en reproduisant l'instant qui précède, le rythme conserve et la mesure qui débute le processus et le recommencement de ce processus avec ses modifications, donc avec sa multiplicité et pluralité. Sans répéter identiquement le 'même' mais en le subordonnant à l'alterité, voire à l'altération, c'est-à-dire, la différence.[17]

Benjamin's description of the modern subject's alienation from *Erfahrung*, its assailment by the non-rhythms of mechanisation, not just in art but also in the printed media that replaces the oral tradition and above all in the machines of the workplace, closely resembles what Lefebvre would diagnose as a state of 'arrhythmia'. Lefebvre draws a sharp distinction between the 'cyclical' rhythms of nature and the cosmos – the rhythms that, according to Eliade, the gift-economy

---

17   Henri Lefebvre and Catherine Régulier, 'Le Projet rythmanalytique', *Communications*, 41 (1985), 191–99 (p.195f).

seeks to replicate[18] – and the 'linearity' of time that predominates in technological, industrial society. Whereas cyclical rhythms are continuous, with neither beginning nor end, linear time is fragmented and discontinuous. The former give rise to a harmonious state of 'eurhythmia' – a term habitually reserved for healthy bodies.[19] The latter, by contrast, is characterised by the 'situation pathologique' of 'arrhythmia', where 'les rythmes se dissocient, se modifient et passent à côté de la *synchronisation*.'[20] The arrhythmia of commodity time is experienced as a disruption to the protective, eurhythmic time of the gift.

With the regime of linear clock-time imposed by the workplace, the natural, cyclical, rhythms of the body are overcoded.[21] For Lefebvre and Benjamin alike, in line with their respective Marxist humanisms, the end result is alienation, moreover alienation from a sense of time and historical destiny. The use of rhythm as a technique of discipline for the creation of a collective archaic subject means that there was no individuated archaic subject who could suffer alienation. The collapse of the eurhythmic, collective archaic subject suggests that the modern individuation of subjectivity is more than just a condition of alienation. The states of alienation and individuation are intrinsically related.

Alienation is accordingly a distinctly modern condition, stemming from the breakdown of rhythm, which exposes the subject in its individuation. This completely transfigures the nature of the political in modernity. We see a shift from the coextension of a (collective) subject with the totality of time to the modern subject as abandoned by time, confined to a present that has access and refers only to itself, where the future announces itself as a shock that cannot be assimilated

18   Mircea Eliade, *Le Mythe de l'éternel retour* (Paris: Folio, 1969), p.112.
19   This is again consistent with Deleuze and Guattari's reading of gift-economic tribes in terms of a pre-individual, unified, collective subjectivity, 'un investissement collectif des organes' organised on the 'corps plein de la terre'. Deleuze and Guattari, *Capitalisme et Schizophrénie I: L'Anti-Œdipe*, p.166, p.181.
20   Henri Lefebvre, *Éléments de rythmanalyse: introduction à la connaissance des rythmes* (Paris: Syllepse, 1992), p.92.
21   Lefebvre and Régulier, 'Le Projet rythmanalytique', p.192.

into experience. We might go further and suggest that this claustro-phobic entrapment in the present is what motivates the now pre-dominant pursuit of multiculturalism and theoretical pluralism, that is to say, the pursuit of difference within identity and a reconfiguration of the present as non-self-identical.

Again, this abandonment of the subject by rhythm, by time, brings us away from structuralism, moreover from the modern idea of the ontological structures of time as interior to the subject. *Contra* Lévi-Strauss's reading of Mauss the proto-structuralist,[22] we find Mauss the post-structuralist, the proto-Foucauldian who moreover anticipates Heidegger's idea of *Geworfenheit*, or thrownness, the interiority of the subject to time. Reading Mauss alongside Benjamin and Lefebvre serves to distance him from earlier structuralist appro-priations of the gift-economy. It also demonstrates a way in which the above might all be thought of as early thinkers of difference and repe-tition, whose ideas presage those of later critics of structuralism.

For Lefebvre, the human body is one '*gerbe* de rythmes' among others;[23] rhythmanalysis is the science that enables us to identify this. We might see it thus as the technique through which to diagnose what Benjamin regards as the crisis of modernity. Turning to rhythm, we might politicise and thereby reappropriate time as the experience that underlies our concept of the political. The experience of time, when viewed in terms of rhythm, is political precisely because it is not reducible to pre-experiential universal structures and social categories; precisely because it is rendered foremost an object of experience, contingent upon a set of disciplinary practices and technological circumstances. Rhythm thus serves to reground the political in experi-ence, above all in the experience and production of temporal identity.

22   Claude Lévi-Strauss, 'Introduction à l'œuvre de Marcel Mauss', in Mauss, *Sociologie et anthropologie* (Paris: PUF/Quadrige, 1950).
23   Lefebvre, *Éléments de rythmanalyse*, p.32.

Gerald Moore

Suggested Reading

Benjamin, Walter, *Illuminations*, ed. Hannah Arendt, trans. Harry
Zohn (London: Pimlico, 1999).
Deleuze, Gilles and Félix Guattari, *Capitalisme et Schizophrénie I:
L'Anti-Œdipe* (Paris: Minuit, 1972).
Husserl, Edmund, *On the Phenomenology of the Consciousness of
Internal Time (1893–1917)*, Vol. 4, Collected Works, ed. Rudolf
Bernet, trans. John Barnett Brough (Dordrecht: Kluwer, 1991).
Lefebvre, Henri, *Éléments de rythmanalyse: introduction à la con-
naissance des rythmes* (Paris: Sylleèpse, 1992).
Lefebvre, Henri and Catherine Régulier, 'Le Projet rythmanalytique',
Communications, 41 (1985), 191–99.

IV Everyday Rhythms

MICHAEL SHERINGHAM

Everyday Rhythms, Everyday Writing: Réda with Deleuze and Guattari

A connection between the dimension, or level, of everyday life and the potentially rhythmical character of lived experience is familiar to us through such realities as circadian rhythms. Moreover, when one tries, on the basis of the set of discourses that progressively shaped this key concept in modern culture, to establish some of the para- meters that define the *quotidien*, rhythm has a prominent place, alongside such ideas as the overlooked, the recurrent, the residual, the self-evident.[1] A central project of Henri Lefebvre's three-volume *Critique de la vie quotidienne* (1947–82) is to establish how 'rhythmic temporalities' – beneficent rhythms, including cyclical time, which blend the heterogeneous array of everyday experience into some sort of homogeneity – subsist within the linear time of modern industrial society, and the 'compressed time' of the modern bureaucratic world.[2] Indeed one of Lefebvre's last publications was *Éléments de rythm- analyse: introduction à la connaissance des rythmes* (1992).[3] In the literature on the *quotidien* one could also cite the many places in Michel de Certeau's *L'Invention du quotidien* (1980) where rhythm is a factor, for example in his accounts of urban walking or of reading.[4] There is also the fascinating discussion of 'idiorrythmie', designating a fluid balance between individual and community, in Roland Barthes's posthumous *Comment vivre ensemble* (2002). Drawing on

1   See Michael Sheringham, *Everyday Life: Theories and Practices from Surrealism to the Present* (Oxford: Oxford University Press, 2006).
2   Henri Lefebvre, *Critique de la vie quotidienne*, 3 vols (Paris: L'Arche, 1947–82).
3   Lefebvre, *Éléments de rythmanalyse: introduction à la connaissance des rythmes* (Paris: Syllepse, 1992).
4   Michel de Certeau, *L'Invention du quotidien* (Paris: Gallimard, 1980).

Émile Benveniste's seminal distinction between *rythmos*, implying pattern and regular cadence, and *rhuthmos*, designating 'une forme improvisée, modifiable', Barthes argues that 'idiorrythmie' is 'par définition individuel' and reflects how the subject engages with social and natural codes: 'l'idiorrythmie [...] renvoie aux formes subtiles du genre de vie: les humeurs, les configurations non stables, les passages dépressifs ou exaltés; bref, le contraire même d'une cadence cassante, implacable de régularité.'[5]

In order to probe the links between the upsurge of interest in the nature of rhythm and the convergence of attention on the quotidian, which both occurred in the period around 1980, I intend to read in parallel the important remarks on rhythm in Deleuze and Guattari's *Mille Plateaux* (1980), and the opening text of Jacques Réda's book of prose poetry, *Les Ruines de Paris* (1977). Although they do not allude to the *quotidien* directly, taken together these texts suggest how the rhythmical can be seen as a key figure for the everyday. For they identify rhythm less with repetition and return than with momentum, divergence, and a constant traversing and subverting of fixed codes, articulations and contexts. Seen in this way, rhythmicity expresses the everyday's multiplicity, and the lack of fixed qualities that make it a place of passage, variation, and layering, which resists codification. At issue here, in the convergence of the everyday and rhythm, is the status of the subject. Although Deleuze and Guattari bracket out the subject in favour of processes and flows, and see *subjectivation* as the imposition of a limitation, they are concerned with the vital experience and rhythms of the human animal. It is, however, useful to have in mind Henri Meschonnic's more or less contemporaneous *Critique du rythme* (1981), which notes its affinities with *Mille Plateaux*'s development of the notion of rhythm, but puts forward the view that rhythm, properly understood, is the key to the essential historicity of the human subject.[6] Based on readings of modernist

5   Roland Barthes, *Comment vivre ensemble* (Paris: Seuil, 2002), p. 39.
6   Henri Meschonnic, *Critique du rythme: anthropologie historique du langage* (Lagrasse: Verdier, 1981), pp.522–3. See also Nicolas Abraham, Nicholas Rand, Maria Torok, *Rythmes: de l'oeuvre, de la traduction, de la psychanalyse* (Paris: Flammarion, 1993).

poetic texts, Meschonnic's *Critique du rythme* and *La Rime et la vie* (1989)[7] also have the virtue of frequently recalling the urban focus of many texts that link issues of rhythm, subjectivity and everydayness.

In *Mille Plateaux*, rhythm is the principle that creates passage-ways between heterogeneous *milieux*. The key factor here is the ultimately aesthetic process of appropriation, or territorialisation, for which the emblem is the 'ritournelle' – a repeated musical phrase separating larger units, a 'petit air', or a snatch of song. A frightened child who hums a jingle in the dark creates order in the face of chaos. When we organise our domestic space – often including aural elements, radio, TV, Hi-fi – we act as 'bricoleurs', managing transition between heterogeneous items. When we leave our interior for the outside world, we have the opportunity to improvise, to vary our established itineraries by adopting new pathways and routines. Drawing on ethnology, the account of the 'ritournelle' in *Mille Plateaux* often chimes with ways of talking about the everyday. For example, Barthes's account of 'idiorrythmie' invokes habitat, the 'espace apprivoisé' where a creature is 'chez lui'. Distinguishing two functions of 'clôture' – as protection, and as a marking out of one's own space or territory, one's distance – Barthes cites E.T. Hall's concept of proxemics which studies 'les espaces subjectifs en tant que le sujet les habite affectivement'[8] – also a reference point for Deleuze and Guattari, and echoing Georges Perec's *Espèces d'espaces* and other texts.

Deleuze and Guattari insist that the 'ritournelle', and the rhythm it makes by punctuating the line of experience, is also a mode that allows the openness of chaos to subsist rather than be denied. Like all living creatures we exist simultaneously in a series of *milieux*, each possessing its own code, determined by periodic repetitions. Yet each code is constantly being 'transcoded', as one milieu – for example that linked to the perceptual apparatus – becomes the host or ground for another, for example the milieu linked to bodily processes: 'Il y a rythme dès qu'il y a passage transcodé d'un milieu à un autre, communication de milieux, co-ordination d'espaces – temps

7   Meschonnic, *La Rime et la vie* (Lagrasse: Verdier, 1989).
8   Barthes, *Comment vivre ensemble*, p.156.

hétérogènes' (p.385).[9] Rhythm is a kind of go-between in that, by virtue of its very in-betweeness, it partakes of chaos itself while at the same time serving as its antidote. Rhythm is not the same as measure or cadence. Measure implies code within a specific signifying milieu, while 'le rythme est l'Inégal ou l'Incommensurable, toujours en transcodage'. For Deleuze and Guattari:

> la mesure est dogmatique, mais le rythme est critique, il noue des instants critiques, ou se noue au passage d'un milieu dans un autre. Il n'opère pas dans un espace-temps homogène, mais avec des blocs hétérogènes. Il change de direction. (p.385)

Rhythm is not on the same plane as the elements it deals with: 'Le rythme se pose entre deux milieux, ou entre deux entre-milieux, comme entre deux eaux, entre deux heures, entre chien et loup, *twilight* ou *zwielicht*' (p.385). This switching of *milieux* is vital as it accounts for how rhythm can involve return and periodic repetition but at the same time not fall back into sterile repetition, single measure. In the economy of rhythm, repetition within a milieu effectively creates another milieu: 'c'est la différence qui est rythmique, et non pas la répétition qui, pourtant, la produit' (p.386).

While it switches *milieux* the operation of rhythm does participate in a process Deleuze and Guattari call territorialisation. Rhythms produce territories when they are expressive, in other words when rhythm works on, or works with, 'matières expressives' such as sounds, colours, or gestures: 'Un territoire emprunte à tous les milieux, il mord sur eux, il les prend à bras de corps (bien qu'il reste fragile aux intrusions). Il est construit avec des aspects ou des portions de milieux' (p.386). The operation of rhythm, via the 'ritournelle', becomes creative of territory when the constituents 'cessent d'être fonctionnelles pour devenir expressives. Il y a territoire dès qu'il y a expressivité du rythme' (p.387). To illustrate this point, Deleuze and Guattari evoke the colours of birds and fish, and how, above and beyond other functions, their colour, in becoming expressive, marks a territory: 'C'est la marque qui fait le territoire [...] La territorialisation

9   Gilles Deleuze and Félix Guattari, *Mille Plateaux* (Paris: Minuit, 1980). Page references will be given in the text.

est l'acte du rythme devenu expressif, ou des composantes de milieux devenues qualitatives' (p.388). But by virtue of being rhythmical, the marking of a territory, even if it produces a dimension, occurs on a different plane from actions: 'il conserve le caractère le plus général du rythme, de s'inscrire sur un autre plan que celui des actions' (p.388). And this means that territorialisation does not produce a subject. Even though this appropriation is aesthetic and expressive in kind, and thus constitutes 'signatures' on the part of the markers, what it produces 'n'est pas la marque constituante d'un sujet, c'est la marque constituante d'un domaine, d'une demeure. La signature n'est pas l'indication d'une personne, c'est la formation hasardeuse d'un domaine' (p.389). Here the aesthetic process, the predilection for qualities, is linked to the production of a space: 'C'est avec la demeure que surgit l'inspiration. C'est en même temps que j'aime une couleur et que j'en fais mon étendard ou ma pancarte. On met sa signature sur un objet comme on plante son drapeau sur une terre' (p.389).

One effect of Deleuze and Guattari's ethological parti-pris is to insist that expressive qualities are not just subjective expressions and emotions but are 'auto-objectives, c'est-à-dire trouvant une objectivité dans le territoire qu'ils tracent' (p.390). This specification with its apparent circularity is very relevant to Réda. As is the account of how expressive materials produce mobile relationships which themselves express the links between the territories they produce, the inner level of impulses, and the outer level of circumstances. And also the proposition that territorial motifs 'forment des visages ou des personnages rythmiques', so that the rhythm is not simply associated with a subject – Réda for example – but becomes that subject, constitutes it: 'c'est le rythme lui-même qui est tout le personnage [...] Non plus des signatures, mais un style' (p.391). We can link this to an earlier chapter in *Mille Plateaux* where Deleuze and Guattari define style – that of Kafka, Beckett, or Godard, but one could say equally that of Réda – in terms of continuous variation: 'un chromatisme généralisé' which stems from the '[mise] en variation continue des éléments quelconques.' Thus 'un style n'est pas une création psychologique individuelle, mais un agencement d'énonciation' (p.123). Later they describe the 'ritournelle' as un prisme, un constant d'espace-temps. Elle agit sur ce qui l'entoure, son ou lumière, pour en tirer des vibrations variées, des décompositions, projections et transformations. La ritournelle a aussi une fonction catalytique: non seulement augmenter la vitesse des échanges et réactions dans ce qui l'entoure, mais assurer les intéractions indirectes entre éléments dénués d'affinités dites naturelles. (p.430)

And thus, 'la ritournelle fabrique du temps' (p.431): rhythmical activity, combining heterogeneous fields and entities, produces temporalities.

A final parameter of territorialisation is its link with distance. The operation of rhythm (as in Barthes's 'idiorrythmie') is as much to do with taking one's distance, steering one's course away from – as with proximity or fusion:

Le territoire, c'est d'abord la distance critique entre deux êtres de mêmes espèces: marquer ses distances. Ce qui est mien, c'est d'abord une distance, je ne possède que des distances. [...] Il y a tout un art des poses, des postures, des silhouettes, des pas et des voix. [...] La distance critique n'est pas une mesure, c'est un rythme. (p.393)

Territorialisation is also an operator of deterritorialisation. Although always involving the 'natal' and the *heimlich*, 'ritournelle' – and rhythm – are also linked to what Deleuze and Guattari call 'lignes de fuite'. This connects with breaking codes:

L'essentiel est dans le décalage que l'on constate entre le code et le territoire. [...] le territoire se forme au niveau d'un certain *décodage* [...] Partout ou la territorialité apparaît, elle instaure une *distance critique* intra-spécifique entre membres d'une même espèce; et c'est en vertu de son propre décalage par rapport aux *différences spécifiques* qu'elle devient un moyen de différenciation indirect, oblique. (p.396)

Let us now look at how Jacques Réda takes his distances, carves out his differential territory but also deterritorialises himself in the everyday city. The back cover of Réda's *Les Ruines de Paris* begins by quoting the opening of the first text, 'Le Pied furtif de l'hérétique' (which will be our main focus), a generic prelude to the forays or searches into what Réda calls elsewhere 'la nébuleuse parisienne':

« Vers six heures, l'hiver, volontiers je descends l'avenue à gauche, par les jardins... » Ensuite, de Belleville à Passy, de Montmartre à la Butte-aux-Cailles [...] il n'y a plus qu'à se laisser guider par les pas d'un promeneur tour à tour (ou ensemble) nuageux, curieux, inquiet, hilare, furibond, tendre, ahuri, à travers les arrondissements et boulevards de Paris.

The impersonal formulation, 'se laisser guider par les pas d'un promeneur' relates first to the reader but also suggests that the 'promeneur' is guided by his own 'pas' (this reversal – the 'promeneur' being 'promené' – recurs constantly in Réda).[10] Rather than an agent, the walking subject is framed as an affective space that is by turns (or at once) 'nuageux, curieux [...]', etc., while Paris is in turn personified as having secrets, desires and morals. Other sorties, beyond the city, are then evoked, always involving styles of motion akin to the walking or strutting bass of the jazz player: 'toujours au rythme de la marche ou des trains, imitant le rebond plein d'espoir de la *basse ambulante*, en jazz, sur bon tempo'. And this, along with the last sentence ('sans cesse on repart...'), invokes a rhythm that is also directional, a momentum that is linked to the endless 'resurgissement' of passage itself.

Turning now to 'Le Pied furtif...' I want to argue that what is rhythmical in this text is not so much its beat or cadence as a cluster of features that can be related to the ideas of Deleuze and Guattari: the switching between or out of codes; the sense of creating a territory based on taking one's distance; the treatment of 'matières expressives'; and the presence of specifically '"ritournelle"-like' elements. And furthermore that, in Réda's case, these facets of the rhythmical can be related to the traversal of everyday space, and to everyday experience when this is seen in terms of an opposition between dead routine – purely mono-coded repetition – and an experience of heterogeneity bound up with a rhythmicity that does not produce or consist in unity but in an endless knitting together of the heterogeneous into provisional ensembles.

Although in prose, like the subsequent shorter texts that make up *Les Ruines de Paris*, a collection that marked Réda's turn towards the

---

10   On this see Sheringham, 'Jacques Réda and the Commitments of Poetry', *L'Esprit Créateur*, 32 (1992) 77–88.

city and the everyday, 'Le Pied furtif...' is more lyrical, more lin-
guistically and poetically supercharged, than the texts which follow.
Yet the poem is essentially the account of a walk through Paris as
dusk descends. The title points to the text's bassline – walking – and
to dissidence: the step is 'furtif' because it is 'hérétique' – and this
counter-orthodoxy is linked to the narrating subject's non-utilitarian
predilections, and his susceptibility to interaction with his surroundings. In the following brief discussion I will focus primarily on
the beginning and end of this highly intricate text (consisting of six
pages without a paragraph break).

In the opening sentence (p.9),[11] we learn of the narrator's
proclivity to follow a particular 'avenue' down its left-hand side, via
some gardens, at nightfall (other poems will link this to the very
Baudelairean motif of the 'crépuscule du soir', and the dangerous
transitional moment it represents: between night and day, but also
between realms, reigns, climates, etc.). The poet seems to slip into
the city via a conduit that is already in-between, and he tells us that
he stumbles and bumps into chairs because – like Johnny-head-in-the-
air – his eyes look upwards to the sky whose quality of incompre-
hensibility is also that of 'l'amour qui s'approche' (love and the poet
as amorous subject will be one of the text's codes). The second
sentence is devoted to the indefinable colour of the sky, a dull shade
of turquoise, and the way this 'aspire tous mes yeux' also involves
an osmosis or reversal, whereby a light that eludes the visible becomes (or reveals) an inner dimension of the experiencing subject. In
the following lines, various sounds, colours and lighting effects – a
stream of perceptions – are evoked in conjunction with the antithetical
qualities of love and night, both portrayed as forces that are driven
to express themselves through concrete entities. Everything in the
walker's path becomes a 'matière d'expression' in a process that is
rhythmical in the way the next item chimes with the preceding one, or
others already mentioned, but at the same time involves another
dimension or order of experience. And if everything that grabs the
'hérétique's' attention along his way is apprehended via qualities that

11   Jacques Réda, *Les Ruines de Paris* (Paris: Gallimard, 1977). Page references
      will be incorporated in the text.

are also, or become, his own, this is seemingly by virtue of an endless capacity for subdivision ('en subdivisions, c'est l'obscur [already a variant on nuit] s'arrachant par la masse des arbres qui chante, qui veut s'y perdre') whereby an entity is grasped – synecdochically or metonymically – via one of its features or parts. Thus the night modulates into 'l'obscur', personified as a sonorous presence actualised by the trees that darken as it tries to cling to them. And this segment ends with an affirmation of affinity, picking up first the sound – 'j'ai la même voix dans la tête et la même épaisseur monotone' (as the trees) – and thus the same capacity to be a 'matière expressive' for the realm of the nocturnal.

The next segment begins by 'explaining' the implicit principle that accounts for this osmosis: 'Car il arrive qu'une obsession de transmutation urgente nous possède: à force de le contempler, passer du côté du spectacle, entrer dans la substance aveugle qui sait, qui resplendit' (p.10). The irresistible desire for transmutation, for becoming other – a part of the 'substance aveugle' – via an act of contemplation so intense that the spectacle allows us to enter it, is seen to be paradoxical given that, as the following sentence observes, the witnessing subject already contains ('débordait') the sky he aims at. And this realisation brings him back to earth with a bump: 'C'est l'instant où je trébuche ...'. Ultimately the process at work here is not ascensional but lateral: the desire is for transmutation itself; and favouring one's own transmutability is seen to be a way of responding to, or participating in, a dimension of experience that is not above or below but constituted via a particular way of processing what comes one's way. There is nothing special about the things the poet encounters; what is special is his mode of encountering them, and the way this mode transmutes them – and him.

As he reaches the Place de la Concorde, the milieu becomes 'tout à coup maritime' (p.10), a transformation that seems to be induced by a combination of factors: the wide open spaces, gusts of wind flapping flags, and a monumentality that conjures up Lorrain's paintings of ships in harbours – artworks already ambiguous insofar as the seemingly vast edifices surrounding Lorrain's ports often seem to make the sea unreal. In effect, the maritime code that transmutes the cityscape is over-determined by a cultural code stemming from classical painting, while the 'ritournelle' here is the walker's visual memory. This is poetic metaphoricity, in the tradition of Baudelaire's 'Le Cygne' ('tout pour moi devient allégorie'), but more markedly a function of the transmutation engendered by transit and the aspiration towards transition. 'Making his way', as if along a beach, the poet acknowledges that it is the 'indécision du soir' – the ambiguity of evening light – that opens up this space. Although as the next segment will testify – in a kind of parenthetical flashback to moments in broad daylight ('plein air') – this bit of Paris always has an estuary-like feel, linked to the quality of light and its interaction with architecture. The stones of Paris, as in the 'blocs et échafaudages', and 'ce Louvre' in 'Le Cygne', become a 'ritournelle', infiltrating other contexts.

In the fourth segment the deserted park which ruminates (we recognise the Tuileries) counters the pompous assertiveness of the 'allée en terrasse [...] qui part droit comme un coup de fanfare étrange de la Raison' (p.11), redolent of fanatical inflexibility and geometric law. The 'ritournelle' here is the earth, the compacted soil, and particularly the blade of grass – a key motif in Réda, and also in Deleuze and Guattari (p.399) – that obstinately refuses to be obliterated in this 'jardin français' and invites only 'le pied furtif de l'hérétique' (the poem's title phrase occurs here). Later in the Tuileries passage, the 'ritournelle' is a snatch of music heard – or rather imagined and interpolated – when the poet comes across a merry-go-round where the fake painted horses invoke animality, childhood and ageing, and where the final strains of Fauré's *Requiem* which come into his mind redirect his attention, once again switching codes.

Let us now fast-forward to the end of the heretic's progress. In what we can construe as its penultimate segment (p.13), the beginning, 'Bien sûr je pense à une Dame', pulls the plug on a flight of fantasy, centred on the moon, which casts the poet as howling wolf and lunatic. If love and desire are part of the picture, it is motion – the walking that love-sickness induces – that is catalytic. Echoing Laforgue, and also Beckett's ruminative narrators (rumination, which favours variousness, is an operator of metamorphosis), the poet specifies the conditions of walking: the key article of the walker's faith is that '[l]e désespoir n'existe pas pour un homme qui marche' (p.14). Hence a need to avoid social exchange that inevitably pins you down, arresting the rhythm of transmutation: 'C'est pourquoi je vais vite et droit devant moi vers la rase campagne à fourrés qui règne autour des Invalides. Déjà rue de Babylone il arrive qu'on croise un lapin' (p.14). Here the switch of milieu invokes the code of the 'campagnard', triggered by the vast expanse of the Esplanade des Invalides, and then by the provincial aura of the streets of the seventh arrondissement which conjure up 'rase campagne', 'des cloches qui tintent derrière les vieux murs', and a wind redolent of 'terre molle.'

Finally, 'Je rentre': the poet gets back to base, rejoining, like Apollinaire at the end of 'Zone', a cosy domestic space: eggs, cheese, wine, lots of records, and a hi-fi system that allows you to turn up the bass. And this leads into a final projection, a last transmutation or role, which axiomatically sums up the process enacted in the walk. In casting himself as the vibrating strings of the double bass ('tendues comme l'expérience'), the narrator sidesteps or sets aside psychology ('Est-ce que je suis gai [...] triste?') and metaphysics ('Est-ce que j'avance vers une énigme, une signification?'), and affirms, in lieu of any wish for knowledge ('je ne cherche pas trop à comprendre'), the pure desire to progress rhythmically ('je continue d'avancer, pizzicato') and thus, through a forward momentum that constantly shifts the scenes, to participate in the wider vibration of the world, of the cosmos as Deleuze and Guattari would put it.

In Réda, as in *Mille Plateaux*, the 'travail de la "ritournelle"' involves an aesthetic process where a minor element that returns brings about a change of gear, a switching of codes, and in doing so constitutes a parallel track, enmeshed with, but also at a distance from the plane of actions and events. Réda's walk through Paris, between day and night, involves recognisable locales and activities – he is in the city we know – but also a parallel universe, a possible world that is a product of the way his progress selects and processes the elements it traverses. It is walking that makes the territory: territorialisation is inseparable from this peripatetic, mobile mode of apprehension. Yet even if we may ask where all the city's usual noises and crowds have gone, the 'promeneur' is not in a solipsistic cocoon: he may pick up stray bits and pieces, but they don't build a cosy nest. The counter-story, the fable he concocts, may have stable elements – and reflect his heretical options – but they are always improvised and *ad hoc*: the 'ritournelle' is a response to a threat, a deviation induced by desire's resistance to constraint. The kind of rhythmicity at work in this prose poem, which I have sought to characterise by way of Deleuze and Guattari, can, moreover, be linked to those ways of experiencing the everyday (as a dimension where freedom balances constraint, and where inventiveness stems from familiarity with the rhythms of constant change) that Lefebvre, Barthes, de Certeau and Perec, along with others, have taught us to recognise.

Suggested Reading

Barthes, Roland, *Comment vivre ensemble* (Paris: Seuil, 2002).
Deleuze, Gilles and Félix Guattari, *Mille Plateaux* (Paris: Minuit, 1980).
Meschonnic, Henri, *Critique du rythme* (Lagrasse: Verdier, 1981).
Réda, Jacques, *Les Ruines de Paris* (Paris: Gallimard, 1977).
Sheringham, Michael, *Everyday Life: Theories and Practices from Surrealism to the Present* (Oxford: Oxford University Press, 2006).

SOPHIE FUGGLE

Le Parkour: Reading or Writing the City?

Over the past ten years, the activity referred to as 'le parkour' has grown from a little known underground movement to a highly respected discipline practised by thousands worldwide. Much of parkour's appeal lies in the challenge it offers to established ways of understanding the urban spaces in which we live and move, inscribing individual, subversive rhythms against the more collective, uniform rhythms of everyday city life. The aim of this essay is to examine how parkour embodies poststructuralist notions of text, author and reader and how it can offer a way of deconstructing architecture which both develops and departs from the work of Jacques Derrida and architects such as Bernard Tschumi and Peter Eisenman. It will also explore how parkour, like other forms of cultural and textual practice, becomes caught up and restricted by attempts to position and define its method and philosophy. Finally, in response to the limits and constraints imposed upon parkour, I suggest that parkour can nevertheless maintain its freedom and originality. In particular I will be looking at how parkour embodies a form of care of the self, as described by Michel Foucault in his later works.

Parkour is frequently described as 'l'art du déplacement'. It involves moving at speed, running, jumping and climbing from one point to another. However, this movement rejects conventional routes and modes of access. The idea is to take the most direct route from A to B, even if this route encounters obstacles such as buildings, walls and barriers. Where this route traverses conventional modes of access such as stairs, these are negotiated in a way intended to disrupt and challenge regular usage. With the example of stairs, this could involve jumping or climbing down a stairwell or vaulting over banisters. Achieving this involves a mental process in which the three-dimensional landscape becomes flattened out. Everything then exists on the same level and as such, nothing is an 'obstacle' and therefore nothing can stand in the way of movement. Coupled with this mental process or state of mind is a series of carefully executed physical jumps and other movements. To jump from the roof of one building to another requires a certain faith, but this is not blind faith. It is more a confidence in one's own ability, an ability acquired as a result of lengthy training and practice. Consequently, parkour involves a break with established, everyday rhythms both in terms of movement and perception. Moreover, in breaking with the rhythms and patterns of movement prescribed by city life, parkour demands that one create one's own rhythm through the dual process of physical effort and mental creativity.

The name 'parkour' has its origins in a form of military training known as 'le parcours du combattant'. This was a technique deployed by the French in Vietnam as a means of crossing difficult and un-known jungle terrain with maximum speed and efficiency. Parkour is also referred to as 'PK' and has been translated into English as 'free running' and 'urban freeflow'. Practitioners of parkour tend to be known as 'traceurs' or free runners. David Belle and Sebastien Foucan are generally recognised as the founders of parkour. They developed the discipline whilst growing up in the suburbs of Paris in the eighties and nineties. Their influences came from gymnastics and martial arts as well as from David Belle's father, Raymond Belle, who had been a soldier in Vietnam.

Parkour cannot really be described in terms of a conventional sport with fixed rules and regulations but more in terms of its 'styles' and 'philosophies' in a similar way to martial arts. The purpose or meaning behind parkour is two-fold. First, it is a question of what David Belle has referred to as 'escape' and 'reach' – the development of quick thinking and physical agility enabling one to get out of difficult situations and to go wherever one wishes.[1] Secondly, it is about elegance. It is not just a matter of travelling from one obstacle

---

1   David Belle and the PAWA Team, Parkour Worldwide Association (2005) <http://web.archive.org/web/20050508021450/www.pawa.fr/Welcome/welcome.html>. Accessed 28 May 2007.

to another but of doing so gracefully. For Sebastien Foucan, parkour is about being 'fluid like water.'[2]

It is worth noting here that much of what is written and said about parkour today – including, to a certain extent, this essay – is both inspired by and indebted to earlier writing and discussion about skateboarding. In July 2000, the architecture magazine *Blueprint* published an article by Iain Borden on how skateboarding offered a new form of interaction with the city.[3] At that time, parkour was a relatively unknown phenomenon especially outside of Paris. Skateboarding, on the other hand, had been around since the 1960s and was already becoming an important topic in the discussion of youth and sub-cultures. Yet, where skateboarding requires the intermediary object of the skateboard, parkour establishes a relationship between the individual and his or her surroundings which depends entirely upon the human body – defined in terms of the body's freedom as well as its physical limitations, and also in terms of the movement of the body across a multi-layered, multi-dimensional space.

Having briefly described parkour and its origins, I wish to ask whether running and jumping around a city can challenge traditional ideas of text and authorship. More precisely, to what extent can parkour be described as a means of both reading and writing the city? We have long been comfortable with a notion of 'text' which extends beyond an isolated work of literature. Textual practice is generally accepted as an exercise involving both reader and writer, terms which since Roland Barthes have become interchangeable. All cultural activities – art, architecture, cinema, television, music, dance and martial arts – can be regarded as forms of text that embody a type of reading and writing.

Moreover, the idea of 'reading' the city, the concept that one's physical surroundings can be read as a form of text, is one which has been around at least since Baudelaire's *flâneur* and perhaps even

2   Dan Jones, 'Parkour: A Natural Perspective', *The Urban Freeflow Network*, (2005) <http://www.urbanfreeflow.com/articles/articles.htm>. Accessed 28 May 2007.
3   Iain Borden, 'Chariots of Ire', *Blueprint: Architecture, Design & Contemporary Culture*, 174 (July 2000), 38–40.

before that. But how exactly does the reading offered by parkour differ from other readings of the city and its architecture? The urban landscape dictates to us how we should interact with its architecture in terms of functionality and accessibility. We visit certain buildings and places with the intention of carrying out certain tasks and achieving certain aims. The way in which we reach and move within these spaces is mapped out for us in relation to these aims. This is not a bad thing in itself since it is a necessary part of the productive forces operating in society. However, when architecture and town-planning focus solely on specific functions, our experience and interpretation of the spaces in which we live and work can become restricted to the extent that all other possibilities become excluded and architecture becomes a more negative form of social control. The façades of office buildings are often designed to be imposing and unfriendly in order to discourage unwanted lingerers. Likewise, big city firms will design their office space to include every thinkable amenity: ATM machines, fitness centres and even areas to sleep. Consequently, employees have little need or reason to leave their place of work and, in some extreme cases, come to forget that a world outside the office exists.

Parkour calls into question these notions of functionality and accessibility since it is the traceur who selects his or her route and the aspects of the architectural landscape with which to interact. It also avoids the monotony often imposed upon individuals as they make their journeys around the city. While traceurs might frequent the same architectural spaces, each encounter will involve interactions with different elements of these spaces. For example, where one day they may choose to travel over a fence or railing using one particular jump, the next time they might use a different jump or traverse the fence at a different point. As a reader of literature gradually becomes more skilled in identifying themes, styles and clues as to the outcome of a particular novel or play, in the same way the traceur's ability to identify new methods of approaching their surroundings improves as he or she becomes more experienced.

But parkour is not only a means of reading the city. Parkour is also a form of writing, constructing a new city from the one presented to us by architects and town planners. It is a form of writing which is both collective and individual. Traceurs often travel in groups, but each traceur must work out his or her own method of traversing the various obstacles encountered. A traceur crossing the city tells a story of this city from a unique perspective. Their story involves elements of adventure, danger and discovery. The narrative provides minute details of everyday things we usually ignore or take for granted, such as handrails and windowsills. These take on a new importance in the journey of the traceur. At other times, the narrative provides a panoramic view of the city as the traceur surveys the landscape from the roof of a high building.

While recognising Foucan and Belle as its founders, parkour nevertheless tends to dispose of notions of authorship. As a form of writing, it completely acknowledges its intertextuality: movements are 'borrowed' or developed from martial arts, gymnastics and athletics. Consequently, parkour incorporates the idea of 'jeu' described in the work of Derrida.[4] A traceur's originality lies not in the choice of route or the movements used but in the infinite number of combinations and permutations that these can produce.

Parkour can also be described in terms of 'unwriting'. A traceur needs not merely move from A to B, but also back to A again. This self-effacing element of parkour, as it demands the traceur retrace his or her steps, represents just one of the ways in which parkour is an affirmation of silence. Silence is also affirmed in a more literal manner: unlike the loud, grating noise associated with skateboarding, the traceur makes little or no sound. Commenting on the audible elements of skateboarding, Borden explains how strident sounds are integral to the urban disorder or disruption sought by the skateboarder, marking the key distinction, as identified by Anne Galloway, between traceur and skateboarder.[5] Perhaps it is this silence which represents the traceur's challenge to the proliferation of noise associated with city life. For a brief moment, the onlooker might glimpse the passing traceurs, but only by knowing where to look before they disappear without a trace. This onlooker, who is also a reader, has their eyes

---

4   See in particular Jacques Derrida, 'La Structure, le signe et le jeu', in *L'Écriture et la différence* (Paris: Seuil, 1967), pp.409–428.
5   Anne Galloway, 'The Sound of Mobility – Part 1', *Space & Culture* (2004), <http://spaceandculture.org/2004_01_01_archive.php>. Accessed 28 May 2007.

opened by the traceur as they are shown a different urban landscape from the one that informs and limits their everyday experience.

In its refusal to conform to the modes of access and functions intended by architectural planning, parkour offers a means of deconstructing the city so that traditional conceptions of architecture and its role within society are no longer assumed or taken for granted. In an essay entitled 'Space versus Program', Bernard Tschumi identifies basic parallels between literature and architecture, questioning how literary and narrative techniques might inform architectural practice:

> If writers could manipulate the structure of stories in the same way as they twist vocabulary and grammar, couldn't architects do the same, organising the program in a similarly objective, detached, or imaginative way? For if architects could self-consciously use such devices as repetition, distortion, or juxtaposition in the formal elaboration of walls, couldn't they do the same thing in terms of the activities that occurred within those very walls? Pole vaulting in the chapel, bicycling in the laundromat, sky diving in the elevator shaft?[6]

Architects such as Tschumi and Eisenman challenge or deconstruct architecture's 'telos', unsettling the conventional relationships which exist between function and structure. Habitation is no longer assumed as the founding principle of an architectural structure. As the notion of habitation is decentred, assumptions as to the form such habitation or dwelling should take are also called into question. For example, Eisenman's House VI, designed and built for Suzanne Frank, is a family house which undermines accepted ideas about what a family living space should be. Yet such attempts to challenge established ideas concerning architectural form and structure often result in functionality being heavily compromised or dispensed with altogether. While conceptually brilliant, House VI proved nevertheless to be a logistical nightmare for the Franks who resided in this space.

Tschumi's Parc de la Villette is perhaps a more successful example of the manner in which architecture can deconstruct its own purpose and meaning yet still maintain this purpose and meaning in an albeit decentred and arbitrary way. La Villette, which formed part of

6   Bernard Tschumi, *Architecture and Disjunction* (Cambridge, MA & London: The MIT Press, 1994), pp.146–7.

an urban renewal plan in the early eighties, was designed by Tschumi around a series of abstract structures known as 'folies.' The project calls into question the image of the public park as a natural, open space amidst the man-made artificiality of the city: all urban parks are equally as artificial and man-made as the city life from which they offer refuge. La Villette is a celebration of this artificiality. In an essay entitled 'Point de Folie – Maintenant l'architecture', published alongside Tschumi's *La Case Vide*, Derrida refers to a form of architecture, embodied by Tschumi and Eisenman, which is perceived not as a monument, or monumental moment, but as an event or a series of experiences. He describes this notion of encounter with particular reference to the Parc de la Villette:

> Le parcours des folies est sans doute prescrit, de point en point, dans la mesure où la trame ponctuelle compte avec un *programme* d'expériences possibles et d'expérimentation nouvelles (cinéma, jardin botanique, atelier-vidéo, bibliothèque, patinoire, gymnase). Mais la structure de la trame et celle de chaque cube, car ces points sont des cubes, laissent leur chance à l'aléa, à l'invention formelle, à la transformation combinatoire, à l'errance. Cette chance n'est pas donnée à l'habitant ou au fidèle, à l'usager ou au théoricien de l'architecture, mais à qui s'engage à son tour dans l'écriture architecturale: sans réserve, ce qui suppose une lecture inventive, l'inquiétude de toute une culture, et la signature du corps. Celui-ci ne se contenterait plus de *marcher*, de circuler, de déambuler *dans* un lieu, *sur* des chemins, il transformerait ses mouvements élémentaires en leur donnant lieu, il recevrait de cet autre espacement l'invention de ses gestes.[7]

Where projects like Eisenman's house of cards and Tschumi's Parc de la Villette involve a form of architecture that questions its own purpose and structure, parkour embodies the 'architectural writing' and 'inventive reading' to which Derrida alludes. The traceur inscribes the body's signature on the routes taken and the points traversed. It is up to individuals, as they creatively engage with architectural spaces, to define their own events and invent their own experiences. Yet it is not within sympathetic architectural spaces which welcome invention and transformation such as La Villette that

---

7   Jacques Derrida, 'Point de Folie – Maintenant l'Architecture', in *La Case Vide – La Villette* (London: Architectural Association, 1985), p.12.

parkour achieves its most effective deconstruction, but rather in its challenge to the limits imposed by a more traditional, or as Derrida describes it, 'nostalgic' architecture which continues to affirm its existence according to principles of 'telos', origin and centre. To a certain extent, the disruptive rhythms of the traceur are only rendered possible by an architecture which evokes a very specific function and mode of use and consequently appears to preclude the very possibility of such disruption.

Despite its confrontation with everyday behaviour and social norms, external pressures and internal struggles perpetually threaten the freedom offered by parkour. Through increasing popularity, disagreements between the parkour founders, Belle and Foucan, led to their separation. Moreover, parkour's growing recognition has, unsurprisingly, been seized as a commercial opportunity. In addition to high profile media attention which includes Foucan's high-speed chase through a construction site in *Casino Royale* (2006), Belle's role in Luc Besson's *Banlieue 13* (2004) and the *Jump London* documentary (2003), there is now a whole series of products associated with parkour: shoes, clothing, DVDs and computer games. Many of these products are endorsed by experienced traceurs, calling into question their integrity, as they become tools of a corporate, consumer world, a world which parkour once claimed to undermine. To some extent, parkour should be a practice open to everybody since it is a question of developing one's individual physical abilities whilst remaining aware of one's own limitations. However, the media's focus on the more dramatic and extreme aspects of parkour has been misleading and is perhaps responsible for restricting its appeal to the wider population. Much of parkour occurs at ground level where obstacles include more surmountable objects such as park benches, rather than a series of jumps from rooftop to rooftop. Thus, as it becomes a marketing tool aimed, like skateboarding, at a certain demographic, parkour itself becomes restricted. Borden has pointed out how skateboarding, in its association with an adolescent male culture, ends up excluding other social groups and, as a result, is often regarded as promoting values which are both sexist and homophobic;[8] parkour risks embodying the same forms of prejudice and exclusion.

But there is another issue which threatens to overshadow the positive, liberating elements of parkour. Grace has always been recognised as a significant element of the discipline, but there is much debate as to whether or not acrobatics, which do nothing to increase the efficiency of the traceur but simply enhance aesthetic appeal, have a legitimate place within parkour. To overemphasise the importance of the acrobatic element of parkour is to risk turning it into a form of exhibitionism. Nevertheless, many groups of traceurs have chosen to concentrate almost exclusively on this aspect of parkour, preferring to practise set pieces on a few well-known obstacles rather than explore a wider area.

This debate is symptomatic of the struggle of a discipline which tries to portray a philosophy that is free from strict definitions, but which also wants to maintain the integrity of its original aims. The problem arises when there is confusion as to what these aims actually are. Should parkour always be about uninterrupted movement? Should it always be practical as well as aesthetic? These questions are unlikely to be resolved easily. What remains to be seen is whether such questions can be positively assumed by traceurs as they work to define parkour for themselves. Since the need for group identity perpetually threatens parkour's freedom by demanding that members conform to prescribed discourses of what the discipline can and cannot be, it falls to the individual traceur with his or her own specific experience of movement and perception to reassert the possibility of freedom.

One such possibility of freedom can be found in parkour's celebration of the death instinct, as it offers the traceur liberation from an existence controlled by the need for self-preservation and the fear of dying. In a society where fear is both created and operated on by government and media alike, any opportunity to confront and exist beyond or outside this fear should be seized wholeheartedly. In 'Beyond the Pleasure Principle', Freud opens his discussion of the death instinct with the maxim that 'the aim of all life is death.'

8   Borden, 'Chariots of Ire', pp.39–40.

Accepting the validity of this statement also means recognising, as Freud notes, that:

> The hypothesis of self-preservative instincts, such as we attribute to all living beings, stands in marked opposition to the idea that instinctual life as a whole serves to bring about death.[9]

As a result, self-preservation, self-assertion and mastery all diminish in their importance and are relegated to what Freud describes as 'component instincts whose functions it is to assure that the organism shall follow its own path to death [...]'.[10] When we stand at the top of a tall building, we are often faced with an overwhelming urge to jump off, but this impulse is kept in check by our instinct for self-preservation. Consequently, we grip the handrail more tightly, step back from the edge and breathe deeply before heading to a safer location. Parkour embraces this urge to jump. It releases the individual from the paradoxical situation where the organism 'struggles most energetically against events (dangers) which might help it attain its life's aim'.[11] It succeeds in both affirming the primacy of the death instinct and also provides the individual with the means to dispense with a fear of death. The mental and physical preparation undertaken by the traceur means that this affirmation of the death instinct is not an irresponsible leap into the unknown. Instead, parkour is an activity which recognises the need for self-preservation, but at the same time questions what form this self-preservation should take.

Yet perhaps a more accurate way of describing parkour, and this is the second possibility of freedom I would like to suggest, is in terms of a care or ethics of the self. The 'care of the self' is an idea discussed by Foucault in his third volume of *Histoire de la sexualité*, *Le souci de soi* and also in his lecture series on *L'Herméneutique du sujet* given at the Collège de France in 1982. In these texts Foucault describes how during the first and second centuries, individuals in Greco-Roman society were encouraged to form their own truths and

9   Sigmund Freud, 'Beyond the Pleasure Principle', in *The Essentials of Psycho-analysis*, trans. James Strachey (London: Penguin Books, 1986), p.246.
10   Ibid., p.247.
11   Ibid., p.247.

ethics about themselves, a process which involved a series of detailed and varied practices, collectively referred to as a 'care' of the self. According to Foucault, a shift occurred in the centuries which followed and truth about oneself became detached from these practices of 'care.' Truth became associated with knowledge, a knowledge produced by and for power as it operated through the religious and social institutions which serve as the focus of Foucault's earlier studies.

However, there are numerous similarities between parkour and the Greco-Roman practices described by Foucault. In particular, Belle has emphasised the role of parkour in training oneself to escape from difficult and dangerous situations and also to assist others in difficulty. Intrinsic to the Greco-Roman notion of care of the self was the idea that in order to govern and help others, one needed first to be able to care for and govern oneself.[12] Practices such as abstinence were a form of training in how to cope with hardship. The same debate between acrobatics and athletics at the heart of parkour was also present in the first and second centuries. Where aesthetics was always an important part of Greek culture, which placed much emphasis on the 'life lived beautifully', to train in gymnastics, was nevertheless to train oneself to deal with the unexpected. Consequently, acrobatics and other exercises that served no purpose beyond the aesthetic were rejected in favour of those which could be applied to everyday situations and potential dangers.[13] At one point in his lectures, Foucault suggests that it is only by a care of the self as exemplified in Greco-Roman culture in the first and second centuries that we can free ourselves from the constraints imposed upon us by society.[14] Parkour is perhaps one type of this care of the self, as it forces us to look more closely at our everyday environment and our own existence within this environment.

The freedom or subversive force of parkour thus lies not so much in an individual's ability to engage with the philosophy or the 'way of life' described by other practitioners of parkour. Inevitably

12   Michel Foucault et al, *L'Herméneutique du sujet: cours au Collège de France, 1981–1982*, Hautes études (Paris: Gallimard/Seuil, 2001), p.27.
13   Ibid., p.435.
14   Ibid., pp.242–243.

such philosophies always risk becoming limited and restricted by their own discourses. Instead, parkour should be regarded as one of many tools which allow us to construct and deconstruct our own discourses, our own 'ways of life' or living. Whether this is as a result of the close proximity with death which is presented to the traceur in terms of the useful survival and rescue skills it provides, or as a celebration of movement in its own right, parkour is an activity which teaches individuals how to find their own rhythm, conceived in terms of their personal reading of the city or space in which they live, as well as how to write their own existence upon and within this space.

Suggested Reading

Borden, Iain, 'Chariots of Ire', *Blueprint: Architecture, Design & Contemporary Culture*, 174 (July 2000), 38–40.

Derrida, Jacques, 'La Structure, le signe et le jeu', in *L'Écriture et la différence* (Paris: Seuil, 1967), pp.409–428.

Derrida, Jacques, 'Point de Folie – Maintenant l'Architecture', in *La Case Vide – La Villette*, (London: Architectural Association, 1985).

Jones, Dan, 'Parkour: A Natural Perspective', *The Urban Freeflow Network* (2005) <http://www.urbanfreeflow.com/articles/articles. htm>. Accessed 28 May 2007.

Foucault, Michel *L'Herméneutique du sujet: cours au Collège de France, 1981-1982*, Hautes études (Paris: Gallimard/Seuil, 2001).

Freud, Sigmund, *The Essentials of Psycho-analysis*, trans. by James Strachey (London: Penguin Books, 1986).

Galloway, Anne, 'The Sound of Mobility – Part 1' in *Space & Culture* (2004)   <http://spaceandculture.org/2004_01_01_archive.php>. Accessed 28 May 2007.

Tschumi, Bernard, *Architecture and Disjunction* (Cambridge, MA & London: The MIT Press, 1994).

LISA VILLENEUVE

The Urban Experience of Placelessness: Perceptual Rhythms in Georges Perec's *Un homme qui dort*

When does a metropolis alter perceptions of time and place, recognition and identity? One of Perec's less familiar works of the 1960s, entitled *Un homme qui dort*, portrays a young *flâneur* who wanders about Paris indifferently and anonymously. The story is a lyrical portrayal of estrangement in the French capital. The title also evokes the image of a somnambulist or of an unconscious man. More precisely, Perec's story is that of a sleeping man's experience of the city – one that is fraught with temporal ambiguity, confusion and identity dissonance. It is also devoid of structure or *peripeteia*. The story begins when an anonymous student at the Sorbonne decides, one morning, not to sit an examination. The young man's decision not to attend classes, not to graduate and not to explain himself to anyone, is an abrupt one. As a result, he relinquishes the strictures of social expectations, schedules and everyday tasks. He cloisters himself in his room by day and wanders the streets at night, randomly observing the city's marginal residents: the ill, the homeless and the destitute, as well as the feral creatures in their midst.

Published in 1967 to little public acclaim, *Un homme qui dort* is Perec's second novel. It straddles his juvenilia and his sociological writings of the early 1970s. The novel drew ambivalent reactions from the publishers of *Les Choses*, Perec's work of 1965. The latter was commercially successful and won that year's Prix Renaudot. *Un homme qui dort* puzzled the same French readership that had been drawn to *Les Choses*. In part, readers had identified with Perec's satirical portrayal of young, upwardly-mobile Parisians in *Les Choses*, whose subtitle –'chronique des années soixante'– placed the work in the context of France's newly-emerging consumer culture. *Un homme qui dort* is a more lyrical text than *Les Choses*, and its narrative action is more subtle. The novel also raises a number of questions relating to the role of the body in the built environment and its movements and sensations in public and private spaces. In particular, these considerations bear upon a number of contemporary lines of inquiry, ranging from those of human geography (Soja, Harvey) to performance theory or musicology. In the early 1970s, Perec chose to adapt his story to screen. For the film version of *Un homme qui dort*,[1] the author commissioned two electro-acoustic musicians to score the work. Their composition transposed sensations of subjectivity, difference and dissonance into strident and arrhythmical sounds. Released in 1974 and acclaimed by Franju, among others, Perec's film garnered the Prix Jean Vigo of that year.

This paper focuses on Perec's novel and film. In the first section, I address the character's relationship with the built environment. Exploring concepts associated with the body, the city and the biorhythmic, I use Henri Lefebvre's *Éléments de rythmanalyse* as a point of reference. In the second section, my discussion addresses the film version of *Un homme qui dort* and focuses on its soundtrack. The haunting composition of Eugénie Kuffler and Philippe Drogoz, both of whom were influenced by the *musique concrète* practices of the fifties and sixties, suggests an arrhythmic evocation of everyday activity and urban wandering.

Perec's story is one of banal experiences, both at home and in the city. The small or otherwise insignificant activities that engage the young hero form the basis of his body's movements in space. These insignificant micro-acts subtend the narrative of *Un homme qui dort*, including examples such as: sipping coffee while staring at elderly gentlemen in the Jardins du Luxembourg, standing outside in the rain, walking toward the Sorbonne for no apparent reason, reading a newspaper that has been left behind in a bistro or standing near the apartment wall, listening to a neighbour open and close his drawers. For Perec, these pedestrian activities also convey a form of depersonalisation in relation to a greater social environment. The novel's title

---

1   *Un homme qui dort*. Dir. Georges Perec and Bernard Queysanne. Dovidis-Satpec. 1974. 78 min.

implies a sleepy or anaesthetised reaction to an external environment. As Perec's protagonist lives and wanders alone, the novel plays off subjective sensations of anonymity and identity in the urban landscape. In addition to this, *Un homme qui dort* is rich in intertextual allusions. These include echoes of Aragon's *Le Paysan de Paris,* Melville's 'Bartleby the Scrivener' and a Roquentin-like revolt led by a lone character. By rejecting social encounters, goals and the concept of productivity, Perec's young hero does not feel anchored in the dominant structures of the industrial era.

Since both novel and film are devoid of *peripeteia* proper, the reader or viewer has difficulty determining when anything begins. The protagonist merely prefers not to sit an examination one day in May. There is an obvious echo of Melville's 'Bartleby' here. By abandoning normative social behaviour and routine social encounters, the young student begins to wander, linger, smoke, play cards and observe others, alone and frequently at night.[2] He does little other than 'traîner', 'flâner' and 'glisser dans les rues'.[3] As mentioned above, Perec's title is suggestive of an unconscious experience of the outside world. It connotes reverie, narcosis, the fantastic and the spectral alike. 'Un homme qui dort' is a phrase borrowed from the first pages of Proust's *À la recherche du temps perdu*.[4] By experiencing the metropolis in an almost clandestine manner, alone and aloof, the student dwells outside the modernist parameters of time and space.

---

2   For an allusion to Melville, see Georges Perec, *Un homme qui dort* (Paris: Denoël/Lettres nouvelles, 1967), p.171: 'Jadis, à New York, à quelques centaines de mètres des brisants où viennent battre les dernières vagues de l'Atlantique, un homme s'est laissé mourir. Il était scribe chez un homme de loi. Caché derrière un paravent, il restait assis à son pupitre et n'en bougeait jamais. Il se nourrissait de biscuits au gingembre. Il regardait par la fenêtre un mur de briques noircies qu'il aurait presque pu toucher de la main.' Note also Perec's reference to 'Bartleby the Scrivener' in Perec, 'Pouvoirs et limites du romancier français contemporain', in *Parcours Perec: colloque de Londres, mars 1988*, ed. Mireille Ribière (Lyon: Presses universitaires de Lyon, 1990), pp.31–40.

3   Perec, *Un homme qui dort*, p.63, p.64, p.97.

4   Marcel Proust, *Du côté de chez Swann* (Paris: Gallimard, 1954), p.11: 'Un homme qui dort tient en cercle autour de lui le fil des heures, l'ordre des années et des mondes.'

He eats, walks, smokes and visits museums, haphazardly. Subject only to the rhythms of his body, the student's sensations – of appetite and fatigue, for instance, or of heat, exhaustion, pain or dizziness – resonate with his experience of the city.

Un homme qui dort (1967) and the Lefebvrian city

The role of the city in shaping an individual's perception of space reflects one of the dominant concerns of twentieth century urban theory. More specifically, some of the works of Henri Lefebvre, David Harvey, David Pinder and Edward Soja – all urban theorists – attempt to address the spatial relations that subtend human movements and interactions in a city. Lefebvre's *La Production de l'espace* (1974) is a seminal study in the analysis of space and movement. It also links the rapid expansion of urban development with the post-war period in particular. For Lefebvre, urbanism emerges in the 1940s with massive rural exoduses in the West. Lefebvre maintains that space has long remained a product of various intellectual traditions that sought to systematise 'space', to address space by opposing it to 'non-space',[5] or to otherwise reify the idea of 'space'.[6] Lefebvre seeks to attend to the body's experience of space by analysing the roles of social space, communication and economic practice which affect it. For him, the study of city space requires contemporary responses that Marx did not envisage at the time of *Das Kapital*.[7] More significantly, Lefebvre reads space as a code. He notes the existence of peculiarly personal experiences of space, or those that are not subject to theoretical reductionism. The idea of a subjective experience of space

5   Henri Lefebvre, *La Production de l'espace* (Paris: Anthropos, 2000 [1974]), pp.197–208.
6   Ibid., pp.13–14.
7   See Lefebvre, *Une pensée devenue monde... Faut-il abandonner Marx?* (Paris: Fayard, 1980), pp.148–150. Lefebvre claims that urban space was of marginal interest to Marx, who mythologised rural life.

bears upon the discussion of random, everyday or habitual uses of city space in Perec's novel. In *La Production de l'espace*, the term 'espace vécu' is used to designate a socially created space that plays upon the notion of *habitus* and the habitual. Lived space is a body or character's mode of experiencing space in an almost natural or bio-rhythmical manner, and it is corporeal in function. It allows for a body's absorption (and experience of) an environment, and runs contrary to the rationalist or abstract practices of theorists who relate to space as an object. For Lefebvre, lived space can be distinguished from both perceived space ('espace perçu') and conceived space ('espace conçu') since, in very broad terms, the latter two are abstracted means of relating to space: they remain divorced from a body's physical movements, and they fail to account for the raw, somatic experiences of a body surrounded by people and structures.[8] For Lefebvre, perceived space and conceived space are rationalist and teleological spatial practices that are similar to the planning projects of figures such as Euclid or Hausmann. Lived space is altogether different, since it is inherently subjective. This means that it is the space of a subject – of his interactions and movements at home and in the city, as well as what Lefebvre terms 'l'espace des performances qu'accomplissent quotidiennement les usagers'.[9] In relation to a work of post-war literature, the concept of Lefebvrian social space underscores the ways in which a metropolis mediates experience. Social space encompasses a body's everyday activities, as well as how a body senses and is shaped by the natural world. For Perec, the anonymous student of *Un homme qui dort* absorbs the spaces of a city through mundane experiences: 'Tu es seul et tu dérives', he writes. 'Tu marches dans les avenues désolées, longeant les arbres rabougris. [...] Tu n'as d'autres rencontres que des fontaines Wallace depuis longtemps taries, des églises gluantes, des chantiers éventrés, des murs blafards.'[10]

In both *La Production de l'espace* and *Éléments de rythmanalyse* (1992), Lefebvre uses the terms rhythm and rhythmanalysis

8   Lefebvre, *La Production de l'espace*, pp.48–50.
9   Ibid., p.49.
10   Perec, *Un homme qui dort*, p.123.

to designate a body's movement in (and occupation of) space. This
occurs on both a conscious and unconscious level. Rhythm and
rhythmanalysis are employed loosely rather than technically. In
reality, it is a body's (arrhythmic) movements within a territory – and
its facilitation of certain movements – that Lefebvre identifies as a
unique rhythm. The term rhythmanalysis refers to the experience of
space in which a body is always the primary mediator and repository
of sensations. This experience can include acts such as rapid
breathing, sweating, bending backwards, gesticulating, shouting or
crouching in certain spaces or territories. For Lefebvre, rhythmanalysis may come to replace psychoanalysis as a way of investigating
human thought. He writes:

> La rythmanalyse appliquerait au corps vivant et à ses relations internes-externes
> les principes et lois d'une rythmnologie générale. Cette connaissance aurait
> pour champ privilégié et terrain expérimental la danse et la musique, les
> 'cellules rythmiques', leurs effets. Le corps polyrythmique ne se laisse com-
> prendre et approprier qu'à ces conditions.[11]

For Lefebvre, a body's orientation in space can be analysed in the
same way as a text since a body by nature acts as an orientational
agent and is endowed with a perceptual horizon. For the 'homme
qui dort', as for Lefebvre, space implies a cognisance of particular
rhythms:

> Un rythme enveloppe des lieux, il n'est pas un lieu; ce n'est pas une chose, ni
> agrégat de choses, ni un simple flux. Il a sa loi en lui, sa régularité; cette loi lui
> vient de l'espace, le sien, et d'un rapport entre l'espace et le temps.[12]

For Perec's wandering student, purposeless journeys differ from
conventional or planned ones because they are centred upon bodily
sensations. For Lefebvre, a conformist journey denies the body: conventional travel is subtended by a spatial practice ('espace conçu') and
it has recourse to cartographic emplacement. For example, the land-
marks of a tourist's map can be included in a tourist's journey from
site to site. Perec's protagonist, however, walks in a perpetually

11   Lefebvre, *La Production de l'espace*, p.237.
12   Ibid., p.238.

random motion. For the 'homme qui dort', time is comprised of trivial or solipsistic activity rather than quantifiable units: 'comme un rat dans la dédale cherchant l'issue. Tu parcours Paris en tous sens.'[13] Calling into question the role of (putatively) meaningful activity, Perec shows how action and agency, which normally define character and identity, are now meaningless. When the protagonist identifies with the city's rats and vagrants, moreover, these 'vieux fous',[14] or those who live outside the fixed coordinates of homes and schedules, come to intersect and enmesh with the student's body: 'ils sont venus à toi, ils t'ont agrippé par le bras.'[15] Paris is shown as an ambiguous space that is neither wholly banal nor grotesque. Furthermore, since the student identifies with rats and vagrants, he implicitly joins those who often live outside organised spaces and times. As the humdrum rhythms of tasks and schedules have now lost their potency for the protagonist, he moves about the city randomly and interminably. This is described as follows:

> Le temps passe, mais tu ne sais jamais l'heure, le clocher de Saint-Roch ne distingue pas le quart, ni la demie, ni les trois quarts; l'alternance des feux au croisement de la rue Saint-Honoré et de la rue des Pyramides n'intervient pas chaque minute; la goutte d'eau ne tombe pas chaque seconde. Il est dix heures, ou peut-être onze, car comment être sûr que tu as bien entendu, il est tard, il est tôt, le jour naît, la nuit tombe ici, tu apprends à durer [...] tu t'enfonces dans l'Ile Saint Louis, tu prends la rue de Vaugirard [...] Tu marches lentement [...] tu vas t'asseoir sur le parapet du pont Louis-Philippe [...] De la terrasse d'un café [...], tu regardes la rue.[16]

By underscoring a subjective negotiation of the experience of place, Perec shows how the physical structures of a city may no longer serve as sites for the *flâneur*. And by experiencing the urban via the mundane, Perec implies, gestures are no longer imbued with a teleology of their own: they no longer resemble the purposeful destinations of a tourist's travels or of a commuter's journey from home to office. Rather, gestures are the whimsical, bodily perceptions of parameters

13   Perec, *Un homme qui dort*, p.133.
14   Ibid., p.130.
15   Ibid., p.130.
16   Ibid., pp.64–65.

that have effectively been subverted. The spatial practice of compart-
mentalising the physical and the temporal, for Lefebvre in particular,
is reduced to a purely sensorial-sensual relationship with ritual, nature
and dance.[17] Time and space come to be measured in the ineffable
time of insignificant moments, such as those of coffee spoons, as
Eliot's Prufrock might say. Time is that of sipping, staring, smoking,
stepping or counting; it is that of tasting or not tasting a particular
steak, and identifying its flavours, as Perec's protagonist does.[18] The
social fabric of the city is absent from the text and the 'homme qui
dort' is left very much identifying with what Perec terms the city's
'bannis, parias, exclus'.[19] These marginal residents are also associated
with the impermanent and the haphazard. And yet, '[les] brutes, les
vieillards, les idiots, les sourds-muets aux bérets enfoncés jusqu'aux
yeux, les ivrognes […] les paysans égarés dans la grande ville'[20]
possess genuine, personalised rituals and rhythms of their own.[21] The
novel emphasises the significance of marginal residents and feral
animals by contrasting them with those who often respond to the built
environment in a static and predictable manner.

Perec's film *Un homme qui dort* (1974)

In 1971, Perec and co-producer Bernard Queysanne began working on
a film adaptation of *Un homme qui dort*. The film was released in
1974, just prior to Perec's work of non-fiction, *Tentative d'épuisement
d'un lieu parisien*.[22] Perec spent time considering the implications
of a score for his film. For both producers, the film's soundtrack is an

---

17   Lefebvre, *La Production de l'espace*, p.244.
18   Perec, *Un homme qui dort*, pp.75–76.
19   Ibid., p.129.
20   Ibid., p.129.
21   Ibid., p.129.
22   Perec, *Tentative d'épuisement d'un lieu parisien* (Paris: Christian Bourgois,
      1975).

integral aspect of its format as sonic elements are meant to imbricate various textual, psychological and sensorial experiences. The most singular feature of the black and white film (the soundtrack of which was broadcast by *France Culture* in 1974) is the use of long, discordant or complex sounds. For Perec, aural sensations that encompass strident or unidentifiable noises, originating in a city or a home for example, differ from those of stock cinematic compositions. The evocation of a raw and natural environment, through a number of arrhythmic sounds, is an important feature of transposing text to film.[23]

The film opens with visual clichés of the French capital. Images of pigeons resting on 'Ville de Paris' bins, for instance, as well as a montage of rooftops, bistros and boulevards, play with ideas of location and recognition. After these introductory sequences, however, the camera fixes on a particular attic-level window. In a close-up, the viewer distinguishes a young man staring at himself in a mirror, standing silently in his small room. The camera subsequently pans across the student's room, lingering upon an alarm clock whose ticking sound is audible for the viewer. At this juncture, Perec's film is silent bar the ticking of the alarm clock. The film's introductory sequence lasts at least five minutes, and it is entirely devoid of dialogue. The images of rooftops, the protagonist, his kitchen, bed and domestic appliances evoke what Adorno terms the 'ghostly effect of the moving image without music'.[24] Perec deliberately echoes the original silent films of the early twentieth century. Yet, by introducing the first sound as a non-human, industrial one – that of a technological apparatus ticking – Perec draws attention to the noises of the modern era. Traditional piano accompaniment has come to be replaced by a banal, technological device that ticks away indefinitely. The film's voiceover, which does not appear in these opening sequences, is also jarring for the viewer. After the sequence of the ticking alarm clock, a

---

23   Perec and Queysanne deliberately subvert the way in which compositions come to evoke a particular place, in contrast to more familiar examples such as Delius's 'Paris – The Song of a Great City' (1899).

24   Theodor Adorno and Hans Eisler, *Composing for the Films* (London: Athlone Press, 1994 [1947]), p.75.

female voice announces: 'ton réveil sonne. Tu ne bouges absolument pas.' In both novel and film, the use of 'tu' is striking. The film is suggesting an external voice or, perhaps, a bifurcated psyche. It also remains dissociated from the protagonist's own voice. By using 'tu', Perec also mirrors Butor's use of 'vous' in *La Modification*, written a decade earlier.[25] In the film, the voice is that of an older actress (Ludmila Mikaël). For Perec, the use of a female voice prevents the viewer from collapsing the voiceover into a possible interior mono-logue, as the former cannot be confused with the voice of the male student (Jacques Spiesser). When the first event of the novel appears on film, the narrator reads directly from the text:

> le jour de ton examen arrive et tu ne te lèves pas. Ce n'est pas un geste prémédité, ce n'est pas un geste, mais une absence de geste, un geste que tu ne fais pas, des gestes que tu évites de faire [...] Ton réveil sonne, tu ne bouges absolument pas, tu restes dans ton lit, tu refermes les yeux.[26]

Some of the everyday activities, however, such as the act of making coffee or smoking, are recorded on film, and thus are observed by the spectator, in real time. Other acts, such as that of entering a cinema and watching a film repeatedly, are merely alluded to verbally. These acts are muted and compressed, since they cannot play themselves out in real time. The film, while stripping bare what Bert States terms the 'actual aspect of performance',[27] however, still toys with the concept of verisimilitude and the idea of a (mock) documentary. Banal and insignificant acts are either filmed in real time or in a chronicled, truncated version voiced by the female narrator. By reproducing most of the novel's prose with a shrill voiceover and by incorporating a score with unmodulated pitches, the film also subverts the dominant use of the scopic as a way of conjuring time or place.

When the voiceover announces mysteriously, 'tu ne sors qu'à la nuit tombée', a number of musical notes can be detected. Beyond certain chords, however, the sounds are often too strident for the

25   Michel Butor, *La Modification* (Paris: Minuit, 1957).
26   Perec, *Un homme qui dort*, p.21.
27   Bert O. States, *Great Reckonings in Little Rooms: On the Phenomenology of Theater* (Berkeley: University of California Press, 1985), p.119.

human ear. The film's score is comprised of the aural experiences that can be gleaned from an individual's movements in a city: traffic sounds, for instance, as well as the noises of domestic appliances; the shuffle of unknown feet on a random stairwell; the sound of water running; the opening of apartment shutters onto other apartment windows; the noises of a construction crew at work. These sounds are often arrhythmic, and they also convey an experience of human density and industrialisation. In an interview in 1974, Perec spoke of 'ce film "parallèle" où l'image, le texte et la bande sonore s'organisent pour tisser la plus belle lecture que jamais écrivain n'a pu rêver pour un de ces livres.'[28] As the film's voiceover becomes more frenzied, it is amplified by sensations of confusion and dissonance found in Perec's prose. The strident shouts of the narrator, however, contrast with some of the more banal urban sounds that are captured on screen. This occurs, for example, when the narrator shouts bizarrely, 'tu ne veux que *durer*!', just as the scene depicts a series of mundane acts, including smoking a cigarette. In another example, the student imagines himself in an examination hall at the Sorbonne, while, in reality, he is in bed. Here, the soundtrack is excruciatingly strident for no apparent reason. Musical dynamics and pitch are used unconventionally throughout the film, often contrasting starkly with the images on screen. The narrator shouts, as if in a panic, 'le temps passe et tu ne sais jamais l'heure', just as her words are drowned out by shrill, percussive sounds. The orchestration of scenes around specific incongruities, notably those of sight and sound, points to the primacy of estrangement in the text.

The musical score by Eugénie Kuffler and Philippe Drogoz, both part of Ensemble 010 in the early 1970s, is an electro-acoustic composition. The two directors and Kuffler (who had studied composition under Nadia Boulanger) were influenced by the unconventional uses of sound in *musique concrète* creations of the 1950s and 1960s.[29] This

28   Perec, 'Un homme qui dort. Lecture cinématographique', *Georges Perec: Entretiens et Conférences 1965–1978*, ed. Dominique Bertelli and Mireille Ribière, 2 vols (Paris: Joseph K, 2002), I (1979–1981), pp.151–152.

29   *Musique concrète* is associated with certain works dating from 1948, which was the year of Schaeffer's 'concert de bruits' (5 October 1948). This concert

school (1948–1965) was formed around Pierre Schaeffer in post-war Paris, and it embraced the production of musical sound by means of mundane, unusual or incongruous noises incorporated into compositional theory. Aural sensations might arise, for instance, by means of birds chirping in a garden surrounded by industrial construction crews at work in the street. The natural world provided a series of musical or sonic elements for Schaeffer, who frequently spoke of the liberation of sound when explaining the function of *musique concrète*. The legacy of the school can be discerned in Perec's film of 1974, well after the period of *musique concrète*, though retaining influences from Varese in particular. Both Drogoz and Kuffler were commissioned by Perec to provide a musical composition for a film that lacked a conventional narrative, in which a body's random movements at home and in the city form the basis of a story. For Drogoz, this was akin to a *mise-en-scène*:

> L'idée des trois récits [texte, images, sons] nous a séduits d'emblée [...] Il fallait faire tout le contraire d'une émission de télévision – où on accumule des faits pour créer un discours –, ici nous partions d'une idée pour ne conserver que des éléments matériels. Ainsi, c'est une voix de femme [...] qui raconte, procédé qui nous permet de réaliser une séparation ontologique entre le discours dit et la lecture cinématographique.[30]

included Pierre Boulez. The end-date (1965) is the death of Edgard Varese, whose electronic works form an important part of *musique concrète*. Certain works by John Cage, Olivier Messiaen, Pierre Henry, and some ballets by Maurice Béjart, are associated with the school. See Pierre Schaeffer, *À la Recherche d'une musique concrète* (Paris: Seuil, 1952), p.218: 'la musique concrète, hors des limitations imposées par les instruments traditionnels, considère que tout son naturel ou artificiel peut, du fait de sa situation dans une structure, prendre un caractère musical.' In works using pre-recorded sounds, in which sounds are divorced from their primary contexts (e.g. a dining-room), John Young notes that such noises 'present a set of ambiguities and complexities' for listeners determined to establish their origin. See Young, 'Imagining the Source: The Interplay of Realism and Abstraction in Electroacoustic Music', *Contemporary Music Review: A Poetry of Reality. Composing with Recorded Sound*, ed. Peter Nelson and Nigel Osborne (Amsterdam: Harwood Academic Publishers, 1996), pp.73–93.

30   Perec, *Georges Perec: Entretiens et Conférences 1965–1978*, I, p.165.

The film also provides a means of exploiting the ambiguities of Perec's text by fusing real and imagined sequences. When a scene shows the examination hall in which the protagonist is not present, for instance, the film conveys a form of fantasy. Yet the overall impact remains predominantly acoustic, the viewer being both intrigued and irritated by an unbearably shrill use of percussion. Like a retina, according to John Gilbert,[31] Perec's protagonist conceives space and time in subjective terms. The *rapports* of both body and time, and body and space, are transmuted by perceptions of familiarity and proximity. Though the student wanders through Paris, from a cinema, to the bistro and to the Jardins du Luxembourg, he lacks a sense of place or an authentic and identificatory *rapport* with the built environment. In an interview in 1974, Perec evokes a phrase used by Franju in reference to the protagonist: '[il] vit au point mort de sa vie'.[32] For Perec, the student's lived space is one of bodily exchange with a territory. It is driven by biological rhythms, gestures, sensations and randomness. The Perecquian 'homme qui dort' experiences the city's spaces as territories left unpunctuated by the periodicity of modernity, transformed by an economic order. By negating the creation of a distinct sense of location within the conventional parameters of time and space, Perec shows how an urban fabric exposes the banal.

Both film and text can be linked, according to David Bellos, with the Situationist notion of *dérive*.[33] In the novel, the term *dérive* occurs no less than four times: 'aller à la dérive' (p.104), 'tu es seul et tu dérives' (p.123), 'la lente dérive des bulles' (p.125) and 'une certaine paix du corps: abandon, lassitude, assoupissement, dérive' (p.103). In the film, the camera fails to linger on any particular location as the student wanders about, and, after its introductory sequences, the camera avoids stock filmic images of Paris. By allowing the rhythms

---

31   John Gilbert, [Review] 'Un Homme qui dort', *Novel: A Forum on Fiction*, 2:1 (Autumn 1968), pp.94–6.

32   Perec, 'Un homme qui dort. Lecture cinématographique', pp.151–152.

33   David Bellos, *Georges Perec: A Life in Words* (London: Harper Collins, 1993), p.281: 'Its [The Situationist International] influence on Perec's attitudes is more certain. He was familiar with the ideas of *dérive* and *détournement* in the early 1960s, and these notions informed his reinvention of the art of seeing as well as the art of writing.'

of his body to fuse with the everyday rhythms of a city, the protagonist of *Un homme qui dort* subverts the conventional, topographical
itineraries of the capital, in which particular sites are selected. In this
sense, the anonymity of the 'homme qui dort' is reflected in (and
refracted by) the generic alocality of a metropolis. By experiencing
the city aimlessly, atemporally and randomly, Perec's Everyman
paints an *anti-map* of the city, in a wholly somatic way.

Edward Casey notes that modern life is 'so place-oriented and
place-saturated that we cannot begin to comprehend, much less face
up to, what sheer placelessness would be like.'[34] Sensations of recognition and identity, normally associated with a familiar or significant
person or place, intersect with the roles of memory and anamnesis in a
community. The student's decision *not* to engage with the environment he once had is described as follows:

> tu dois te déshabituer de tout: d'aller à la rencontre de ceux que si longtemps tu
> as côtoyés, de prendre tes repas, tes cafés à la place que chaque jours d'autres
> ont retenus pour toi.[35]

The release from past routine gives way to random, unstructured
movements through the city. For this, Perec frequently uses expressions such as 'tu traînes', 'tu flânes', 'tu te laisses aller' and 'tu
glisses'.[36] Activities which used to be associated with specific sites of
memory, such as a well-known café, are now cloaked in mundane gestures. Living by his own dictates, Perec writes how the student shapes
time and place as he sees fit: 'parce que tu es seul, il faut que tu ne
regardes jamais l'heure.'[37] The marked absence of fixed boundaries in
relation to a character's body, mind and living environment mirrors
the intersection of spatial and temporal paradigms in the modern city.
This produces what Celeste Olalquiaga qualifies as 'psychasthenia':

34   Edward S. Casey, *Getting Back into Place: Toward a Renewed Understanding
     of the Place-World* (Bloomington: Indiana UP, 1988), p.ix, p.xiii.
35   Perec, *Un homme qui dort*, p.62.
36   Ibid., pp.63–67.
37   See also Perec, *Un homme qui dort*: 'ta vie ralentie' (p.33); 'tous les instants se
     valent' (p.98); 'tu n'existes plus: suite des heures, suite des jours, le passage des
     saisons, l'écoulement du temps, tu survis' (p.87).

> A disturbance in the relation between self and surrounding territory, psy-chasthenia is a state in which the space defined by the coordinates of the organism's own body is confused with represented space. Incapable of demarcating the limits of its own body, lost in the immense area that circum-scribes it, the psychasthenic organism proceeds to abandon its own identity to embrace the space beyond.[38]

Left to wander as a 'spectre' or 'monstre', as he is often referred to, the protagonist of *Un homme qui dort* is almost disembodied. In-capable of demarcating the 'limits of his own body', as Olalquiaga terms it, the student's experience of proximity and distance in relation to others is reduced to somatic reactions: everyday fatigue, hunger, dehydration and physical discomfort prevent him from determining where he himself begins and ends. Rather, as Perec writes, 'seul existe ta marche, et ton regard, qui se pose et se glisse, ignorant le beau, le laid, le familier, le surprenant'. The Situationist undertones are un-deniable here. As Serge Daney writes, the city for Perec is:

> [non pas] la ville sociale – cet espace encombré, mis en scène par la bourgeoisie. Pour celui qui vit « en autarcie » […] la Ville est ce sein qui l'enveloppe toujours avec la même indifférence, indifférence entre la vue d'ensemble et le détail […] [39]

The use of an alocal metropolis or *unheimlich* space runs as a sort of Ariadne's thread throughout the text. It points to the body's unconscious rhythms among city residents, streets and structures, and it speaks to contemporary perspectives on identity as a relational pro-cess, mediated by a *rapport* with an environment. For the 'homme qui dort', identity and recognition are subsumed under a generic form of placelessness that is not a mental condition but the sum total of every-day sensations. Like a Vertovian camera roving amongst 'les brutes, les vieillards, les idiots, les sourd-muets',[40] Perec's story evokes the

---

38   Celeste Olalquiaga, *Megalopolis: Contemporary Cultural Sensibilities* (Min-neapolis: University of Minnesota Press, 1992), pp.1–2.

39   Serge Daney, *La Maison cinéma et le monde. 1. Le Temps des Cahiers 1962–1981*, ed. Patrice Rollet (Paris: P.O.L., 2001), pp.152–154 (p.153). Daney's review of the film is from the *Libération*, 9 May 1974.

40   Perec, *Un homme qui dort*, p.129.

ways in which a body intersects and enmeshes with the spatial coordinates of a city.

Suggested Reading

Lefebvre, Henri, *Éléments de rythmanalyse: introduction à la connaissance des rythmes* (Paris: Syllepse, 1992).
—— *La Production de l'espace* (Paris: Anthropos, 2000 [1974]).
Perec, Georges, *Un homme qui dort* (Paris: Denoël/Lettres nouvelles, 1967).
—— *Un homme qui dort*, dir. Georges Perec and Bernard Queysanne, Dovidis-Satpec, 78 min.
Schaeffer, Pierre, *À la Recherche d'une musique concrète* (Paris: Seuil, 1952).

V   Cinematic Rhythms

IAN JAMES

The Rhythm of Technology?
Paul Virilio on Temporality and Modern Media

Paul Virilio is a thinker whose publications over the past thirty years have sought to interrogate the impact of new technologies on society, state power, war and geopolitics. His work has also sought to describe the way in which technologies have transformed perceptions of space and time, their overriding concern perhaps being the question of speed and the ever increasing speed of transmission afforded by modern modes of communication and transport.[1] In certain respects, Virilio's work can appear to be marginal in relation to some of the major currents of French thought since the 1970s. As will become clear, Virilio's analyses are firmly rooted in the concerns of phenomenology, in particular the thinking of Edmund Husserl and Maurice Merleau-Ponty. At key points his work remains very much attached to a notion of phenomenological presence albeit an experience of presence which, he believes, is threatened by the modes of perception which modern media and communications make available.[2] So in this sense Virilio's work diverges from that of perhaps better known philosophers of difference who, in the latter half of the twentieth century, sought to deepen, exceed or deconstruct phenomenological notions of

---

1   For introductions to Paul Virilio's work see: Ian James, *Paul Virilio* (London: Routledge, 2007), Steve Readhead, *Paul Virilio: Theorist for an Accelerated Culture* (Edinburgh: Edinburgh University Press, 2005) and John Armitage, *Paul Virilio: From Modernism to Hypermodernism and Beyond* (London: Sage, 2000).

2   See for instance Virilio, *L'Inertie polaire* (Paris: Christian Bourgois, 1990), p.16 and *L'Espace critique* (Paris: Christian Bourgois, 1984), p.105. This has been well noted in critical responses to Virilio's work. See, for instance, Scott McQuire's essay 'Blinded by the (Speed of) Light' in Armitage, *Paul Virilio: From Modernism to Hypermodernism and Beyond*, p.152.

presence and subjectivity, most notably of course Deleuze and Derrida. In Anglophone academic work, Virilio has mostly been read by those involved in the study of media and culture but also by political scientists, as important work in international relations by James Der Derian shows.[3] However, Virilio is interested in art and contemporary artistic production (although he offers a rather negative or pessimistic account of this) and, in particular, his analyses are likely to be of strong interest to those working in the area of film criticism and theory.

What follows will interrogate Virilio as a thinker of time and temporality and, in particular, will explore the way in which he perceives a transformation in the temporal rhythms of modern life which has its roots in the different ways of seeing the world offered firstly by cinema and then by contemporary televisual and other media. It is, of course, Henri Lefebvre in his work on rhythmanalysis who reminds us that rhythm is inseparable from a temporal dimension and from the question of repetition in time and space: 'Pas de rythme sans répétition dans le temps et dans l'espace'.[4] According to the phenomenological perspective adopted by Virilio, the way in which the world of sensible appearances is made manifest to us or is perceived in vision is inseparable from a spatial and temporal situatedness of the perceiving body. Here, he relies very much on the Merleau-Pontean notion of the body-subject: those familiar with *Phénoménologie de la perception* will know that Merleau-Ponty's body-subject experiences the world as meaningful only insofar as it is orientated in space, has a certain experience of temporality and is inserted into more or less diffuse horizons of sense and purpose. These horizons exist in a certain manner prior to conscious intentionality or will and constitute the 'intentional arc' of the body-subject, that is, the field of purposeful engagements on the basis of which meaningful experience can occur.[5]

3   See James Der Derian, *Antidiplomacy: Spies, Terror, Speed, and War* (Oxford: Blackwell, 1992) and *Virtuous War: Mapping the Military-industrial-media-entertainment network* (Boulder: Westview Press, 2001).

4   Henri Lefebvre, *Éléments de rythmanalyse: introduction à la connaissance des rythmes* (Paris: Syllepse, 1992), p.14.

5   Maurice Merleau-Ponty, *Phénoménologie de la perception* (Paris: Gallimard, 1945), p.158.

Virilio's concerns relating to modern technology and the manner in which speeds of transmission transform both perception and also the structure of social, political and military space are wide-ranging. The focus of this discussion will be on the manner in which Virilio views cinema and then television and video as media which alter our collective experience of time and duration. The advent of cinema and, in particular, the creation of cinema halls at the end of the nineteenth and beginning of the twentieth century inaugurated a more general mode of perception in which '[une] nouvelle vérité de la vue méta-morphosait les rythmes de la vie'.[6] Virilio argues not only that the viewing of cinema implies a different mode of perception but that this led at a specific historical juncture to a more generalised trans-formation in collective habits of perception and shared temporal rhythms of life.

In speaking about cinema Virilio draws a distinction between an 'aesthetic of appearance' on the one hand and an 'aesthetic of dis-appearance' on the other. The former describes the manner in which we encounter works of art such as painting or sculpture, the latter the manner in which we view the images of film. Virilio is interested in the way in which sculpture and painting appear as stable forms which persist through time by virtue of their materiality. For example, the Venus de Milo or the Mona Lisa both remain as they are, they remain unique and durable because of the stone, canvas, paints and pigments from which they are made. The manner in which the film image appears is quite different. No such stability exists since its material support is not the fixity of carved stone, paint or pigment but rather the rapid movement of celluloid passed in front of a projection lamp. As viewers of film we have a sense of continuity from one passing image to the other and therefore an experience of a moving image. Virilio explains the illusion of movement given to us by the cinematic image by reference to the now outdated theory of 'retinal persistence'. This theory was once used by scientists to explain why we see a rapid succession of still images as a moving image. The assumption was that visual stimuli were stored in the memory for a few hundred milli-seconds after they had disappeared, and that this retention allowed the

6   Virilio, *L'Esthétique de la disparition* (Paris: Galilée, 1980), p.69.

intervals of darkness between individual film images to be filled in. Each new visual stimulus would register on the eye before the preceding visual impression had entirely passed and would thus give rise to a sense of continuity and therefore of movement. The illusion of movement given by film is nowadays explained with reference to what is known as the 'phi effect'. It is now thought that certain neurons exist in the retina which specialise in detecting movement and that it is due to these, and not the retention of past visual stimuli, that a succession of still images can appear to give an image in motion.

The main point for Virilio in this context is that, in the shift from traditional plastic art to film, what was a stable, material presence in, say, sculpture or painting gives way to an unstable, fleeting presence in the cinematic image. The duration of the cinema image is that of its passing or disappearance. This shift from an aesthetic of appearance to one of disappearance is described in *L'Espace critique* in the following terms:

> De l'esthétique de l'apparition d'une *image stable*, présente par sa statique même, à l'esthétique de la disparition d'une *image instable* présente par sa fuite (cinématique, cinématographique...), nous avons assisté à une transmutation des représentations. À l'émergence de formes, de volumes destinés à persister dans la durée de leur support matériel, ont succédé des images dont la seule durée est celle de la persistance rétinienne [...][7]

What is at stake here is not simply a difference in the way we view different types of art but rather modes or ways of seeing which can begin to structure our more generalised habits of perception and, in particular, time perception, in new and perhaps unforeseen or indiscernible ways.

For Virilio an aesthetic of disappearance is radically different insofar as visible images are constituted in the material absence of the object which is represented, but most importantly because the very fleeting nature of their appearance structures the temporality of perception differently. In *La Machine de vision*, Virilio discusses this in terms of the different process by which the cinematic image is 'objectivised', that is, actualised as a visible figure of form:

7   Virilio, *L'Espace critique*, p.29.

Le problème de l'objectivisation de l'image ne se pose donc plus tellement par rapport à un quelconque *support-surface* de papier ou de celluloïd, c'est-à-dire par rapport à un espace de référence matériel, mais bien par rapport au temps, *à ce temps d'exposition qui* donne à voir ou qui ne permet plus de voir.[8]

What is at stake in the shift Virilio identifies from an aesthetic of appearance to an aesthetic of disappearance is a loss of spatial and material reference in favour of a dominant reference to a temporal dimension of exposure. A temporal structure of duration (that of the material stability and persistence of stone, canvas, paint etc.) gives way to one in which the appearing form only appears in the instant in which it is 'lit-up' or exposed to light (as emitted by the projector) and indeed only appears in an instant which is also that of its continual disappearance.

Virilio identifies a shift from what might be called 'chronological time' to 'light-time'. We all understand very easily our everyday conception of temporal experience. We are situated in a present moment or a 'now' which we feel slipping away into a series of past moments and moving forward purposefully into a future moment or 'now'. This experience we translate easily into chronological time as measured by clocks in hours, minutes and seconds. From the phenomenological perspective this experience of time passing, or of duration, is intimately connected with the appearance of perceived objects as Husserl makes clear in his *Thing and Space* lectures of 1907.[9] The phenomenological account of time also thinks the present, or an experience of presence, as something which is constituted in a relation to a retained past and an anticipated future. This is an account developed by Husserl throughout his thinking on time, gathered together in the volume *On the Phenomenology of the Consciousness of Internal Time*.[10] According to Husserl, the flow of sensory data which forms the basis of perceptible appearances has a tenseless ordering which becomes tensed only in the temporality of conscious experience. In

8   Virilio, *La Machine de vision* (Paris: Galilée, 1988), p.129.
9   Edmund Husserl, *Thing and Space*, ed. and trans. Richard Rojcewicz (Dordrecht: Kluwer, 1997).
10   Husserl, *On the Phenomenology of the Consciousness of Internal Time (1893– 1917)*, trans. John Barnett Brough (Dordrecht: Kluwer, 1991).

our apprehension of the present we retain sensations of the immediate past just as we anticipate future sensations. Our experience of a present moment or 'now' and of time passing only occurs therefore on the basis of this retention of an immediate past and anticipation of a future possibility (what Husserl refers to as protention). What we think of as linear or objective time, that is time as thought and measured by science, is, Husserl would argue, always secondary in nature, just as the conception of space as three extended dimensions is secondary in relation to our embodied experience of spatiality.

Virilio relies heavily on this phenomenological account of time in his analysis of an aesthetics of disappearance and the manner in which it transforms the rhythm of lived temporality. If, as this account suggests, the experience of duration is constitutively bound up with our relation to sensory and spatial experience, then changes in the structure of sensory and spatial orientation will necessarily have an impact upon time perception.

In *L'Inertie polaire*, Virilio suggests quite explicitly that our experience of temporality is inseparable from the way things come to appear to us and, in particular, from the manner in which they are 'lit-up' or exposed to vision by light. He puts this in the following terms:

> Au « mouvement » chronologique: passé, présent, futur, il faut désormais associer des phénomènes d'accélération et de décélération [...] changements de vitesse qui s'apparentent à des phénomènes d'éclairement, à une exposition de l'étendue et de la durée de la matière à la lumière du jour.[11]

Time, Virilio asserts, should no longer be understood as an order of duration, of the succession of past, present and future moments, but should, rather, be understood as an order of 'exposure', that is of the instant in which phenomena are lit-up or exposed.

Now, this new concept of a 'time of exposure' or 'light-time' is perhaps one of Virilio's most difficult. In order to think through what is exactly meant by such a concept, we need to remind ourselves carefully that we are talking about an experience of lived time perception rather than any scientific concept of time. We also need to pay careful attention to the way in which, for Virilio, the intensivity of

11   Virilio, *L'Inertie polaire*, p.77–8.

light-time is opposed to the extensivity of duration. Light-time is intensive rather than extensive because it is, as it were, only in the intensivity of the instant or moment of illumination that appearance occurs and does so as a field of temporally and spatially perceived forms. So the aesthetics of disappearance proper to cinema gives us an image of the world of sensible appearances in which spatial and temporal perception is transformed: spatial and material extension is lost in favour of what Virilio terms an 'intensivity' of a temporality of exposure.

One way of putting this would be to say that the cinematic image offers a different kind of window on the world. For Virilio the motorised passage of celluloid in front of a projection lamp represents nothing other than a different way of 'lighting' the world, that is, of making it accessible to vision and therefore to conscious apprehension. In this context he speaks of the 'appearance of the motor', and here a double meaning can perhaps be inferred: motorised film-projection appears or emerges as a technology of viewing, but it also has a mode of appearance which belongs or which is proper to it: 'Avec l'apparition du moteur, un autre soleil s'est levé, changeant radicalement la vue; son éclairage ne tardera pas à changer la vie'.[12] On one level, this alteration in life is quite straightforwardly related to social habit: the gathering together of masses of people in a darkened room to view a film is different from a gathering in a church or theatre. Where the latter offer either a sacred ritual or a theatrical performance involving actually present bodies (priests or actors), the former is a spectacle of light only projected onto the screen and reflected back onto the spectators so that they themselves become 'fluorescents, dégageant eux aussi une mystérieuse clarté'.[13] Within this spectacle of light the spaces of the world can be made present in their very absence; the speed and fleeting movement of the images of film liberate vision from the constraints of distance, of time and space. With the advent of the cinema hall:

---

12   Virilio, *L'Esthétique de la disparition*, p.58
13   Ibid., p.68.

Tout se passait dans la multitude *des voyants lumineux* d'un transport en
commun [...], moment d'inertie où tout est déjà là, dans *le faux jour* d'une
vitesse de libération de la lumière qui nous libère effectivement du voyage au
profit de l'attentive impatience d'un monde qui ne cesse plus d'arriver, que
nous ne cessons plus d'attendre.[14]

This is a way of viewing the world in which the intervals of time and
space which might separate, say, an audience in the east end of
London from the Taj Mahal in India are annihilated in favour of a
seeing at a distance, literally a tele-vision, which negates the need to
depart or to travel in order then to see, and does so in favour of an
arrival of a visible image when no departure has ever occurred. The
notion of 'false day' plays a key role in Virilio's account of the transformation of time perception effected by the experience of cinema.
He is interested in the way various technologies over the centuries
have allowed humans to light up the world differently. In order to
supplement the light of the solar day, we have used candles, torches,
lamps and then finally electrically powered sources (light-bulbs, neon
tubes etc.). The cinema image, as a 'window on the world' which
abolishes the temporal and spatial intervals which separate us from
distant visible forms, marks a decisive shift beyond these various
means of supplementing the solar day towards an alternate structure of
vision. Here, it is not the reflection of light emitted from a direct
source which 'lights up' visible forms, rather it is the passage of light
as mediated by the rapid motion of film which gives, as it were, an
indirectly illuminated visible form, one which is present by virtue
of its absence, one whose appearance is predicated on its very disappearance.

The aesthetic of disappearance of the cinema image and the
impact it has on both the temporality and spatiality of seeing is perceived by Virilio to be a precursor to the contemporary world of
television and modern media more generally. If cinema represents the
dawn of a false day which begins to exist alongside the solar day, then
television and contemporary media represent the light of that false day
risen to its highest point. Virilio is once again primarily interested in
the way in which the *false day* of the electronic image restructures the

14   Ibid., p.68.

temporality and spatiality governing the perception of visible forms. In *L'Espace critique*, he explicitly compares television to the window of a house:

> depuis que l'on n'ouvre non seulement les volets mais aussi la télévision, le jour s'est modifié: au jour solaire de l'astronomie, au jour douteux de la lueur des bougies, à la lumière électrique, s'ajoute maintenant un *faux-jour électronique* dont le calendrier est uniquement celui de « commutations » d'informations sans aucun rapport avec le temps réel. Au temps *qui passe* de la chronologie et de l'histoire, succède ainsi un temps *qui s'expose* instantanément.[15]

The rhythm or structure of temporality is as it was in Virilio's description of cinema. It is no longer a question of the rapid movement of film before a projection lamp but rather of 'lumière électrique'. Light-time once again becomes the lived temporality of perceptual experience, here as it is mediated by the technologies of television and digital media. It is the time of the false day of electronic tele-images.

As has been argued, the central concern within Virilio's account of technological rhythms is that cinema and now contemporary media have effected a shift from the spatial and the extensive (the spatiality of bodily experience, the extensivity of temporal duration) to the temporal and the intensive (the exposure of light-time and the intensivity of the exposed instant). This shift appears most often to be described in negative terms. The day of light-time is *false*, the temporality of exposure Virilio identifies is always one which is associated with loss: the loss of sensory experience, the loss of the persistence or duration of a material element, the loss of a bodily orientation within space where material reality is 'within reach' and where the delays of time and distance give us a sense of physical rootedness in our environment.

Yet if Virilio's account appears to be overly pessimistic or negative, it perhaps also draws our attention to aspects of our technologically transformed experience which we do not easily discern and for which we have few conceptual tools or interpretative strategies

15   Virilio, *L'Espace critique*, pp. 14–15.

that might allow us to respond to the pace and speed of technological change. Straightforward or everyday notions of time passing, or traditional notions of history and linear historical time do not, perhaps, offer adequate conceptual tools to understand the way in which collective perceptions and experiences have been altered in a world transformed by information technology.

It is arguable that the pace and speed of technological change, from the nineteenth century onwards, has been such that it outstrips our capacity to think or conceive the impact it has had, and continues to have, upon collective experience. The interest of Virilio's account of a time of exposure in which our relation to the past and the material world is subtly altered is that it allows us to begin to think in a different manner the underlying rhythms of technological modernity, rhythms in which we may be held and carried along whether we like it or not, and with that thinking respond differently and reclaim another temporal beat, another rhythm of everyday life.

Suggested reading

Armitage, John, *Paul Virilio: From Modernism to Hypermodernism and Beyond* (London: Sage, 2000).

Der Derian, James, *Antidiplomacy: Spies, Terror, Speed, and War* (Oxford: Blackwell, 1992).

—— *Virtuous War: Mapping the Military-industrial-media-entertainment network* (Boulder: Westview Press, 2001).

Husserl, Edmund, *On the Phenomenology of the Consciousness of Internal Time (1893–1917)*, trans. John Barnett Brough (Dordrecht: Kluwer, 1991).

—— *Thing and Space*, ed. and trans. Richard Rojcewicz (Dordrecht: Kluwer, 1997).

James, Ian, *Paul Virilio* (London: Routledge, 2007).

Lefebvre, Henri, *Éléments de rythmanalyse: introduction à la connaissance des rythmes* (Paris: Syllepse, 1992).

Merleau-Ponty, Maurice, *Phénoménologie de la perception* (Paris: Gallimard, 1945).

Readhead, Steve, *Paul Virilio: Theorist for an Accelerated Culture* (Edinburgh: Edinburgh University Press, 2005).

Virilio, Paul, *L'Espace critique* (Paris: Christian Bourgois, 1984).

—— *L'Esthétique de la disparition* (Paris: Galilée, 1980).

—— *L'Inertie polaire* (Paris: Christian Bourgois, 1990).

—— *La Machine de vision* (Paris: Galilée, 1988).

JENNIFER VALCKE

Rhythmical Images and Visual Music: Montage in French Avant-Garde Cinema

Rythmes.
La toute-puissance des rythmes.
N'est durable que ce qui est pris dans des rythmes.
Plier le fond à la forme et les sens aux rythmes.
— Robert Bresson

During the 1920s, avant-garde filmmakers and theoreticians saw montage as a sort of visual equivalent to musical rhythm. It was thus that scansion, far from being perceived as artificial rupture, became an instrument capable of generating emotion and complex dramatic effect. These filmmakers echoed expressions borrowed from musical vocabulary to reflect their personal conceptions of what cinema ought to be. This was largely in response to the strong influence of theatre, painting and literature, which was predominant in most other film-makers' work at the time. These avant-garde artists questioned problems of *tempo* and *rhythm* in film: the flux of images, the incessant movement of bodies and light on the screen, the necessary succession of 'impressions'. These problems were essential when analysing the relationship with and correlations between filmic images: since film is by definition the art form of moving images, it is logical to assume that movement should play a preponderant role in its understanding.

Movement is defined as a succession of regularly recurring elements, and it is the perception of these elements that introduces rhythmical patterns. The analogy between the rhythm of sounds in music and the rhythm of the movement of form and colour viewed through a succession of images became central to the concerns of French avant-garde filmmakers. Significantly, the organising principle foreshadowed by such an analogy became known as montage. This essay will endeavour to describe the emergence of this parallel between music and cinema in order to demonstrate how rhythm – the movements and variations that visual form undergoes – played a major role in the parallel via the concept of montage.

Movement: montage and cinematic rhythm

Very early on, avant-garde filmmakers and theoreticians questioned the issue of movement and rhythm in film, the succession of images and their intrinsic relation. Rhythm is initiated by a sequence of elements regularly provoked through the production of movement itself and is a dominant feature exploited by avant-garde filmmakers. Ideas emanating from and around movement and rhythm infused the conceptions of avant-garde artists during the 1920s. By correlating ideas of music and cinema, avant-garde theorists aptly pointed to the musical aspect of images unfolding on the screen. Through cinematic devices such as montage, their interests focused on the creation of slow and fast movements as well as the rhythmical sensations they provide.

Ideas and concepts encompassing such notions of movement and rhythm became central to many avant-garde filmmakers during the first decades of the twentieth century: Abel Gance (*La Roue* 1923, *Napoléon* 1927), Jean Epstein (*Coeur fidèle* 1923, *La Chute de la maison Usher* 1928), Marcel L'Herbier (*L'Inhumaine* 1924), Germaine Dulac (*La Souriante Madame Beudet* 1923, *L'Invitation au voyage* 1927, *La Germination d'un haricot* 1928, *La Coquille et le clergyman* 1928) and Jean Grémillon (*La Photogénie mécanique* 1924, *La Croisière de l'Atalante* 1926, *L'Etrange Monsieur Victor* 1938). They all sought to utilise the possibilities which stemmed from coupling internal volumes with visual rupture in order to model cinematographic material. Since a film can be constructed following the same rules as those of musical composition, a film might thus be understood as a symphony of images, in which shots correspond to musical phrases. A number of theoreticians, some of whom were avant-garde filmmakers like Germaine Dulac and Albert Guyot, celebrated this analogy. The first to have noted the resemblance between filmmaking and musical composition was the critic Emile Vuillermoz. A confirmed musicographer and an authority in the field of music, he was also, significantly, a well-respected film critic. Discussing music and film in 1927, he writes:

> Car la composition cinégraphique obéit, sans s'en douter, aux lois secrètes de la composition musicale. Un film s'écrit et s'orchestre comme une symphonie. Il faut savoir harmoniser ces phrases plastiques, calculer leur courbe mélodique, leurs rappels, leurs interruptions.[1]

Vuillermoz indicated that a film, surreptitiously and without awareness, follows the same rules that govern musical composition. The cinema orchestrates images and scores our visions according to a strictly musical process: the film chooses its visual themes, renders them expressive, meticulously regulates their exposition, their opportune return, their measure and rhythm, develops them, breaks them down into parts, reintroduces them in fragments, and so on. Vuillermoz compared filmic images to visual phrases; the latter parallel becomes an analogy for musical phrases. For Vuillermoz, the shot is likened to a musical chord, in which the notes correspond to specific features of the *mise-en-scène* and framing. Thus, a scene or a sequence of shots is analogous to several bars of music, or even a stanza or movement.

In 1927, Vuillermoz's writings further investigated the analogy between filmic composition and musical composition. He states:

> Il y a des rapports fondamentaux exceptionnellement étroits entre l'art d'assembler et celui d'assembler des notations lumineuses. Les deux techniques sont rigoureusement semblables.[2]

---

1   Emile Vuillermoz, 'Devant l'écran – Lueurs', *Le Temps*, 21150 (4 June 1919), 3a–3d (p.3b).
2   Vuillermoz, 'La Musique des images', in *L'Art cinématographique*, 8 vols (Paris: Librairie Félix Alcan, 1927), III, pp.39–66 (p.59).

The expression 'rigoureusement semblables' underlines the perfect similarities of the two techniques of composition. Vuillermoz possessed an extremely rigorous formula when comparing musical composition with the technique of filmic montage:

> On peut donc retrouver dans la composition d'un film les lois qui président à celle d'une symphonie. Ce n'est pas un jeu de l'esprit, c'est une réalité tangible. Un film bien composé obéit instinctivement aux préceptes les plus classiques des traités de composition du Conservatoire.[3]

This statement again leaves little doubt as to the kinship that exists between music and cinema. According to Vuillermoz, both art forms observe the same rules of composition; the montage of a film is then similar to musical composition. Germaine Dulac reiterated this concept in 1927: 'Musique, cinéma technique semblable, jusqu'ici inspiration dissemblable. Deux arts causant l'émotion par des valeurs suggestives.'[4] No longer a mere grouping of ideas, in the second half of the 1920s the analogy between cinema and music developed into a concrete theory shared by a number of avant-garde artists. Among the advocates was the filmmaker Albert Guyot who wrote in support of this fundamental theory in 1927 (the same year as Vuillermoz and Dulac):

> Le rythme est assimilable à la mesure et toutes les règles de la composition cinématographique – l'ouverture de l'iris, la surimpression, le renchaîné, le fondu, etc. – ont leur [sic] correspondantes musicales.
>   Ouvrir en quatre, fondez en huit; six tours de réserve... Le réalisateur est un monsieur qui compte. Quand il ne compte pas, il mesure. La précision mathématique est à la base du cinéma comme elle est à la base de la musique.[5]

Underlining this new conceptual theory, Guyot demonstrated that both cinema and music follow the same rules of composition and supported this claim by citing examples of film technique. He referred specifically to the work of the cameraman who regulates the *duration* of

3   Ibid., p.60.
4   Germaine Dulac, 'Les Esthétiques, les entraves, la cinégraphie intégrale', in *L'Art cinématographique*, II, 29–50 (p.50).
5   Albert Guyot, 'Éditorial – Réflexions sur le cinéma pur', *Cinégraphie*, 3 (15 November 1927), a single page editorial (p. 41).

the cinematic processes used by the filmmaker. Cinema and music also share characteristics of time, calling on the use of the time signature – itself founded on mathematics. Guyot is right in highlighting that mathematics is at the root of both music and cinema. Thus the avant-garde – under the guise of one of its least well-known protagonists – sees, in cinema, an art form as precise in its use of means as music.

By this point, the avant-garde had already produced works that attempted to resemble musical pieces. Theoreticians found similar traits between rhythm in the cinema and rhythm in music since, as noted above, music and cinema are both art forms unfolding in time – one through the means of sounds and the other through images. In 1924, Dulac stated: 'Tous les arts sont mouvement puisqu'il y a développement, mais l'art des images est, je crois, plus proche de la musique par le rythme qui leur est commun.'[6]

After repeatedly studying a film made by Henri Chomette, entitled *Cinq minutes de cinéma pur* (1925), Guyot likened the film to a well-known musical form: the sonata. To illustrate this, Guyot explains:

> Je suis convaincu qu'une salle spécialisée, projetant uniquement des films de cinéma pur, aurait rapidement son public – comme les grands concerts ont le leur. J'introduis à dessein la musique dans cette affirmation. La bande de Chomette est une sonate aimable que l'on éprouve sans le moindre désir de *l'interpréter*. Ce qui prouve sa perfection.[7]

He also added that the spectator should *feel* the film without seeking to interpret it, strengthening once again the analogy to music where the listener is not asked to understand, but rather to feel a sensation. Avant-garde cinema, which is close to music, or which identifies itself with it, must touch the sensitivity of the spectator. Vibrations of light should emotionally move the sense of sight, triggering sensations or feelings in the same way that music stimulates the sense of hearing.

6   Dulac, 'Conférence de Madame Dulac –   Faite à la séance des « Amis du cinéma » donnée le 7 décembre dans la Salla [sic] du Colisée', *Cinémagazine*, 1 (December 1924), 516–518 (p. 516b).
7   Guyot, 'Éditorial – Réflexions sur le cinéma pur', p.41.

For Dulac, then, cinematic rhythm corresponds to musical rhythm. The function of the filmmaker is thus closely aligned with that of the composer; the former negotiates images while the latter considers musical phrases. The product of the two artistic techniques is endowed with intense emotion, and it is this emotion that constitutes the ultimate goal of both the filmmaker and the composer. It is therefore not surprising that film images should themselves suffice without any recourse to text or title. The use of titles in avant-garde film can even be qualified as something of a heresy since images, as a result of their rhythmical structure, penetrate the very core of the spectator's sensitivity with maximum force. And this purely visual and rhythmical emotion can spring from the mere acceleration of film as seen in Dulac's *La Germination d'un haricot* (1928). This abstract film demonstrates the accelerated development of a bean sprout. Thus, the film embodies her theory: the rhythm of movement, with its lines and forms, is the very essence of cinema.

Cinema and music: theories of musicality in film

Tracing the origins of these avant-garde film theories, the analogy between music and cinema first gained momentum in 1925, although the relation had nonetheless been hinted at previously. As early on as 1921, Riccioto Canudo had already attempted to establish connections between cinema and music. Canudo even indicated that it was music that brought about the dawn of cinema as an art form:

> C'est bien la prestigieuse évolution de la Musique qui a permis à l'esprit humain, averti par la Science, de se créer cet art à nul autre pareil, et qui est bien l'Art du XXe siècle.[8]

But for Canudo, cinema stemmed not only from musical parallels, but also from scientific influence. For Canudo, cinema represents the

8   Riccioto Canudo, 'Cent versets d'initiation au lyrisme nouveau dans tous les arts (Suite et fin)', *La Revue de l'époque*, 17 (May 1921), 927–932 (p.927).

fusion of the arts of time and the arts of space, that is to say music (and its counterparts, poetry and dance) and architecture (and its counterparts, painting and sculpture). It is therefore not surprising that, in Canudo's system, cinema originates from music.

Louis Delluc, an avant-garde filmmaker and writer, also wrote on the relations between cinema and music. It is worth noting that his writings chronologically precede those of Canudo, a point that has seldom been emphasised in the literature.[9] Delluc described the filmmaker as a composer of moving images and compared the actor to 'une note dans la grande composition du musicien visuel.'[10] Film, whether the work of a visual musician or a composer of images, is therefore considered as a musical piece and a genuine symphony. Like the musician, the filmmaker must be precise, as Delluc stated in 1919: 'Cet art prodigieux qui vit, comme la musique, de précision mathématique et de mystère, est en butte à toutes les contraintes.'[11] Although Delluc, like Guyot, wrote of the mathematical precision common to both cinema and music, he also spoke of its mystery. Filmic images are sometimes open-ended, allowing the viewer's imagination to wander, in the same way that musical sounds are immaterial. When discussing mathematics, Delluc often spoke of montage: he believed that montage incorporated elements of algebra.

9   Canudo was an Italian film theoretician. In his manifesto *The Birth of the Sixth Art*, published as early as 1911, he argued that the cinema synthesised the spatial arts (architecture, sculpture and painting) with the temporal arts (music and dance). He later added poetry in his seminal manifesto *Reflections on the Seventh Art* of 1923 (which went through a number of earlier drafts, all published in Italy or France). He has traditionally been considered as the very first theoretician of cinema. Louis Delluc used and illustrated the theories of Canudo, which aimed at imposing the autonomy of film as an art form. Delluc, in his writings more than in his films, attempted to impose the taste and perhaps even the snobbery of what Canudo had proposed to call the 'seventh art' to French intellectuals. With regard to the relation between film and music, Delluc's writings preceded those of Canudo by two years.

10   Louis Delluc, 'Cinégraphie', *Le Crapouillot* (16 February 1921), Numéro spécial sur le cinéma, 3–6 (p.5).

11   Delluc, *Cinéma et Cie: Confidences d'un spectateur* (Paris: Bernard Grasset, 1919), p.68.

Here, the term algebra most likely refers to the word's original Arabic meaning of *reunion* and *combination*:

> Et quand le film est tourné [...] qui sait *monter* les scènes? Un petit nombre seulement ont le sens voulu pour couper ces kilomètres de pellicule et savoir l'algèbre musical qui préside au dosage des vignettes enregistrées.[12]

Having compared the filmmaker to a visual musician, Delluc transformed the perfect *monteur* into a genuine composer. Here the French term *monteur* will be preferred to *editor*, since we are dealing with the technique of montage in avant-garde film and not the mainstream technique of editing. The cinema is thus an entirely musical construct, spanning the film's initial outline, shoot and final assembly in a montage sequence, where rhythm is created, endowing the film with a poetic quality. Delluc equated the work of the filmmaker to that of the composer, while the *monteur* was compared to the conductor who provides the composed and written work with *rhythm* and *tempo*.

Further research into testimonies around the relations between cinema and music reveals that Vuillermoz was the first to initiate a close comparison of the two art forms. As a result of his musical training and his intimate knowledge of the cinematic genre, he laid the foundations for a fruitful and relevant comparison of the two media. As early as 1916, he wrote:

> Cette forme de développement de la pensée, avec ses rappels de thème, ses motifs conducteurs, ses allusions, ses insinuations rapides ou ses lentes sollicitations, mais c'est celle de la symphonie! Le cinéma orchestre les images, instrumente nos visions et nos souvenirs par des procédés strictement musicaux: il doit choisir ses thèmes visuels, les rendre expressifs, en régler minutieusement l'exposition, le retour opportun, la mesure et le rythme, les développer, les morceler, les présenter par fragments, par « augmentation » ou « diminution », comme disent les traités de composition; plus heureux que la peinture et la sculpture, le cinéma a, comme la musique, toutes les inflexions et toutes les nuances de la beauté qui marche: le cinéma fait du contre point et de l'harmonie...mais il attend encore son Debussy![13]

---

12   Delluc, *Photogénie* (Paris: Maurice de Brunoff, 1920), p.72.
13   Vuillermoz, 'Chroniques – Devant l'écran', *Le Temps*, 20234 (29 November 1916), 3a–3b (p.3b).

The work undertaken by Vuillermoz in terms of popularising the analogy between cinema and music was enormously successful since, as I examine next, a movement pushing for symphonic cinema was at the heart of the avant-gardes.

From visual symphonies to *cinéma intégral*

Prestigious names contributed to the specifically musical analysis of renowned films, with Dulac as one of the key proponents. As she described Abel Gance's 1922 film *La Roue*: 'Mouvement d'yeux, de roues, de paysages, noires, blanches, croches, double [sic] croches, combinaison d'orchestration visuelle: le cinéma!'[14] Upon viewing the film, Dulac equated a filmic image to a single note or sound, describing *La Roue* as follows: 'Poème symphonique où, comme en musique, le sentiment éclate non en faits et en actes, mais en sensations, l'image ayant la valeur d'un son.'[15] By comparing a filmic shot to a musical note, Dulac directly opposes Vuillermoz's analogy which likens a shot to a phrase of music. However, the shots in *La Roue* are so short that they might momentarily be equated with notes. Furthermore, when Dulac relates certain excerpts of *La Roue* to a kind of symphonic cinema, she underlines the duration of time: she writes of crotchets, minims (which are twice the length of crotchets), and quavers (which last half the length of crotchets). The film composer is therefore someone who arranges, counts and measures.

Dulac perceives an intricate link between music and film as they both deal with the succession of elements in time: sounds, in the case of music, and images, in the case of film. The layout of images in a film strongly resembles the organisation of sounds in a symphony. The image can be as complex as the musical phrase since it is also made up of multiple movements combined together. Dulac is a fervent

14   Dulac, 'Films visuels et anti-visuels', *Le Rouge et le noir*, Cahier spécial 'Cinéma', (July 1928), 31–41 (p.33).
15   Dulac, 'Les Esthétiques, les entraves, la cinégraphie intégrale', p.43.

supporter of the visual symphonic poem where vibrations are pure and comparable to the symphonic poems of music. She wrote: 'Poème symphonique, où le sentiment éclate non en fait, non en acte, mais en sonorités visuelles.'[16] Thus, the fruitful comparison between music and film brought about the theory of pure visual symphony.

It must be noted that the advent of sound put an end to visual cinema. The invention of the 'talkie' was thus perceived by some as a catastrophe, since it cut short the evolution of a cinema built on the visual rhythm imposed by the filmmaker. The theories emanating from the concept of visual symphony are thus far richer than the actual filmic works presenting these ideas. In any case, French theorists and artists in the 1920s all questioned whether the cinema could not be oriented towards pure visual symphony. Dulac initiated this movement, as Vuillermoz reported in 1927:

> Il est bien évident qu'on peut espérer arriver dans un avenir plus ou moins prochain à orienter certains cinégraphistes, particulièrement bien doués, vers ce que Germaine Dulac appelle si justement la symphonie visuelle pure.[17]

For Dulac, visual symphony is different from the theory of *cinéma intégral*, which she considers to be 'plus synthétique et plus forte [...] musique de l'oeil'.[18] She considers them to be two distinct theories: while the theory of *cinéma intégral* stems from that of visual symphony, the latter is more specifically inspired by an analogy with music. Dulac appears to have founded her conception of visual music after viewing *La Roue* at the end of 1922, where the racing of the locomotive is expressed through the rhythm of short shots and fast montage. Apart from Gance's film, Dulac must have seen the series of four *Opus* films in Ruttmann and Eggeling's seminal *Diagonal Symphony*. These films were inspired by musical techniques trans-

---

16   Dulac, 'Les Œuvres d'avant-garde cinématographique: leur destin devant le public et l'industrie du film', in *Le Cinéma des origines à nos jours* (Paris: Éditions du Cygne, 1932), pp.357–364 (p.360).
17   Vuillermoz, 'La Musique des images', p.63.
18   See Dulac, 'Du Sentiment à la ligne', *Schémas*, 1 (February 1927b) and 'Les Œuvres d'avant-garde cinématographique: leur destin devant le public et l'industrie du film', p.27.

posed to the cinema and strongly influenced Dulac in the elaboration of her theory. Until 1926, Dulac defended her ideas on paper and could only come up with parsimonious examples, along with her 1929 *Arabesque*. Her theory uses music as a simple model, with a simple analogy: the images dominate and their visual character in particular is emphasised. Only rhythm is transposed from music to cinema.

As we have seen, the theory of visual symphony was a stage in the development towards *cinéma intégral* in 1926, which feeds off cinema through movement only. It has often been reported in critical literature that Dulac only created a general theory. In fact, she progressed from narrative cinema to visual cinema by developing the notions of visual symphony and *cinéma intégral*. Visual symphony is inspired by music and thus founded on principles outside the filmic realm, whereas pure cinema or *cinéma intégral* is solely based on cinematographic movement. An abstract, 'symphonic' cinema offers little possibility of representational figures. Instead, only pure forms and the use of light play a prevailing role. Dulac's 1927 film *L'Invitation au voyage* reveals the subjective world of its heroine through a succession of slow shots using effects of superimposition. Here, montage works through associations with a strict economy of movement. The music flows into the poetry of the images without ostentation and aptly illustrates the rites of transient desire. Thus, visual symphony evades any link to literature and, as in musical symphony, only plays with sensations.

Techniques of visual rhythm

In order to represent musical rhythm onscreen, French avant-garde filmmakers used a variety of techniques. One of the first tools was 'accelerated montage',[19] labelled 'precipitated montage' by many of

---

19   A series of cuts are used over a short period of time, moving rapidly from one shot to another so as to produce a rhythmically chaotic effect. D. W. Griffith, for example, used this effect to create suspense at the end of his films.

its detractors in order to convey the surge of images it creates. This montage technique was used to striking effect by Gance in *La Roue* and influenced many subsequent films:

> Le montage rapide, écrit Epstein, existe en germe dans l'œuvre géante de Griffith. C'est à Gance que revient l'honneur d'avoir à ce point perfectionné ce procédé, qu'il mérite de passer pour son inventeur génial. *La Roue* est encore ce monument cinématographique formidable à l'ombre duquel tout l'art cinématographique français vit et croît [...] Aujourd'hui on abuse du montage rapide jusque dans les documentaires; chaque drame possède une scène montée par petits bouts, quand ce n'est pas deux ou trois.[20]

Parts of the action of *La Roue* take place on a train, where the emotions of the passengers are linked to the train's speed, and thus to the manner in which it has been filmed. 'Filmer la vitesse' is precisely the challenge of this type of cinematic expression. For speed to be added *a fortiori* to dramatic intensity, neither the frame nor the elements it contains suffice. Gance uses the resources of montage to work with visual oppositions, ruptures of lines (tracks running towards one another, locomotives travelling in all directions through a very rapid succession of shots on the screen) and the acceleration of sequences themselves. As Gance suggests:

> C'est en exécutant *La Roue* que j'ai compris que le cinéma était réellement la musique de la lumière. Et à partir du moment où j'ai pensé au mot musique et au mot cinéma, j'ai construit toute me vie de cinéaste. Dans le montage, dans l'accélération, les images ont des syncopes, ont des mouvements de plus en plus rapides, et je montais absolument comme si une image était un violon, une autre était une flûte, et tout cela s'organisait en fonction de cette idée de la « musique de la lumière » [...] J'ai spéculé à ce moment-là sur la perception rapide et simultanée des images au quart et même au huitième de seconde.[21]

From this perspective, the creation of clashes as well as associations occurs explicitly by the same process, since the brevity of the shot 'slashes' perception through jerky effects on the one hand, while the

---

20 Jean Epstein, *Pour une avant-garde nouvelle*, conference given in 1924, printed in *Écrits sur le cinéma* (Seghers: Paris, 1974), vol 1, pp.147–151 (p.148–149).
21 Interview with Abel Gance, *Histoire du cinéma français* (Armand Panigel, 1974), documentary film.

speed of succession yields false superimpositions on the other. These figures of montage are comparable to what video is able to create today on a larger scale. In video clips, for example, or in certain short films, such effects of visual transformation (the fast succession of images) simultaneously produce rhythm, either through ruptures and links or through associations.

Marcel L'Herbier's *L'Inhumaine* is more radical, integrating, in particular, accelerated montage sequences of totally abstract shots. When the heroine is 'resuscitated' in the workshop of a mad scientist, we witness a succession of movements whose function is solely sensory, devoid of any intention to represent in concrete terms. Pistons and a metal pendulum abruptly change lights to yellow, black or even some entirely white shots, articulating vision separately. The displacement of light, the visual harmonies and the abstract movements all seek to make an appeal to the spectator's senses.

It is important to note, however, that this highly formalistic approach is different to that of the school of Soviet montage. The multiple ruptures found in the bridge episodes of *October* (1927) or the Odessa step sequence of *Battleship Potemkin* (1925) stage figurative elements. These are destructured, certainly, but hold the value of what they represent. This is quite different from the vision of musical montage shared by the French filmmakers discussed here. The Soviets emphasised intellectual montage whereby meaning was generated through the association of images. For the French theorists, the montage process was far more intuitive and relied on superimpositions, split screens and the speed of succession of certain shots. French filmmakers aimed at provoking in their spectators the same sensitivity as when listening to a musical piece. Visual rhythm and its visual effects work on the spectator as much as, if not more than, the logical and emotional development of a particular film narrative.

This sensory montage, inspiring Henri Langlois to coin the filmic movement 'impressionist',[22] is based on the *legato* – the flow formed

22   The 'French Impressionists', also referred to as the 'First Avant-Garde' or the 'Narrative Avant-Garde', is a somewhat anachronistic term applied loosely to the group of films and filmmakers discussed in this essay. Theorists have had much difficulty in defining this movement or, for that matter, deciding whether

by the succession of fragments rather than their separate entities. It emerges through frequent recourse to dissolve and superimpose. The former is a collage effect which intimately links shots which, for the duration of a few images, appear simultaneously on the screen, blending their volumes before following one another. Filmmakers L'Herbier and Epstein used these figures repeatedly, while Jean Vigo, who later inherited this legacy, used superimpositions until his last film *L'Atalante* in 1934. Dissolves and superimpositions sometimes complemented accelerated montage, especially to highlight its role of aesthetic synthesis even further.

Rather than a *montage of shots,* superimpositions are actually a *montage of surfaces*, defined as the confrontation or marked difference between diverse entities within the same shot. In Abel Gance's *Napoléon*, one can see up to eight or even twelve superimposed shots. Crowds are associated with storms, without any anecdotal relation. With visual effects preferred over identifiable figurations, once again, form prevails over representation in montage sequences. Commenting on some of these extracts, Abel Gance explains: 'Il faut juguler l'intelligence du spectateur, l'empêcher de reprendre ses esprits.'[23] Neither story nor discourse justifies the shot's unity and articulation in respect to others. It does, however, legitimise the relations of sensitivity that develop between them and the synthesis of movement that only this process can highlight. We can recall Gance's earlier comparison with an orchestra: if each image is like an instrument, the montage of surfaces truly becomes a visual symphony.

it should be considered a movement at all. David Bordwell, for example, has attempted to define a unified stylistic paradigm and set of tenets. See Bordwell, *French Impressionist Cinema* (New York: Arno Press, 1980). Richard Abel criticises these attempts and groups the films and filmmakers more loosely, based on a common goal of 'exploration of the process of representation and signification in narrative film discourse.' See *French Cinema: The First Wave 1915–1929* (New Jersey: Princeton University Press, 1984), p.21. Dudley Andrew struggles with awarding enough credibility to these artists and films to define them as a 'movement'. See *Mists of Regret* (New Jersey: Princeton University Press, 1995).

23   Vincent Amiel, *Esthétique du montage* (Paris: Éditions Nathan, 2001), p.85.

The montage theories elaborated by the French avant-garde during the 1920s, especially by the second wave of *impressionists*, have long remained in the shadows. French avant-garde filmmakers did not systematise the technique of montage in the same way as their Soviet counterparts. Nonetheless, very early on, French filmmakers certainly understood the value and importance of montage. The theories centring on the notion of music, and particularly musical or symphonic montage, were certainly the most fertile and rich of all the concepts developed by France's filmmakers in the 1920s. The search for a visual equivalent of music led these avant-garde artists to conceive film as a symphonic poem: imperceptibly, narrative and the performance of the actor lose their isolated value in favour of a broad orchestration of rhythm created by shots, framing, angles, lighting, proportions, contrasts and harmonies of images. French avant-garde filmmakers constantly returned to the evocative power of the filmic image, the harmonious emotional qualities of *rhythm* and *movement*. For these artists, this was the very essence of cinema, possessing the power to project the viewer into an emotional state that remained unrivalled.

Suggested Reading

Abel, Richard, *French Cinema: The First Wave 1915–1929* (Princeton: Princeton University Press, 1984).

Brenez, Nicole and Christian Lebrat, *Jeune, dure et pure! Une Histoire du cinéma d'avant-garde et expérimental en France* (Paris: Cinémathèque française and Milan: Mazzotta, 2001).

Ghali, Noureddine, *L'avant-garde cinématographique en France dans les années vingt: idées, conceptions, théories* (Paris: Paris Expérimental, 1995).

Grieveson, Lee and Peter Krämer, *The Silent Cinema Reader* (London: Routledge, 2004).

Wees, William, *Light Moving in Time: Studies in the Visual Aesthetics of Avant-Garde Film* (Berkeley: University of California Press, 1992).

JENNY CHAMARETTE

A Short Film About Time:
Dynamism and Stillness in Chris Marker's *La Jetée*

> *Ceci est l'histoire d'un homme marqué par une image d'enfance. La scène qui le troubla par sa violence, et dont il ne devait comprendre que beaucoup plus tard la signification, eut lieu sur la grande jetée d'Orly, quelques années avant le début de la troisième guerre mondiale.* [1]

These are the opening lines of Chris Marker's 1962 short film, *La Jetée*, spoken in voiceover. They point towards the marking of an anonymous man by some kind of revised primal scene – a mark that is only made meaningful many years later. So reflexive is this process of marking that it resonates even with the name of the film-maker. Marker's work invokes such marks and representational difficulties, addressing critical issues between cinema, subjectivity and temporality. His oeuvre itself oscillates between writing and critique, filmmaking and photography, video installation and poetic monologue. His work continually questions: what constitutes cinema? What constitutes subjectivity? Or indeed temporality? *La Jetée*, perhaps the most remarkable of Marker's fictional work, absolutely refigures notions of cinematic continuity and cinematic temporality.

La Jetée's image montage of photographs or photogrammatic images is accompanied by a voice-narrated story: one set in the future but staged as a series of voyages to a past contemporary with Marker's making of the film, and an unrecognisable, illegible post-futural landscape. A series of predominantly static images, the film could equally be described as a visual photographic novel played out

---

1   Chris Marker, *La Jetée: ciné-roman* (New York: Zone Books, 1992). No page number given.

on-screen. Nonetheless, each image is carefully staged within a set of cinematic conventions that 'read' as a film, in spite of the stillness at work in each image.

The events of *La Jetée* occur in a fictional time, somewhere between our past (the film was made in 1962) and an imagined post-apocalyptic future, where atomic war has ravaged the earth to the extent that the only remaining survivors live in subterranean caverns below Paris. The protagonist, an unnamed *lui*, is coerced into a form of psycho-physical time travel, induced by injections of an unknown, unnamed drug, in order to travel into the future to ask for help from the future generations. His psychical journeys initially throw him back into a pre-apocalyptic time (thus contemporary with the production of the film), where he meets an unnamed woman, with whom he subsequently falls in love on his fleeting visits to the past. The film culminates in his doomed attempt to escape from the post-apocalyptic present into the ambrosian past of his childhood, where his fate has always been sealed. The childhood image that marks him is also the instant of his own death, which he comes to realise only at that moment. The narrative is consequently locked into a perfect cycle, where beginning is end and end is beginning.

La Jetée is not the only 'photo-roman' of its kind to have emerged in French filmmaking of the 1960s. Philippe Dubois contextualises this in his article '*La Jetée* de Chris Marker ou le cinématogramme de la conscience'. He cites Agnès Varda's 1963 film *Salut les Cubains*, which is entirely made up of 1800 photographs that she took on a visit to Cuba in the winter of 1962–63, and Philippe Lifchitz's film *X.Y.Z.*, made from postcards.[2] Like Marker, Varda accelerates and decelerates the shifts between photographs, and accompanies the images with real-time sound, in order to give the impression of animation or de-animation. There are also numerous polemical film-photo-montage projects from the Montreal animator Arthur Lipsett, dating from the early 1960s, such as *Very Good, Very Good*. However, as many critics have explained with reference to

2   Philippe Dubois, '*La Jetée* de Chris Marker ou le cinématogramme de la conscience', in *Recherches sur Chris Marker*, ed. Philippe Dubois (Paris: Presses Sorbonne Nouvelle, 2002), p.11.

La Jetée, the film is not photographic, as are both *Salut Les Cubains* and *Very Good, Very Good*, but rather *photogrammatic*, as will be explained in further detail later.[3]

La Jetée's rhythms of halting continuity and relentless linear narrative are both engaging and slippery, and move outside the bounds of narratival cause and effect. Thus, the film engages with questions of psychical and subjective relations to time, both in its content and its inter-textual medium. In particular, *La Jetée*'s specific interrelation between dynamic sound and still image, between the rhythm and duration of the image on screen and the temporal shifts of the narrative, make this film particularly influential upon questions of contemporary cinema more than forty years after its release. *La Jetée* intersects between film and photomontage, between linear narrative and disrupted subjective temporality. However, what is at stake in the internalised temporality of *La Jetée*, both represented and subjective, are the kinds of movement that this oscillation takes: from the rhythmic form of a regular pendulum, to a more halting, stuttering rhythm, without resolution or conclusive pattern.

Rhythm and (dis)continuity

As both Mary Ann Doane and Laura Mulvey have pointed out, the effectiveness of cinema rests upon an illusional logic, where the projection of twenty-four still images or frames per second 'moves' objects through filmic space and time, creating a fundamentally discontinuous but nonetheless highly effective simulacrum of our own subjective space-time. A pertinent issue is raised by Mulvey in her most recent book, with regard to what she describes as new forms of

3   To name but a few, Barthélemy Amengual, 'Le Présent du futur: sur *La Jetée*', *Positif* (March 1997), 96–98. See also Dubois, '*La Jetée* de Chris Marker ou le cinématogramme de la conscience', and Nora M. Alter, *Chris Marker* (Urbana and Chicago: University of Illinois Press, 2006).

cinema spectatorship enabled by new technologies' emphasis upon the possibilities of the freeze frame, the still and so on. She states:

> When narrative fragments, and its protagonists are transformed into still, posed images to which movement can be restored, the rhythm of a movie changes. The supposed laws of smoothly distributed linear cause and effect are of minor aesthetic importance compared to another kind of, more tableau-oriented, rhythm.[4]

It is important to note at this point that Mulvey does not discuss Chris Marker's experimental works; rather she is referring to the effect of new digital technology upon iconic film images, particularly those of golden age Hollywood cinema. However, the intersections between this analysis and an examination of Marker's film *La Jetée* are striking.

The images of *La Jetée* retain all the traces of cinematographic *mise-en-scène*, lighting, close-up, even including extra- and intra-diegetic sound. Nonetheless, the rhythm of this 'film' is composed via processes of fragmentation and reassembly. The flow of narration is inherently detached from the diegesis – the on-screen events – and the protagonists and images are still and posed. Movement, or dynamism, then, is produced diegetically via apparent movement and extra-diegetic sound, only to be disassembled once that dynamic moment returns to the englobing narration of the voiceover and stillness of the photogramme. Thus, the cinematographic-photogrammatic forms and narrative drive of Marker's 'photo-roman' fundamentally disrupt the illusional logic of cinematic time. In spite of this, the diegetic rhythms of *La Jetée* do not quite adhere to the fragmentary qualities set out by Mulvey as examples of tableau-oriented rhythm. Is *La Jetée*, then, a pre-emptive example of a different kind of tableau-oriented rhythm in film, while still retaining a relentlessly linear narrative – the kind of narrative, in fact, that Mulvey first posited in her 1975 essay on Hollywood narrative cinema?

Patrick ffrench points out in his article, 'The Memory of the Image in Chris Marker's *La Jetée*':

---

4   Laura Mulvey, *Death 24x a Second: Stillness and the Moving Image* (London: Reaktion, 2006), p.166.

> The withdrawal of the images of the film from the illusion of continuous motion induced by shooting and projection at twenty-four frames a second serves to emphasise, not to deny, the dynamism inherent in cinema. One might say, with Deleuze, that in the classical Hollywood film the movement of the image becomes frozen in the stereotype of movement and that it takes the stillness of the photogram to make visible, through montage, the dynamic gesture in movement.[5]

ffrench's counterintuitive logic of the dynamism invoked by stillness seems to have historical echoes both backward to cinema's origins in the tracing of the moving image, and forward, towards a cinematography of stillness as described by Mulvey. In revealing the dynamic gesture of movement, the stillness of *La Jetée*'s images allow for a deeper, less momentary contemplation of what it is to think time in the cinema, or in other words, to examine cinematic temporality.

The presentation of temporality in the film is very much part of the dichotomy between dynamism and stillness. One could argue that Marker's move away from illusional cinematic movement and continuity in the photogrammatic film *La Jetée* makes obvious the impossibility of a pure representation of time. The photogrammatic image-moments are not displayed on the screen as inseparable and are not even necessarily linked sequentially or indexically. It is quite the opposite, in fact: each image serves its carefully structured purpose as a *tableau vivant* within the narrative frame. Consequently, the manner in which the narrative is told – rather appropriately defined by Bakhtin as the *suzhet* – constructs the temporal journeys, indeed, the time travel, of its central protagonist, while guiding our personal cinematic experience through linear time. As a result, both subject matter and medium invoke an exploration of a subject-in-time. They do so through a narrational and image-based temporality that is deliberately striated, separated, made unreal and cut into moments. Furthermore, the artificiality of each of these moments is foregrounded by the slow pace of the changing images and the compositional distinctness of each photogramme.

---

5   Patrick ffrench, 'The Memory of the Image in Chris Marker's *La Jetée*', *French Studies: A Quarterly Review*, 59 (January 2005), 31–37 (pp.32–33).

A stilled cinema?

As Catherine Lupton points out in her text on Marker, *La Jetée*'s photogrammatic images cite the technical aesthetics and *mise-en-scène* of the cinema:

> Like shots in a conventional film, the photographs are separated by straight cuts, fades and dissolves of varying duration, while individual sequences are broken down into the recognisable patterns of classical narrative cinema, with establishing shots, eyeline matches, shot-countershot, close-ups and so forth, all working to create a sense of narrative coherence and momentum.[6]

Consequently, duration is conceived of across the cut and the dissolve so that the cinematic form emerges from a 'momentum', rather than a temporality represented by the moving cinematic image. Editing becomes the means to access the film's own temporality, alongside the inexorable linearity of the narrative. This position also aligns itself with Mary Ann Doane's assessment of film theory from an early theoretical and historical position. Doane suggests that the possibility of a production of meaningful cinematic temporality can come into being via editing technique, in particular the cut:

> Ultimately it is editing, the possibility of a *cut* in the temporal and spatial continuity of the shot, that is fetishised as the semiotic imperative of the cinema. For general cultural theorists such as Walter Benjamin and Siegfried Kracauer, the cut was *the* incarnation of temporality in film, and it constituted the formal response to the restructuring of time in modernity.[7]

In this respect, Marker's film not only invests in a temporality distinguished by the cut, and by the gaps between images, but also has perhaps the most marked investment in multiple qualities of tem-

---

6   Catherine Lupton, *Chris Marker: Memories of the Future* (London: Reaktion, 2005), p.91.
7   Mary Ann Doane, *The Emergence of Cinematic Time: Modernity, Contingency, the Archive* (Cambridge, Mass. and London: Harvard University Press, 2002), p.184.

porality – that is, in durational distinctions between photographs, photogrammes and cinematic images.

Filmic space is cut, framed and pasted together in accordance with the content. However, this content is drawn together by a voice-over that dictates the signifying power of the image. The narrative voice forces the spectator through the images without apparent permission of divergence or reflection, forging an inviolable bond between narration and image. There is however, an affective charge to this inviolable narrative bond – one of viol-*ence*. When narrative is forced and forged onto the images, the tranquility that might be associated with a still, non-moving, undynamic image is ravaged, generating an affectively dynamic image in the face of its stillness.

This stuttering, affective rhythm seems absolutely in excess of the montage construction, it exists on a plane – indeed, a tableau – which is both within and between the sound, image and spectatorial reception of *La Jetée*. Furthermore, its affective intensity is more specific than the violent re-production of time and space that Walter Benjamin highlights in that well-used phrase from his essay 'The Work of Art in the Age of Mechanical Reproduction', where film 'burst this prison-world asunder by the dynamite of the tenth of a second [...].'[8] Rather than a violence of the contingent, the cinematic narrative within *La Jetée* forges a painterly or authorial interpretation upon the image, re-inscribing the supposed contingency of the photo-grammatic film still onto a carefully bound cinematic object – in this case, the protagonist's passage through time.

This carefully composed and almost obsessively precise montage seems to be in exact opposition to the possibilities of both total and chance representation that a contingent, moving, mass-mediated image might bring, and which early twentieth-century theorists such as Siegfried Kracauer and Walter Benjamin suggest.[9] *La Jetée* is

---

8   Walter Benjamin, 'The Work of Art in the Age of Mechanical Reproduction', in *Illuminations*, ed. Hannah Arendt, trans. Harry Zohn (London: Pimlico, 1999), pp.211–44 (p.229).

9   See Benjamin, 'A Small History of Photography', in *One-Way Street and Other Writings*, trans. Edmund Jephcott and Kingsley Shorter (London and New York: Verso, 1979), pp.240–57. See also Benjamin, 'The Work of Art in the

totally legible – in some ways, it is the perfect narrative, tied at both ends into a perfectly circular story. Thus, paradoxically, the images of *La Jetée*, which bear such resemblance to photographs, are, unlike the photograph, tightly bound to a narrative construction. *La Jetée*'s photogrammes leave no visual or diegetic space for contingency or the chance event, the possibilities which Benjamin expounds both in 'The Work of Art in the Age of Mechanical Reproduction' and in 'A Small History of Photography', and which Roland Barthes gestures towards in *La Chambre claire*.[10] In driving away contingency via the inexorable *driving forward* of narrative, the dynamic of *La Jetée* reveals its visual cartography as definitively, regularly, rhythmically conceptualised.

In terms of its total legibility, forged narrative and the iconic significance of each image to the forward thrust of the narrative, *La Jetée* seems to construct itself within a highly conventional set of linear storytelling forms; closer indeed to a novel than to a film. In his discussion of the photogrammatic images of *La Jetée*, Philippe Dubois takes care to note that the subtitle 'photo-roman' of the film is altered to 'ciné-roman' in the printed version of the screenplay and story-board, published in 1992 by Zone Books – a slippage that crosses between media and which traverses the communicative strategies of each art form: novel, photography, film. Dubois is quick to point out this inter-imagery, calling upon Raymond Bellour's text, *L'Entre-images*,[11] while retaining his own interpretation:

> conformément à sa stratégie permanente de brouillage des pistes et de refus des cloisonnements, Marker a joué d'emblée et délibérément sur le double support (non pas *ou* mais *et*), tournant à la fois en photo et en film, et sur les deux effets, photographiques et photogrammatiques, tressant inextricablement un film d'entre-images entre les deux dimensions.[12]

Age of Mechanical Reproduction', and Siegfried Kracauer, *Theory of Film: The Redemption of Physical Reality* (Princeton: Princeton University Press, 1997).

10   Cf. Roland Barthes, *La Chambre claire: note sur la photographie* (Paris: Gallimard, 1980).

11   See Raymond Bellour, *L'Entre-images: photo, cinéma, vidéo, Les essais* (Paris: Éditions de la Différence, 2002).

12   Dubois, '*La Jetée* de Chris Marker ou le cinématogramme de la conscience', p.12.

La Jetée takes on an intermediary quality, between photography and film, between layers of temporality, and between qualities of the cinematic. This intermediary quality seizes upon the narrative positions of the protagonists, while also acknowledging the crucial role of the stilled image in imbricating one layer of temporality upon another.

Affect and matrices of memory

In addition to the complex temporalities played out between *La Jetée*'s form and content, its *suzhet* and *fabula*, another complex network of qualities enters into and between the photographic, narrative and filmic elements of the film. Affect saturates each image in this intensely structured photo-roman, the effects of which emerge even on a notional level in terms of the strategies of narrative coercion already discussed. In Barthesian terms, the *studium* of the photograph[13] – its narrative purposiveness – is privileged over all other aspects in Marker's photogrammes. Consequently, our emotional and affective journey is guided, or indeed, coerced by the narratival construction of image and voiceover. This coerced psychical act of moving into and out of the past is interestingly analogous to a number of descriptions of memory. For instance, in his article on *La Jetée*, Dubois argues that the inviolably ordered and precisely narrated montage of images represent a psychical matrix of memory:

> De l'enfance à l'homme, et de l'homme à l'enfance, il ne peut y avoir que des trajets, un jet et un rejet, une pro-jetée et une re-jetée. Donc un voyage dans le temps entre soi et soi, qui, comme tous les voyages dans le temps, ne peut être qu'un voyage par les images et dans la pensée, un voyage en image-pensée. C'est ce qu'on appelle la Mémoire. Chez Marker elle fonctionne exactement comme matrice narrative et discursive, tant diégétiquement (elle est le thème du

---

13   Cf. Barthes, *La Chambre claire.*

scénario) que formellement (elle incarne l'entre-deux visuel du cinéma et de la photographie).[14]

Dubois thus argues that Marker's project is a matrix of thought-images, which move through the multidimensional narrative, discursive and diegetic theme of time and temporality. Effectively, there is no *present* moment represented by the photogrammes, as image dissolves into image and as the pace of the montage quickens and slows. On a primary narrative level, as the protagonist's mind (and a photogrammatic representation of his body) moves between past, present and future, the sole visual, rather than diegetic, clues to temporal location are the repetitions of images – faces, birds, trees. Nonetheless, in spite of the roles of past images as memory-images, present images as inter-mediary and inter-mediatory images, and the ethical and philosophical complexities of the faces represented in the protagonist's travels into the future, each image must also inevitably be 'read' as part of the sequential narrative. Each image, one by one, offers the possibility of a reading that does not reduce itself to the individual, 'photographic' *studium* of the content of each image, but rather the quasi-indexical traces that each prior images leaves upon the next. The legibility of the images of *La Jetée*, then, is entirely reliant upon the rigid narrative, in spite of the role of individual photogrammes as thought-images in the course of this process of narrativisation.

Rhythm, in/animation and subjectivity

In its rupture of the rhythms of cinematic convention, *La Jetée* approaches a kind of anti-representation of time: a metaphysical, rather than an actual representation of movement. Even at the instant of the protagonist's death, the image is deeply resonant, affectively

14   Dubois, '*La Jetée* de Chris Marker ou le cinématogramme de la conscience', p.17.

dense, but set in an impossible instant that nonetheless fixes our gaze upon it as spectators and retains an affective afterimage that remains after the screen has faded to black. The impossible instant of death brings about the culmination of a perfectly (impossibly) cyclical account of time, beginning with the obsession of a lived moment and ending in death, sealing together the 'sole' protagonist's subjectivity within his perfect psychical loop. Just as the cyclical and circadian rhythms of human subjectivity begin and end with birth and death, with day and night, past and present, so these cyclical rhythms dictate the beginning and end of the protagonist's subjectivity. As such, one could argue that *La Jetée* moves beyond an illusory representation of time, whose condition of possibility is the very *im*possibility of representing time itself. Instead, the film embraces this impossibility, towards a representation of an agent of psychical time (the protagonist). *La Jetée* is a film fully aware of its own impossibility, unrepresentability and caesura between moments.

Time and temporality are crucial in the formation of Marker's psychical and animate subjects. The male protagonist always remains subject to and within a series of psychical temporalities, necessarily stilled within the photogrammatic sequence itself. He is constantly in the process of becoming what inevitably he always was – the signal of his own death and his own subjective coming-to-be. In the sense of a Deleuzian becoming, his subjectivity paradoxically attempts to escape and recuperate itself from within the inevitability of the psychical loop. The only possibility for this is via the destruction of temporal flux, of syncopation and rhythm itself. The still photogram, a passage between present, past and future, serial and changing, but nonetheless halted and discontinuous, is constantly in tension with the flight of psychical subjectivity. The photogram coexists in a stuttering, rhythmic, antagonistic relation with the psychical temporal loop that ultimately either destroys the subjectivity of the protagonist in death, or condemns him to a cycle of constantly interrupted becoming, where he may never be still, or indeed, just be.

Such an interpretation of *La Jetée* is somewhat pessimistic: the protagonist is locked within a temporal loop that both creates and destroys his subjecthood. There is, however, a moment within the film, when the temporally and diegetically structured subject is momentarily able to escape the confines of the static image. Significantly, it is only at a moment of awakening – and indeed not the awakening of the central male protagonist, but of the woman he amorously pursues – that the images are elided and sped up to the extent that they teeter on the brink between moving and still image. In this set of photogrammes, a woman stirs and begins to wake. The extra-diegetic birdsong animates the still image even before the female figure opens her eyes. Movement, or dynamism, then, is restored, both physically, literally, for the duration of the blink of an eye, and diegetically via narrative and extra-diegetic sound. The movement of the woman's eyelids from closed to open serves both as a visual metaphor sliding between non-vision and vision, dream and consciousness, but also opens up the possibility of an animated subject that exceeds the photographic or photogrammatic frame into a cinematic and temporal one.

By highlighting this particular moment between sleep and the inanimate, between wakefulness and the animate, Marker toys with the raw material of cinema – its moving image – in order to make a subjective encounter with this image of a woman 'come to life' all the more poignant. While the male psychical subject-in-time is trapped within the circadian and cyclical rhythms of a singular, temporally-closed destiny, this woman, immobile, stilled by her unconsciousness, by the spectatorial fetishisation of her body and by her inability to move at will through past, present and future, is in fact the only subject of the photogrammatic images to be able to exceed her inviolable temporal rhythm. If *La Jetée* is a short film about time, then it may suggest that time travel is *not* an escape if one cannot escape from one's own temporal rhythms – be they dynamic or still.

For Victor Burgin, the female protagonist lacks subjectivity or narrative force – instead her image is nothing more than an affectively invested object driving the desire, and consequently the narrative, of the masculine protagonist:

> Alternately fully present and fully absent, like the object in the fort/da game, she is nothing other than that with which the man seeks to be (re)united. Making no demands of her own, compliant signifier of the man's desire, she is pure function: precipitating the cause of the narrative. For both the man and for

his torturers, all the mortified and somnambulistic movements of the underground prison camp come to turn around this single fixed point.[15]

However, such a reading ignores the complexities of a 'single fixed
point' that is also the sole moment of animation. The wakeful, un-
thinking female protagonist emerges also as an animated subject who
gazes back at the viewer, about whose psychical agency we know
nothing at all. Consequently, her momentary dynamism, and the halting rhythms of stillness and dynamism in *La Jetée* itself, paradoxically
point towards an *escape* from fixity, allowing a different kind of
subjectivity to emerge – a subjectivity not rooted in the psychical
temporal loop, but always moving, always shifting, not even located
specifically in a body in space and time, but in the stuttering form of
dynamism itself. The ecstatic moment of this relational subjectivity is
perhaps where Marker's film can take us in viewing contemporary
cinematic theory. Indeed, Catherine Lupton highlights the moment of
the female protagonist's awaking as a moment of dynamism and a
realisation of the possibility of cinematic transformation:

> For a few seconds, normal film duration is established: the woman opens her
> eyes to look into the camera and smiles. The moment is echoed on the sound-
> track by a rising pitch of birdsong, which heralds this brief flight into life, out
> of the fixed frames and inexorable logic of the fated narrative.[16]

The transformative moment fulfils the cinematic promise of Marker's
film, a moment exceeding the narrative temporality imposed upon the
framed images. The subtlety of movement within the frame makes this
moment of dynamism unsteady and uncertain. Paradoxically, it is a
flight from the narrative voice – a momentary diegetic and dynamic
remove from the unavoidable drive toward a conclusion. But it is also
the ultimately cathected moment of cinematic desire – the woman's
partially occluded face is unavoidably fetishised via the close-up,
immobilised in order to retain the precarious delineation between
stillness and movement. Although this moment of dynamism escapes

15   Victor Burgin, *The Remembered Film* (London: Reaktion, 2004), p.99.
16   Catherine Lupton, *Chris Marker: Memories of the Future*, p.91.

the inexorability of the narrative, it is still party to the same limitations
to representations of temporality in the moving image.

By contrast, D. N. Rodowick describes a kind of subjective temporal freedom in the very stillness of the image in *La Jetée*:

> Movement, drained from the image and divorced from the representation of
> action, has relinquished its role as the measure of time [...]. The painful binding
> of the subject – physically stilled no less than movement is frozen in the image
> – liberates him briefly in time, just as the image of time is released from its
> subordination to movements linked to physical actions.[17]

If *La Jetée* functions as a presentation of cinematic dynamics or
movement, but does not aim to *represent*, then Rodowick argues that
subjective temporality in the film is released from its binds to the
representational image. In other words, there is some subjective release when 'the image of time' no longer needs to be linked to the
movement of time – the image takes on a different, subjective, affect-
tive quality. To extend this line of thought, the female protagonist's
awakening presages an ecstatic moment of escape from the fixed
rhythmic exchange of one still image for another. In effect, only she is
capable of moving beyond the inexorably committed temporality that
constitutes the male protagonist's world.

Temporality is crucial in the formation of Marker's animate and
psychical on-screen subjects – whether this is a cinematic temporality
in the case of the former, where the woman is an animated subject that
gazes back at the viewer, or a psychical 'function' temporality animated in order to disturb the photogrammatic sequence. The still
photogramme, as a passage between present, past and future, is both
serial and changing, but nonetheless halted and non-continuous, and is
constantly in tension with the psychical temporal loop of the central
protagonist. Consequently, Marker's film enables a loosening of
notions of the cinematic, of subjectivity and of the intersections where
these two meet amongst a matrix of temporalities that permeate the
material image, the temporal gaps between images, and the durational
experience that we have as viewers watching the film. Perhaps the

17   D. N. Rodowick, *Gilles Deleuze's Time Machine* (Durham and London: Duke
      University Press, 1997), p.4.

most that we can hope the rhythms of *La Jetée* can do is to shed a little more light onto the flickering screen of cinematic temporality and its subjective encounters.

Suggested Reading

Alter, Nora M., *Chris Marker* (Urbana and Chicago: University of Illinois Press, 2006).

Amengual, Barthélemy, 'Le Présent du futur: sur *La Jetée*', *Positif* (March 1997), 96–98.

Barthes, Roland, *La Chambre claire: note sur la photographie* (Paris: Gallimard, 1980).

Bellour, Raymond, *L'Entre-images: photo, cinéma, vidéo*, Les essais (Paris: Éditions de la Différence, 2002).

Benjamin, Walter, 'The Work of Art in the Age of Mechanical Reproduction', in *Illuminations*, ed. Hannah Arendt, trans. Harry Zohn (London: Pimlico, 1999), pp.211–44.

Doane, Mary Ann, *The Emergence of Cinematic Time: Modernity, Contingency, the Archive* (Cambridge, Mass. and London: Harvard University Press, 2002).

Dubois, Philippe, '*La Jetée* de Chris Marker ou le cinématogramme de la conscience', in *Recherches sur Chris Marker*, ed. Philippe Dubois (Paris: Presses Sorbonne Nouvelle, 2002).

ffrench, Patrick, 'The Memory of the Image in Chris Marker's *La Jetée*', *French Studies: A Quarterly Review*, 59 (January 2005), 31–37.

Lupton, Catherine, *Chris Marker: Memories of the Future* (London: Reaktion, 2005).

Marker, Chris, *La Jetée: ciné-roman* (New York: Zone Books, 1992).

Mulvey, Laura, *Death 24x a Second: Stillness and the Moving Image* (London: Reaktion, 2006).

Notes on Contributors

Helen Abbott is a lecturer in French at the University of Wales, Bangor. She completed her PhD entitled 'The Aesthetics of Voice in the works of Baudelaire and Mallarmé' in 2006, and is currently revising her thesis for publication. She continues to research relationships between voice, poetry and music 1850–1950, with particular emphasis on song settings.

Jenny Chamarette is a doctoral student in the Department of French at the University of Cambridge. Her thesis examines the conditions of temporality, spatiality and embodiment that allow cinematic art to be envisaged as a locus for subjectivity, making particular reference to post-structuralist phenomenological thought in the work of Gilles Deleuze, Paul Virilio and Jean-Luc Nancy.

Sophie Fuggle is currently researching a PhD at King's College London on the subject of power and ethics in the work of Michel Foucault and the letters of Saint Paul.

Brenda Garvey is a lecturer in French at the University of Chester and is completing a PhD at the University of Oxford on 'Dynamics of time and space in recent French fiction: selected texts by Annie Ernaux, Patrick Modiano, Jean Echenoz and Marie Darrieussecq'. She has taught literature at the University of Oxford and has given a series of guest lectures on Annie Ernaux at the University of Warwick.

Louise Hardwick is completing a doctorate examining depictions of childhood in Francophone Caribbean literature at Trinity College, Oxford. She has published an article on postcolonial haunting in Maryse Condé as well as interviews with Condé and Raphaël Confiant.

Ian James completed his doctoral research on the fictional and theoretical writings of Pierre Klossowski at the University of Warwick in 1996. Since then he has been a Fellow and Lecturer in French at Downing College, University of Cambridge. He is the author of *Pierre Klossowski: The Persistence of a Name* (Legenda, 2000) and *The Fragmentary Demand: An Introduction to the Philosophy of Jean-Luc Nancy* (Stanford University Press, 2006). He has just completed a book on the writing of Paul Virilio (Routledge, 2007).

Ariane Kossack is completing a doctoral thesis in musico-poetic studies at the University of Cambridge. Her research explores music and questions of the sublime in the works of Stéphane Mallarmé and Rainer Maria Rilke.

Elizabeth Lindley is studying her doctoral thesis in the Department of French, University of Cambridge. Her research investigates notions of voice and identity in women's contemporary French theatre, exploring the writings of Hélène Cixous, Marguerite Duras, Nathalie Sarraute and Marie NDiaye.

Laura McMahon is a doctoral student in the Department of French at the University of Cambridge. Her thesis explores questions of touch in cinema, examining the films of Robert Bresson, Marguerite Duras and Claire Denis in relation to Jean-Luc Nancy's work on the body and the image. Her publications include articles on Denis and Duras.

Gerald Moore has recently completed a PhD at Downing College, Cambridge on the reception of Marcel Mauss by post-structuralism. Having translated works by Foucault and Lefebvre, including notably, with Stuart Elden, Lefebvre's *Rhythmanalysis: Space, Time and Everyday Life* (Continuum, 2004), he is now writing a book on the concept of life as rhythm, particularly in relation to stock markets.

Dee Reynolds is Professor of French at the University of Manchester. Her work has appeared in numerous publications, including *Dance Research*, *Body, Space and Technology Journal*, *Dance Theatre Journal, Forum for Modern Language Studies, French Cultural Studies, French Forum* and *Journal of European Studies*. She is the author of *Rhythmic Subjects: Uses of Energy in the Dances of Mary Wigman, Martha Graham and Merce Cunningham* (Dance Books,

2007), *Symbolist Aesthetics and Early Abstract Art: Sites of Imaginary Space* (Cambridge University Press, 1995) and co-editor, with Penny Florence, of *Feminist Subjects, Multi-Media: Cultural Methodologies* (Manchester University Press, 1995).

Michael Sheringham is Marshal Foch Professor of French Literature, University of Oxford. He has written extensively on André Breton and Surrealism, on modern and contemporary French poetry and fiction, and on autobiography and related genres. He is the author of *French Autobiography: Devices and Desires* (Oxford University Press, 1993) and *Everyday Life: Theories and Practices from Surrealism to the Present* (Oxford University Press, 2006), editor of *Parisian Fields* (Reaktion Books, 1996), and co-editor, with Johnnie Gratton, of *The Art of the Project* (Berghahn, 2005).

Luke Sunderland is a Junior Research Fellow at Gonville and Caius College, Cambridge. His research interests include Old French narrative cycles and the rebel baron epic.

Jennifer Valcke is working on the final stages of a PhD entitled 'Static Films and Moving Pictures: Montage in Avant-Garde Art and Film', under the supervision of Professor Martine Beugnet at the University of Edinburgh. Currently living in Brussels, she has set up ESP and CLIL programmes for the Faculty of Applied Sciences at the Université Libre de Bruxelles, Belgium.

Lisa Villeneuve is at Balliol College, Oxford, completing a PhD on economic modernisation and dwelling space in French fiction of the post-war period, which examines the work of Camus, Sollers and Perec.

Matthias Zach studied French and Philosophy at Wadham College, Oxford, and German, French and Comparative Literature at the University of Tübingen and the Université de Paris III-Sorbonne Nouvelle. He is currently working on a doctoral thesis on Yves Bonnefoy and Paul Celan, which examines the interplay between translation and poetic creation.

Index

Modern French Identities

Edited by Peter Collier

This series aims to publish monographs, editions or collections of papers based on recent research into modern French Literature. It welcomes contributions from academics, researchers and writers in British and Irish universities in particular.

Modern French Identities focuses on the French and Francophone writing of the twentieth century, whose formal experiments and revisions of genre have combined to create an entirely new set of literary forms, from the thematic autobiographies of Michel Leiris and Bernard Noël to the magic realism of French Caribbean writers.

The idea that identities are constructed rather than found, and that the self is an area to explore rather than a given pretext, runs through much of modern French literature, from Proust, Gide and Apollinaire to Kristeva, Barthes, Duras, Germain and Roubaud.

This series reflects a concern to explore the turn-of-the-century turmoil in ideas and values that is expressed in the works of theorists like Lacan, Irigaray and Bourdieu and to follow through the impact of current ideologies such as feminism and postmodernism on the literary and cultural interpretation and presentation of the self, whether in terms of psychoanalytic theory, gender, autobiography, cinema, fiction and poetry, or in newer forms like performance art.

The series publishes studies of individual authors and artists, comparative studies, and interdisciplinary projects, including those where art and cinema intersect with literature.

Volume 1   Victoria Best & Peter Collier (eds.): Powerful Bodies.
            Performance in French Cultural Studies.
            220 pages. 1999. ISBN 3-906762-56-4 / US-ISBN 0-8204-4239-9

Volume 2   Julia Waters: Intersexual Rivalry.
            A 'Reading in Pairs' of Marguerite Duras and Alain Robbe-Grillet.
            228 pages. 2000. ISBN 3-906763-74-9 / US-ISBN 0-8204-4626-2